IT Architecture

FOR

DUMMIES®

IT Architecture

FOR

DUMMIES®

by Kalani Kirk Hausman
and Susan L. Cook

WILEY

Wiley Publishing, Inc.

IT Architecture For Dummies®

Published by
Wiley Publishing, Inc.
111 River Street
Hoboken, NJ 07030-5774

www.wiley.com

Copyright © 2011 by Wiley Publishing, Inc., Indianapolis, Indiana

Published by Wiley Publishing, Inc., Indianapolis, Indiana

Published simultaneously in Canada

For general information on our other products and services, please contact our Customer Care Department within the U.S. at 877-762-2974, outside the U.S. at 317-572-3993, or fax 317-572-4002.

For technical support, please visit www.wiley.com/techsupport.

Wiley also publishes its books in a variety of electronic formats. Some content that appears in print may not be available in electronic books.

Library of Congress Control Number: 2010937819

ISBN: 978-0-470-55423-4

Manufactured in the United States of America

10 9 8 7 6 5 4 3 2 1

WILEY

About the Authors

Kalani Kirk Hausman is employed as an Assistant Commandant at Texas A&M University and specializes in enterprise architecture, security, information assurance, business continuity, and regulatory compliance. His background includes varied topics from digital forensics and WMD response, pandemic response planning, technology audit practices, and IT governance strategies. His experience includes application design, data resource management, network architecture, server and storage virtualization, strategic technology modernization, network and backup centralization, research computing, and large network BCP/DR planning. With a Master's degree in Information Technology, Kirk has served as a senior research scientist in the fields of cyber terrorism, cybercrime, and cyber security, and he regularly lectures on uses of technology in education, solutions for persons with disabling conditions, and strategic architectural planning to improve enterprise efficiencies. Kirk's professional certifications include the CISSP, CGEIT, CRISC, CISA, CISM, and CCP together with a wide assortment of technology- and regulatory-specific designations.

Susan L. Cook is a Senior IT Policy and Security Programs Administrator at Texas A&M University, specializing in enterprise risk assessment and compliance. She has a master's degree in Information Technology, additional graduate work in Security Management, and more than a decade of experience in the field. She has also worked as a compliance auditor in the financial industry and as a licensed private investigator.

Dedication

This book is dedicated to the many talented IT professionals faced with supporting enterprises in which the only constant is change.

Authors' Acknowledgments

We would like to acknowledge the tremendous help in preparing this book provided by the excellent editorial staff at Wiley, in particular our Project Editor, Blair Pottenger; Development Editors, Kelly Ewing, Jodi Jensen, and Kathy Simpson; Copy Editors, Teresa Artman and Maryann Steinhart; and Tech Editor, Chris Leiter. Special thanks are also due to Katie Mohr, our Acquisitions Editor for the Dummies series, and to our agent and all-around-guide, Carole Jelen of Waterside Productions.

Publisher's Acknowledgments

We're proud of this book; please send us your comments at http://dummies.custhelp.com. For other comments, please contact our Customer Care Department within the U.S. at 877-762-2974, outside the U.S. at 317-572-3993, or fax 317-572-4002.

Some of the people who helped bring this book to market include the following:

Acquisitions and Editorial

Project Editor: Blair J. Pottenger

Development Editors: Kelly Ewing, Jodi Jensen, Kathy Simpson

Acquisitions Editor: Katie Mohr

Copy Editors: Teresa Artman, Maryann Steinhart

Technical Editor: Chris Leiter

Editorial Manager: Kevin Kirschner

Editorial Assistant: Amanda Graham

Sr. Editorial Assistant: Cherie Case

Cartoons: Rich Tennant (www.the5thwave.com)

Composition Services

Senior Project Coordinator: Kristie Rees

Layout and Graphics: Carl Byers, Erin Zeltner

Proofreaders: Tricia Liebig, Lindsay Littrell

Indexer: BIM Indexing & Proofreading Services

Publishing and Editorial for Technology Dummies

    Richard Swadley, Vice President and Executive Group Publisher

    Andy Cummings, Vice President and Publisher

    Mary Bednarek, Executive Acquisitions Director

    Mary C. Corder, Editorial Director

Publishing for Consumer Dummies

    Diane Graves Steele, Vice President and Publisher

Composition Services

    Debbie Stailey, Director of Composition Services

Contents at a Glance

Introduction 1

Part I: Developing the Architecture 7
Chapter 1: Planning for Enterprise Realignment 9
Chapter 2: Exploring Tasks, Roles, and Tools 17
Chapter 3: Pondering Platform Pros and Cons 29

Part II: Defining the Role of IT Architecture 41
Chapter 4: Reducing Complexity through Standardization and Consolidation 43
Chapter 5: Planning Enterprise Information Security 65
Chapter 6: Complying with Mandates and Managing Risk 81

Part III: Creating an Enterprise Culture 93
Chapter 7: Developing Identity and Access Management Strategies 95
Chapter 8: Developing a Network Culture through Collaboration Solutions 113
Chapter 9: Reviewing Communication Methods 127

Part IV: Developing an Extended Network Enterprise 141
Chapter 10: Managing Data Storage 143
Chapter 11: Managing Application Development 163
Chapter 12: Planning for the Mobile Enterprise 175

Part V: Obtaining Value beyond the Basic Enterprise 193
Chapter 13: Virtualizing Enterprise Systems 195
Chapter 14: Facilitating High-Performance Computing 207
Chapter 15: Enabling Green IT 219

Part VI: Protecting the Enterprise 229
Chapter 16: Planning Technology Updates 231
Chapter 17: Planning Security Strategies 247
Chapter 18: Planning Business Continuity and Disaster Recovery 261

Part VII: The Part of Tens 273

Chapter 19: Ten Challenges for Redesigning an Existing Enterprise 275

Chapter 20: Ten "Low-Hanging Fruit" Opportunities 281

Glossary 289

Index 313

Table of Contents

Introduction 1

   About This Book 1
   Conventions Used in This Book 2
   What You're Not to Read 2
   Foolish Assumptions 2
   How This Book Is Organized 3
      Part I: Developing the Architecture 3
      Part II: Defining the Role of IT Architecture 3
      Part III: Creating an Enterprise Culture 3
      Part IV: Developing an Extended Network Enterprise 4
      Part V: Obtaining Value beyond the Basic Enterprise 4
      Part VI: Protecting the Enterprise 4
      Part VII: The Part of Tens 4
   Icons Used in This Book 4
   Where to Go from Here 5

Part 1: Developing the Architecture 7

Chapter 1: Planning for Enterprise Realignment 9

   Defining an Enterprise 9
   Finding the Best Solution 10
   Providing Leadership 10
   In the Traditional Enterprise, Everything May Be Independent ... 11
      Too many resource silos 12
      Too many platforms 12
      Too many people with root access 13
   In the Modern Enterprise, Everything Is Connected 13
   Defining Success 14
   Using Maturity Models 15
   Preventing Failure 15

Chapter 2: Exploring Tasks, Roles, and Tools 17

   Examining Common Enterprise Architecture Tasks 17
      Identifying data requirements 18
      Integrating existing resources 18
      Defining technical standards 18
      Justifying changes 19
      Communicating effectively 19

Knowing the Roles of Enterprise Architecture 20
   Chief architect 20
   Lead architect 21
   Technology architect 21
   Software or application architect 21
   Business architect 22
   Data architect 22
Using the Right Tool for the Right Job 23
   IT governance 24
   Enterprise architecture frameworks 25
   Project management 27

Chapter 3: Pondering Platform Pros and Cons 29
Standardizing Your Platform — or Not 29
   Recognizing the benefits of standardization 30
   Overcoming challenges in standardization 31
Making the Hard Software Choice: Open Source
   or Closed Source 33
   Open source 34
   Closed source 36
Working with Open Standards 38
Looking Past Specifications to Business Needs 39

Part II: Defining the Role of IT Architecture 41

**Chapter 4: Reducing Complexity through
Standardization and Consolidation. 43**
Recognizing Complexity in the Enterprise 43
   Common sources of complexity 44
   Complications of complexity 46
Planning for Consolidation 47
   Applying the 80/20 rule 48
   Finding value 49
   Planning for technology end of life 49
   Maintaining the help desk 51
   Consolidating skills 51
Addressing Concerns about Standardization 53
   Reduced functionality 53
   Decreased productivity 54
   Incompatibility with existing applications 54
   Risk of technology monoculture 55
   Preparing for opposition 55

Consolidating the Data Center...56
    Identifying the benefits 57
    Reducing complexity through virtualization.....................................59
    Implementing desirable redundancy 60
    Planning the centralized facility 61
Automating the Data Center...61
    Patches and updates 62
    Image-based deployment...62
    Backup solutions...63

Chapter 5: Planning Enterprise Information Security 65
Protecting Enterprise Data..66
Creating a Security Plan..67
    Design a workable program..68
    Use a layered framework 68
    Implement security standards 70
    View security as a program, not as a project............................71
    Keep security simple 71
Developing a Security Policy..72
    Classifying data to be secured 72
    Addressing basic security elements..72
    Getting management approval...74
    Maintaining the policy...74
    Training employees 75
Using Technology to Support Security Operations 75
    Use collaborative technologies...76
    Remain flexible...77
    Plan for partner relationships 77
    Outsource only when necessary..78

Chapter 6: Complying with Mandates and Managing Risk 81
Keeping Your Company Compliant...81
    Legal mandates that affect the organization.............................82
    Discovery and retention 83
    Additional requirements..83
Planning to Manage Risk...84
    Identifying threats...84
    Identifying vulnerabilities 86
    Assessing risk...87
Addressing Risk..89
    Prioritizing threats...89
    Reducing probability...90
    Reducing impact 91
    Choosing appropriate mitigations..92

Part III: Creating an Enterprise Culture 93

Chapter 7: Developing Identity and Access Management Strategies 95

Introducing Identity and Access Management (IAM) 95
Identifying Users 96
  Something users know: Password 97
  Something users have: Access token 98
  Something users are: Biometric identification 99
  Something users do: Behavioral identification 101
Authenticating Users 102
  Authentication standards 102
  Directory 103
  Central authentication 103
  Federated authentication 104
  Single sign-on 104
  Cross-realm authentication 105
Authorizing Access 106
  File and database rights 106
  Service rights 107
  Application rights 107
Creating an Identity Management Strategy 108
  Reviewing technologies 108
  Assigning aggregate rights 108
  Meeting legal requirements 108
  Keeping it simple 109
  Finding benefits 109
Implementing an Identity Management Solution 110
  Identification 110
  Authentication 110
  Authorization 111
  Additional functions 111

Chapter 8: Developing a Network Culture through Collaboration Solutions 113

Establishing Networks of Trust 113
  Creating a team from a mob 114
  Developing strong lines of communication 115
  Calculating the value of networks with Metcalfe's Law 115
Developing Network Culture through Social Media 116
  Using social networking 117
  Employing collective intelligence 118
  Setting social-media policies 119
Employing Groupware 120
  Considering the benefits of groupware 120
  Selecting a groupware solution 121

Working with Enterprise Portals 123
    Activating common features of portals............................ 123
    Developing network culture with portals 126
    Integrating business intelligence tools 126

Chapter 9: Reviewing Communication Methods **127**
Identifying Classes of Communication............................... 127
Messaging 128
    Chat.. 128
    Electronic mail (e-mail).. 129
    Instant messaging 131
    Text messaging 132
Community Sites.. 132
    Blogs 133
    Discussion boards and forums 133
    Wikis 134
Conferencing 135
    Videoconferencing.. 135
    Virtual reality.. 136
    Voice over Internet protocol (VoIP)..................... 137
    Web conferencing 137
Broadcast Communications... 138
    Podcasting 139
    Really Simple Syndication (RSS) 139
    Streaming media 140

Part IV: Developing an Extended Network Enterprise **141**

Chapter 10: Managing Data Storage **143**
Determining Storage Requirements 143
    Conducting a storage survey................................. 144
    Interviewing personnel 145
Identifying Important Data Categories............................. 145
    File repositories 145
    File versioning 146
    Databases... 146
    Multimedia... 147
    E-mail.. 147
    Logging 148
    Virtual servers 149
Creating a Storage Policy... 149
    Addressing specific storage topics....................... 150
    Distributing the policy 151

Designing a Storage System 152
    Selecting appropriate storage configurations 152
    Exploring enterprise-level storage strategies 153
    Dealing with expanding storage needs 155
Protecting Stored Data 157
    Fault tolerance 158
    Backup and recovery 158
    Data removal 159

Chapter 11: Managing Application Development **163**

Exploring the Software Development Life Cycle 164
    Waterfall 165
    Prototype 166
    Spiral 167
Rapid Application Development Strategies 168
    Agile programming 169
    Extreme programming 170
    Scrum programming 170
Designing Application Architecture 171
    Multitiered architecture 171
    Service-oriented architecture 172
Including Accessibility 173

Chapter 12: Planning for the Mobile Enterprise **175**

Introducing Mobile Computing 175
    Laptops 176
    Netbooks 176
    Tablets 176
    Cell phones 177
    Bluetooth 177
    Long-range wireless 177
Exploring Mobile Computing in the Enterprise 178
    Device interaction 179
    Boosters and dead zones 179
Going Mobile beyond the Enterprise 182
    Navigation 182
    Connectivity and bandwidth 183
    VPN and SSL access 183
    Remote desktops 184
    Power 184
Planning for SmartPhone Computing 186
    Familiarity 186
    Planning ahead 186
    Device locking 187
    On-device encryption 187
    Kill pills 188
    Laptop LoJack 188

Defining Mobile Access Policy 189
  Mobile computing policies 190
  Remote access policies 190
  Wireless use policies 191

Part V: Obtaining Value beyond the Basic Enterprise 193

Chapter 13: Virtualizing Enterprise Systems 195
Getting the Scoop on Virtualization Technology 196
Virtualizing Servers 197
  Hosting virtual machines 198
  Separating hardware and software tech refresh planning 199
  Emerging best practices 200
Virtualizing Workstations 201
  Using thin and thick clients 202
  Virtual desktops 202
  Remote desktops 203
  Client hosting 203
Virtualizing Applications 203
Cloud Computing 204
  Private clouds 205
  Best practices 205

Chapter 14: Facilitating High-Performance Computing 207
Supercomputers Rule the World 207
  Desktop computing 208
  Parallel computing 210
  Distributed computing 210
Everyday High-Performance Computing 211
  Computing clusters 212
  Visualization clusters 214
  Grid computing 215
  Volunteer computing 216
  Compute farms 217
Desktop High-Performance Computing 217

Chapter 15: Enabling Green IT 219
Practicing Green Technology 219
  Extended replacement cycles 220
  Telework and telecommuting 220
  Data center location 220
  Energy tax credits 221
  ENERGY STAR 221
Considering Alternative Energy 222
Reducing Consumables 223

Selecting Green Hardware..224
Configuring Green Settings...225
Virtualizing Hardware..226
Ensuring Green Disposal 226

Part VI: Protecting the Enterprise 229

Chapter 16: Planning Technology Updates 231
Reviewing Hardware Update Strategies 231
Keeping systems until they fail 232
Using defined replacement cycles 232
Riding the cutting edge 236
Employing trickle-down replacement 237
Relying on surplus technology..................................238
Using technology as a reward 238
Replacing technology in an ad-hoc manner 239
Planning for Sub-System Updates......................................240
Upgrading components...240
Updating firmware 241
Updating device drivers...241
Planning Software Updates...242
Understanding the need for testing...........................242
Exploring deployment strategies...............................243
Planning for software maintenance...........................245

Chapter 17: Planning Security Strategies 247
Identifying Threats to the Enterprise.................................247
Malware...247
Application vulnerabilities 249
Directed network attacks...250
Selecting Appropriate Countermeasures 250
Malware protection 250
Secure application development 251
Data loss prevention..251
Encryption 252
Firewalls 254
Intrusion detection and prevention 256
Network address translation......................................257
Network monitoring 260

Chapter 18: Planning Business Continuity
and Disaster Recovery 261
Defining Business Continuity and Disaster Recovery.........261
Keeping Your Business in Business: Continuity Planning.....262
Participating in a business impact analysis 262
Participating in risk assessment 264

Preparing a Recovery Plan 264
 Developing scenarios 264
 Incorporating virtualization strategies 265
 Testing the plan 267
 Updating the plan 267
Using Alternative Sites 268
 Selecting the right type of site 268
 Managing the alternative site 269
Communicating During a Disaster..270

Part VII: The Part of Tens................................. 273

Chapter 19: Ten Challenges for Redesigning an Existing Enterprise 275

Dealing with Lack of Executive Support 275
Handling Opposition to Change..276
Deciding on a Platform: Open Source versus Closed Source/Commercial Off-the-Shelf 276
Eliminating Resource Silos 277
Integrating Legacy Systems..277
When Change Doesn't Happen Fast Enough 278
Maintaining Compliance throughout the Process...............278
Dealing with Separate Revenue Streams 279
Supporting Personally Owned Equipment 279
Know Your Limits 280

Chapter 20: Ten "Low-Hanging Fruit" Opportunities..............281

Eliminate Resource Silos 281
Standardize the Workstation Environment...........................282
Create a Centralized Data Center 282
Consolidate Resources Already Within the Data Center.....283
Implement Automated Update/Patch Management Solutions.....283
Implement Enterprise-Level Anti-Malware Solutions...........284
Use Risk Assessment Results to Find Easily Fixed Vulnerabilities 285
Schedule Workstation Replacement 285
Implement Virtualization...286
Reduce Cost from Consumables by Implementing Green IT Practices...286

Glossary 289

Index 313

Introduction

● ●

*T*he enterprise begins when you carefully put the first two computers together, and complexity grows with every step thereafter. Haphazard IT building practices can easily lead to an enterprise network that is poorly planned or composed of random, one-off projects undertaken as standalone goals. An e-mail consolidation project can unexpectedly derail concurrent licensing projects intended to vastly reduce expensive software licensing costs by carving the authentication domain into separate silos unable to share resources. A server virtualization project may run into difficulties if not coordinated properly with server consolidation projects to make sure that sufficient bandwidth and host resources are available when systems are transferred from physical to virtual states.

Obviously, these scenarios are simply examples of potential conflicts that may occur when enterprise realignment and cost-saving strategies drive independent projects without coordination and guidance at the strategic level. Many other conflicts are much more subtle and not apparent until well along a new path, such as an incompatibility between communications protocols that support new equipment or a lack of executive support that leaves adoption of enterprise practices in a loose "opt in by choice" state.

After reading this book, you'll have a better grasp of the interconnected nature of enterprise architecture realignment. We hope the information we provide encourages you to look around your own enterprise and find some low-hanging fruit opportunities for quick savings or other proof of value to help develop executive support for additional changes. Few enterprises lack such opportunities because technology and its uses tend to fall into stable practices users describe as "the way we've always done it" rather than changing to adopt the best or most efficient ways.

About This Book

This book is not a checklist for efficiency, although it does present some strategies that may improve cost and operational efficiencies. It is not a step-by-step guide that will lead to a secure and risk-free network, although it provides some examples of projects that may help to reduce risk. Instead, this book introduces you to enterprise architectural planning from the theoretical viewpoint and then drills down to the meat and bones of enterprise technologies and functions.

You should recognize elements of your own environment reflected here and take advantage of my past experience in dealing with challenges faced during realignment, consolidation, and other re-engineering practices within an extended enterprise network. Although the content of this book is suitable for globally distributed enterprises of significant scale, the topics covered are useful for resource and availability planning in networks of any size.

Conventions Used in This Book

This book is, after all, a reference book, and we expect that using conventions will make it easier for you to find exactly what you're looking for by quickly scanning through chapters. The conventions for this book are as follows:

- ✔ *Italics* emphasize important terms the first time they're defined.
- ✔ Web site addresses, or *Uniform Resource Locators* (URLs), are provided for Web sites referenced in this book and appear in a special typeface, such as www.dummies.com.
- ✔ Because the Web is such a dynamic environment, provided URLs may change at any time.

What You're Not to Read

In order to make a technical topic more interesting, we include interesting tidbits of information and anecdotes based on our professional experiences. You can find this information in sidebars throughout the book. You don't have to read the sidebars to understand IT architecture, but if you do, we hope you find them as interesting as we do.

Occasionally, we're guilty of outright techno-babble, but fortunately we mark those discussions with Technical Stuff icons so that you can skip right over them if that sort of thing makes your eyes glaze over.

Foolish Assumptions

We assume this book is going to be read by CIOs, chief architects, network planners, IT operation managers, and front-line technical implementers. We don't delve deeply into specific technologies, but instead present considerations for integration of whatever technologies are already in place.

We also assume that you're not looking for someone to tell you exactly what hardware and software to buy. We won't tell you that open-source is the best solution for every problem, any more than we'll suggest that a particular vendor's commercial off-the-shelf line of products is best. In general, the best choices for technology are based on those already in place and familiar to users and support staff alike.

Finally, we assume that you need help identifying areas of focus and strategies for sustaining your enterprise year to year in the face of constant technological evolution. We trust this will spark many ideas you can leverage toward management of your extended enterprise. By starting at the theoretical level and progressing through the book into ever-more-direct technology approaches and strategies, you can develop a better framework for evaluation of your own enterprise setting.

How This Book Is Organized

We divide this book into several parts based on topic. The following sections describe what you can expect to find in each part.

Part 1: Developing the Architecture

Part I establishes the fundamental concepts of what defines an enterprise and then examines the value provided by this definition.

Part II: Defining the Role of IT Architecture

Part II addresses the identification of challenges and advantages in enterprise reconfiguration. It further examines the need to prove value to the organization as a result of change.

Part III: Creating an Enterprise Culture

Part III discusses the fundamental aspects of identity management, developing an enterprise culture, and specific collaborative options that can be used to reinforce this cultural evolution.

Part IV: Developing an Extended Network Enterprise

Part IV covers elements of a distributed network and its resources, identifying areas of planning that must play a part in enterprise reorganization and long-term operational strategies.

Part V: Obtaining Value beyond the Basic Enterprise

Part V examines technical considerations and projects that may or may not apply to some enterprises, although many of the strategies listed can be applied at any level.

Part VI: Protecting the Enterprise

Part VI defines strategies for protecting resources and services within the enterprise network environment.

Part VII: The Part of Tens

Part VII offers lists of ten useful items in enterprise architectural planning, together with references to areas of the book focusing on each.

Icons Used in This Book

The familiar *For Dummies* icons offer visual clues about the material contained within this book. Look for the following icons throughout the chapters:

Whenever you see a Tip icon, take note and pay particular attention. Tips address special-case items or strategies that come up often.

The Remember icon points out key concepts that will be helpful in understanding later topics in this book. And here's your first thing to remember: There is an online cheat sheet for this book that you can find at www. dummies.com.

Warning icons draw your attention to potential pitfalls and particularly difficult challenges. Pay attention to these factors in your enterprise because they
have a habit of coming back to bite you.

 Although this book attempts to avoid advocating specific technologies or
alternatives in favor of a more generally useful examination of architectural
strategies appropriate to any enterprise, technical details are indicated with
a Technical Stuff icon. These items may prove of greater use to implementers
than to pure strategists, but you will likely wear many hats over the course of
enterprise realignment. It can't hurt to review a few technical details!

Where to Go from Here

The goal of this book is to get you thinking about your own enterprise and
the opportunities it presents to the users, partners, and clients who access
its resources. You don't have to read this book cover-to-cover, although
you can, if you want. Either way, we hope that you walk away with dozens of
ideas for improvements in your own setting, whether your server room is a
converted broom closet or you support hundreds of thousands of users scat-
tered around the globe.

Part I
Developing the Architecture

The 5th Wave   By Rich Tennant

"Don't laugh. It's faster than our current system."

In this part . . .

This part offers a high-level overview of enterprise architecture. If you're not intimately acquainted with the topic of enterprise architecture, you may find this part particularly helpful. In addition to covering basic concepts, we include guidelines for determining success and preventing failure, establishing proper IT governance and management practices, and using enterprise architecture frameworks.

Chapter 1

Planning for Enterprise Realignment

. . . .

In This Chapter

▶ Defining the enterprise

▶ Defining success

▶ Preventing failure

. . . .

*1*nformation technology (IT) is everywhere in the business world, and you'd be hard pressed to find a business larger than a sole proprietorship that does not utilize some type of IT. When an IT decision is made, its effect can be felt throughout the organization. Poor decisions, such as those made without consideration of the impact on other elements of the enterprise, can create both immediate and long-term problems.

In this book you focus on enterprise architecture strategies and mechanisms that support both immediate and long-term (three to five years) planning. These strategies are used successfully in all types of enterprises, including small to mid-sized offices, educational institutions, and global commercial enterprises.

Defining an Enterprise

The *enterprise* is a fluid term encompassing all technologies and tech-related policies that relate to services provided to clients, partners, and customers during operation of the organization. The more the enterprise interconnects elements, the more it becomes like a living organism — growing to meet emerging opportunities; consuming resources for sustenance; and generating piles of outdated, outmoded, or outright broken equipment that must be disposed of carefully. The enterprise requires planning to control its growth into useful areas, guidance to maintain its security and integrity during operation, and leadership to face the myriad personal preferences users will bring to their expectations of service value and function.

The strategies you explore in this book enable the enterprise to be stable but agile, which allows for both continuity of operations and the integration of new technologies.

Finding the Best Solution

There's no perfect solution, no one-size-fits all strategy for enterprise architecture. As long as the technology meets the requirements, performs efficiently, supports business processes, is cost-effective, and can be supported and maintained, it's an acceptable solution, perhaps even a good one. There is no "best" technology, only the best technology for your enterprise.

Technology supports business, not the other way around. Technology should support business processes and align with strategic goals of your organization. Your technology choice should not limit your organization's functionality or future goals.

The strategies you look at in later chapters will help you make the right decisions for your organization, minimize cost, foster long-term planning capabilities, and create a stable and agile enterprise.

Providing Leadership

To be an effective enterprise architect, you must provide leadership for the decision-making process; understand the impact generated by each technology selection; and facilitate communication of strategies, policies, and controls to implementation staff and clients.

An enterprise architect must possess both business alignment and broad technological skills in order to filter through user requirements and separate user preferences ("wants") from requirements ("needs,") while also seeing past the technobabble jargon that tech savvy clients and IT staff members often use when dealing with normal mortals.

As an architect, you must identify future technology trends, up-and-coming opportunities, and evolving security requirements to ensure that the current-state enterprise is properly prepared to meet emerging solutions and technologies. If not planned carefully and tested thoroughly, integrating new items like the immensely popular Apple iPad can be catastrophic on enterprise networks.

You must have the strength of vision necessary to stand firm and persuade concerned individuals and key stakeholders that some choices have got to be made from a larger perspective in order to reap the greatest benefits for the organization overall. You must be able to speak comfortably with chief officers and end-users, but also have sufficient technical credentials and understanding to be taken seriously by front-line technical staff members.

The worst thing you can do is present strategies to technical implementers and display a lack of real-world implementation experience, without sufficient updated and personal technical ability to be taken seriously. When lost, respect and support from the IT geeks may be impossible to recover, and the best possible strategies ignored or circumvented as a result. To perform effectively, you are obliged to continually extend your own IT skills through study and training. A purely nontechnical managerial staff member should never attempt to dictate technical policies or strategies because they lack understanding of the complex web of interconnection that forms the modern enterprise network.

The technical lead who fails to keep his skills current rapidly becomes a non-technical lead due to the rapid evolution of both technologies in use and the manner in which they're consumed by clients and knowledge workers. As an example, consider an IT architect whose skills were developed prior to the evolution of service-oriented architectural design, cloud computing, virtualization of storage and hardware, VDI implementation, Green IT initiatives, privacy and encryption regulatory mandates, and a myriad of other emergent options. This architect won't be able to effectively recognize the potential value these technologies can add to the organization's operations — or understand the limitations, cost, and impact of integrating them into the existing enterprise.

We discuss many of the IT leadership roles that may be present in an enterprise architectural project, together with a review of common IT governance and architectural frameworks, in Chapter 2.

In the Traditional Enterprise, Everything May Be Independent

Many organizations still have traditional networks that are structured the same way they were 10 or 20 years ago — often due to a lack of technical knowledge update within the senior technical staff members, leading to a simple repetition of the same outdated functionality simply on updated hardware. Even if your organization isn't that old, chances are that unless modern enterprise architecture principles were involved in its initial design, you will still run into some of these old-school issues:

✔ Too many resource silos

✔ Too many platforms

✔ Too many people with root access

Too many resource silos

In a traditional enterprise, it isn't unusual for each business unit to maintain control over its own information systems, including servers, workstations, data, and even networking hardware. Along with information systems, each unit also has its own technical personnel, makes its own purchases, and is responsible for backing up its own data. In essence, each business unit is its own autonomous network. This autonomy creates difficulties when anyone tries to access resources in another silo or share data between business units. It also leads to excessive duplication of resources and efforts, as each unit may have its own database server, file server, or e-mail server. As an example, I (Kirk) have seen multiple million-dollar-plus document imaging systems implemented by different business units using incompatible technologies, only because there was no enterprise-level coordination of an IT project portfolio. As enterprise architect, one of your tasks will be to consolidate these resource silos into a single, centralized data center.

Because local silos of information resources create inefficiencies and barriers to architectural design, we address the elimination of silos in many chapters throughout the book. Deal with this pervasive problem early in enterprise planning.

Too many platforms

In information technology, a *platform* refers to a hardware or software framework. Examples of platforms include operating systems, hardware, programming environments, database management systems, and desktop or server configurations. In the old-school enterprise, you may find that many different platforms are in use. Administrators all have favorite technologies, and without a directive for standardization, administrators will push management to purchase these favored technologies. You may have to deal with a wide variety of operating systems, both server and workstation; multiple database solutions; or each programming team using a different programming language.

Another task will be to standardize platforms, which requires your vision and understanding of the organization's business requirements in order to keep the realignment process going even through the conflicts that will surely arise.

Chapter 3 includes an examination of technology standardization and its attendant benefits. Standardization is also key to adoption of new technologies enterprise-wide and to disaster recovery procedures, where complexity and customization can extend the recovery window significantly.

Too many people with root access

Often, too many administrators have high levels of administrative access. This type of access is referred to as *root, superuser, enterprise admin, supervisor,* or *admin,* depending on the operating system or application in use. These accounts may even be used as the administrator's normal logon account, in defiance of security best practices. Unfortunately, root accounts are sometimes considered a status symbol and an indicator of the organization's trust. You may even find that nontechnical staff possesses this access. Managers may insist on root access simply because they're managers or because they want to keep an eye on their administrators, even though they don't have the skills or knowledge to actually do so. Yet another of your tasks will be to remove root access from people who don't truly need it.

In the Modern Enterprise, Everything Is Connected

You can't decide on one particular technology without considering how it will affect all other technologies used in your enterprise now and in the future. For example, the selection of a new e-mail platform may seem simple, but it affects more than just how users get their e-mail. It also concerns the following:

- ✔ Directory services and authentication
- ✔ Network fax or voice mail solutions
- ✔ Instant messaging solutions
- ✔ Existing and future e-mail integrated applications
- ✔ Backup and recovery
- ✔ Data storage
- ✔ Security solutions

Selecting a particular application or programming language can affect your enterprise's future agility and impact business operational procedures. You have to base your technology selection on more than just user requirements and cost analysis; it must align with your organization's strategic business plan. Unless you have full understanding of both technical and business requirements, you risk limiting your organization's options. This understanding is necessary for success.

We discuss common collaborative technologies in Chapter 8. However, these technologies are not alone. A central set of standards should drive selection of platforms, standards for interoperability and communication, identify and access management, and all other functions within the enterprise to ensure that you can effectively integrate all existing functionality as well as newly emergent options into the enterprise fabric.

Defining Success

To be successful, enterprise architecture must provide value to the organization. Change for the sake of change alone is counterproductive.

Although some criteria for success may be specific to your organization, enterprise architecture may generally be considered successful if it does the following:

- ✔ Reduces support and operational costs
- ✔ Defines technical standards
- ✔ Reduces risk
- ✔ Improves continuity of operations
- ✔ Reduces undesirable redundancy while retaining fault tolerance
- ✔ Facilitates business processes
- ✔ Allows for a clear upgrade path to future technologies

These indicators are all fairly straightforward, but another sign of successful enterprise architecture is that the organization sees it as valuable. Because enterprise architecture can have a significant effect on your organization's current and future capabilities and opportunities, your organization needs to be aware of the value provided by the architecture so that costs remain justifiable in the overall business plan.

Using Maturity Models

Maturity models measure how your organization is progressing through an improvement process, and they're used extensively in process improvement, project management, and software development. The models consist of a number of levels, and as your organization matures and improves, it moves up in level. For example, the lowest level of maturity may be None, but when your organization begins to establish processes, even informally, it rises to the next level, which may be Informal or Initial. This process continues until the final level is reached, which is usually Continuously Improving, Audited, Measured, or something similar to indicate that the process is reviewed. Carnegie Mellon's Capability Maturity Model Integration (CMMI) is an example of such a model.

You can also use maturity models for enterprise architecture. Following are some of the more well-recognized enterprise architecture maturity models:

✔ Carnegie Mellon - Capability Maturity Model Integration (CMMI) (`www.sei.cmu.edu/cmmi`)

✔ National Association of State Chief Information Officers (NASCIO) - Enterprise Architecture Maturity Model v1.3 (`www.nascio.org/publications/documents/NASCIO-EAMM.pdf`)

✔ United States Department of Commerce - Enterprise Architecture Capability Maturity Model (ACMM) v1.2 (`ocio.os.doc.gov/ITPolicyandPrograms/Enterprise_Architecture/PROD01_004935`)

✔ United States General Accounting Office - Enterprise Architecture Maturity Management Framework (EAMMF) v1.1 (`www.gao.gov/new.items/d03584g.pdf`)

Maturity models are undoubtedly useful, but you may find that no published maturity models are a perfect fit for your organization. If that's the case, tailor the maturity model to your organization.

Preventing Failure

Unfortunately, not every enterprise architecture project is successful, but how do you know if you're on the path to failure? Some of the indicators to watch for include

✔ **Allotting too much time to respond to problems and too little to planning and actually architecting.** If you're constantly putting out fires, you can't make progress.

✔ **Poor leadership skills.** To be an effective enterprise architect, you must be a leader. It isn't enough to have the technical knowledge; you must be able to take charge when necessary, foster open communication, and think strategically.

✔ **Neglecting to include business staff.** Remember that information technology supports business processes, and you must include business staff in enterprise architecture decisions in order to ensure that technology is aligned with business goals.

✔ **Lack of executive support.** For any enterprise architecture project to succeed, it must have the support of executive staff. Executives have got to understand the value of enterprise architecture so that they can provide proper support. When your executives back the project, corporate culture dictates that the changes to come are not optional.

If you notice any of these problems, it may be time to take a step back and re-evaluate your methods.

Chapter 2

Exploring Tasks, Roles, and Tools

··

In This Chapter

▶ Discovering common tasks

▶ Identifying enterprise architecture roles

▶ Investigating enterprise architecture frameworks

··

*I*n transforming the theoretical concept of the enterprise into concrete components, the enterprise architect brings together a wide assortment of business guidelines, rules, and framework elements. You may work alone or as the head of a team, depending on the enterprise's size and complexity.

In this chapter, I identify common enterprise architecture tasks and the operational roles responsible for them. I also explain the rich set of tools for the enterprise architect: information technology governance, enterprise architecture frameworks, and project management techniques.

Examining Common Enterprise Architecture Tasks

As an enterprise architect, you perform many tasks when you design and implement an enterprise architecture plan, and those tasks vary widely in scope and focus. For example, finding ways to align technology and business needs is a high-level strategic task, whereas determining which anti-malware product to use is more of a focused operational task. The exact tasks depend on the organization and the scope of the plan, but the following sections list some general tasks that the architect should do.

As you read through the following sections, make notes regarding the relevancy of each task to your business environment. That'll help you identify what you need to do when you implement your own enterprise architecture plan.

Identifying data requirements

An organization's business processes are built around its data, and changes to the way data is handled (for example, how it's input, stored, moved, archived, and eliminated) can improve (or harm) those processes. To ensure that changes result in improvement, you must incorporate the organization's data requirements into the plan. Start by identifying the following three items:

- ✔ **Classifications of data used by the organization.** This determines the appropriate security measures.

- ✔ **Location of the data, such as on desktop computers, on servers, or in databases.** This identifies redundancy.

- ✔ **Users of the data, including employees, customers, partners, or the general public.** This aids in defining security controls and mechanisms for availability and access management.

Integrating existing resources

Technology resources, including everything from servers to applications and the people who manage them, are used to support business processes. You must identify the resources currently in use in order to see whether they're being used effectively and whether they'll be integrated into the new architectures. Even resources that are not the "best" choice may need to be integrated into the new architecture for legal, regulatory, or contractual reasons, or because they're impractical to replace in a short time frame.

You also have to identify embedded systems, such as security systems, telecommunications systems, network infrastructure components, and highly specialized systems like medical or manufacturing equipment that you may integrate into your new architecture. These systems have special security needs that are often overlooked, such as hard-coded device authentication mechanisms or fixed communications protocols used for device-to-device coordination of large SCADA environments.

Defining technical standards

It's the enterprise architect's responsibility to define the organization's *technical standards,* which are the rules and guidelines that the organization uses when making decisions regarding information technology and related acquisitions, procedures, configuration specifications, and policy.

Here are some examples of technical standards:

- ✔ Workstation and server configurations, including fair use and storage limitation policies.

- ✔ Approved software, from operating systems to business productivity suites, including malware defense policies.

- ✔ Network hardware components, such as routers and switches, together with remote access and mobile access policies.

- ✔ Application development methodologies, including policies for documentation and code review.

- ✔ Networking and communication protocols, in addition to VPN and RADIUS policies.

These standards are also used when your organization creates or modifies information security and computer-use policies.

Justifying changes

Enterprise architects make changes that have the potential to affect every employee in an organization. So you must ensure that changes aren't made simply for the sake of making changes. Changes have to provide value to the organization in some fashion, such as direct cost savings, reduction in administrative overhead, or improvements to business processes. (Chapter 4 shows you how to find value in architecture, particularly standardization and consolidation initiatives.)

Communicating effectively

Designing and implementing an enterprise architecture plan involves so many tasks that you may need more than one architect to complete them. Communication is essential to all phases of enterprise architecture planning. You must explain the benefits of the plan to the stakeholders (interested and/or affected parties) in both technical and nontechnical terms. In addition, the enterprise architect has to develop plans that define how changes will be communicated to the users, how directions will be communicated to the implementers, and how feedback will be gathered from everyone.

Knowing the Roles of Enterprise Architecture

The larger the enterprise, the more difficult it can be for a single person to manage all the tasks that must be performed when structuring an IT architecture. It isn't uncommon for multiple architects, each with a particular area of expertise, to work together under a chief architect. The following sections identify some of the types of architects that are commonly found in medium to large organizations.

Chief architect

The *chief architect* identifies opportunities for improvement in technology and ensures that technology aligns with business requirements. Depending on the structure of the organization, a likely candidate for the chief architect is the CIO (Chief Information Officer). The CIO should have the background to move effortlessly between business and technology and be able to communicate equally well with executives and technical staff while aligning technology selections with business requirements.

In addition to the general tasks discussed in the "Exploring Common Enterprise Architecture Tasks" section, earlier in this chapter, the chief architect is responsible for the following specific tasks:

- Identifying and analyzing risk factors, such as the potential of exposing protected data or creating security vulnerabilities during transition from one solution to another
- Acting as the final arbitrator in solution negotiation for conflicts that arise from changes
- Providing leadership

Essentially, the chief architect is the individual ultimately responsible for planning, directing, and monitoring the process of enterprise architecture and its associated business processes and technologies.

Significant problems can arise in the project if the chief architect's technological knowledge is lacking or is out of date. Lack of personal technical skills may cause the architect to make uninformed decisions or rely too heavily on advice from others who may have their own personal agendas. Similarly, a lack of soft skills may impair effectively aligning technologies with business needs or prevent conveying the value of technical changes to nontechnical stakeholders.

Several operational roles support the chief architect. They require special-ized knowledge and skills that the chief architect may not possess or have time to use.

Lead architect

Typically found only in larger enterprises, a *lead architect* provides assistance and support to the chief architect. Acting as the chief architect's executive officer, the lead architect may attend meetings and resolve issues in the chief architect's place, which requires close communication with the chief architect.

The lead architect's other duties may include

- Leading implementation teams
- Establishing operational standards
- Coordinating change management

Technology architect

A *technology architect* is useful when the enterprise involves multiple tech-nology solutions, and members of this role must have extensive knowledge of the enterprise's infrastructure and technology requirements. Technology solutions must meet the organization's operational requirements. As a result, the technology architect is concerned with elements such as the following:

- Network components, including routers, switches, and firewalls
- Enterprise software solutions, including e-mail, messaging, and content management
- Computing platforms and operating systems
- Integration of dissimilar technological components into a single func-tioning architecture, such as servers with different operating systems or a mixture of open source and commercial enterprise applications (see Chapter 3)

Software or application architect

A *software* or *application architect* is responsible for higher-level aspects of application design and development, ensuring that they're aligned with the chief architect's plans and the organization's business processes. The duties of the application architect include, but aren't limited to, the following:

rmining the software development process to use

ting application deployment strategies

grating applications

iding data resource management and coordination between software development and resources managed by the data architect role

✔ Specifying requirements for reusable components

The technology architect and the application architect must work very closely
together to achieve proper integration of applications and infrastructure.

Business architect

A *business architect* may be necessary for organizations with complex line-of-
business applications (critical applications that are crucial to the operation
of the business, such as inventory control); e-commerce solutions; or executive information systems such as business intelligence software, dashboards,
and decision support systems. This architect's primary duty is to analyze
business processes and strategies and determine the related technology
requirements. Here are some examples:

✔ Identifying the need for a customer relationship management (CRM)
   solution and determining its appropriate use

✔ Deciding whether to extend the organization's intranet to business partners, thereby creating an extranet

✔ Identifying the need for a network fax solution to replace standalone fax
   machines

Data architect

A *data architect* is a highly specialized role that may be necessary in organizations that have large amounts of data, utilize business intelligence or data
warehousing solutions, or receive data from multiple sources. The data architect performs data management functions such as these:

✔ Analyzing the organization's data requirements and designing appropriate data repositories (as in data modeling)

✔ Creating and maintaining data dictionaries

✔ Defining and designing the flow of data internally (between applications)
   and externally (to and from a customer or partner)

✔ Planning data migrations

✔ Providing guidance to database administrators

Outsourcing and offshoring

Your organization may find that it doesn't have personnel with the necessary skills or knowledge to fulfill the supporting architect roles or to implement the plans. When this challenge occurs, the organization can choose to either outsource roles in which skills are lacking or train its employees to fulfill those roles.

In general, you should outsource only if there is a benefit beyond cost-saving, as the initial cost of outsourcing is often lower but the long-term costs are greater. Additional benefits to outsourcing may include the following:

✔ Allowing your organization's IT staff to be trained while contractors handle migration to or implementation of a particular technology

✔ Adding legitimacy to compliance or security audits by having them conducted by an uninvolved entity

✔ Avoiding internal bias and preference during technology testing

✔ Saving time and cost training employees in skills that won't be used except during the migration

Outsourcing firms may in turn outsource some of their functions, requiring all contracts involving sensitive data to have provisions restricting secondary outsourcing.

Even if benefits exist, be cautious if you're considering outsourcing enterprise architecture functions to an offshore company (a practice called *offshoring*) for the following reasons:

✔ Some laws and regulations restrict where sensitive data can be moved or stored, particularly to foreign countries. This limitation may prohibit offshoring any functions that deal with protected data.

✔ Your organization's internal operational mandates or contractual obligations may also place restrictions on the capability to offshore some functions.

✔ Prosecuting legal action across geopolitical boundaries can pose a problem for businesses whose data becomes exposed in foreign countries.

 The data, application, and business architects work closely together to ensure that data and application requirements are complementary and support business processes.

Using the Right Tool for the Right Job

"The right tool for the right job" is a well-known principle in construction that has spread to information technology. This adage also applies to enterprise architecture, and the right tools for that job are these:

- IT governance
- Enterprise architecture frameworks
- Project management

These three tools are distinct elements, and you should keep them as separate as possible. While you may have some overlap in personnel, ideally the same individual or team is not in charge of all three because the skills and knowledge needed for each of these elements vary widely.

IT governance

You can't make technology-related decisions in a vacuum; you must coordinate and communicate with other business roles. You have to skillfully and consistently manage technology so that all IT decisions align with strategic and operational business requirements. This management is referred to as *information technology governance,* and it helps to ensure the following:

- Communication among the following organizational roles, with regard to information technology:
  - Strategic (chief officers, vice presidents, directors)
  - Operational (managers, team leaders, partner representatives)
  - Infrastructure (technology implementers, training staff)
- Technological decisions in alignment with business requirements
- Mitigation of IT risks
- Proper management of technological resources
- IT performance measurement

IT governance has many models, each with its own strengths, weaknesses, and specific areas of focus. The following sections introduce a few of the best-known models.

Technology doesn't determine business mandates; business mandates determine technology. IT governance helps make sure that technology and business align.

COBIT

Control Objectives for Information and related Technology (COBIT) is a highly detailed governance model developed by the Information Systems Audit and Control Association (ISACA) and managed by the IT Governance Institute (ITGI). COBIT defines control objectives (high-level requirements) for 34 processes to assist with managing and controlling information in order to support business objectives. It also provides guidance on using metrics to determine a maturity model for your organization's IT processes.

ITIL

Developed by the Office of Government Commerce (United Kingdom), _Information Technology Infrastructure Library (ITIL)_ is a framework of best practices covering IT services and operations management. This model requires strong management support and commitment, and it may take three to five years to implement fully. Proponents of ITIL are currently working to adapt its use for "black box" cloud computing service environments. For more information, visit www.itil-officialsite.com.

ISO/IEC 38500:2008

ISO/IEC 38500:2008 is a standard for IT governance, published by the International Organization for Standardization (ISO) and the International Electrotechnical Commission (IEC) in 2008. This high-level standard provides guidance to management on the role of the governing body and the use of information technology in your organization. It's applicable to public, private, and not-for-profit corporations, as well as government entities, regardless of size. The ISO Web site offers more information on this standard:

    www.iso.org/iso/iso_catalogue/catalogue_tc/catalogue_detail.htm?csnumber=51639

Enterprise architecture frameworks

Formal architecture supplies guidance, verification, and structure for long-term enterprise viability. In support of this goal, formal frameworks have developed criteria that you can use to establish value from proposed changes to the enterprise. Many frameworks exist, but the following sections describe some of the more well-known ones.

Not every framework is a one-size-fits-all model. Some organizations may find it beneficial to mix and match elements from multiple frameworks to suit a specific environment.

A number of more complex frameworks, such as those in the following sections, may require training to implement effectively; your organization may want to consider bringing in a trained or certified consultant for assistance with the appropriate framework. A number of enterprise architecture certifications are available, including both framework-specific certifications (Zachman and TOGAF), which are managed by the developing organizations, and vendor-specific certifications, such as Microsoft Certified Architect and Sun Certified Enterprise Architect. In addition, some educational institutions, such as The Ohio State University and California State University, offer certification and training as part of their continuing education or engineering programs.

Zachman Framework

The *Zachman Framework* is a high-level model developed by the Zachman Institute. It contains no methodology or processes; instead, it focuses on views, definitions, relationships, and objects, both physical (such as equipment or facilities) and conceptual (such as a business unit or an enterprise). It asks the simple questions of who, what, how, when, where, and why as they apply to concepts such as scope, business processes, requirements, solutions development, and deployment. The Zachman Framework is an excellent starting point for mapping out architecture processes and for identifying gaps. More information on the Zachman Framework is at www. zachmaninternational.com.

TOGAF

The Open Group Architecture Framework (TOGAF) was developed by the Open Group, a platform-neutral, vendor-neutral consortium whose members include vendors, colleges and universities, and technology companies. *TOGAF* consists of a methodology as well as a modeling system and is compatible with other enterprise architecture frameworks. Its architecture development method begins with analysis and ends with an implemented enterprise architecture. For more information on the TOGAF framework, go to www.opengroup.org/togaf.

FEAF

The *Federal Enterprise Architecture Framework (FEAF)* is designed for federal agencies. FEAF includes comprehensive modeling and methodology components that are designed to work in highly complex environments. Its modeling components focus on business; IT system components, technologies, and standards; data; and performance. Its methodology includes analysis, definition, funding, and project management. The FEAF may not be useful to private sector companies unless they do business with the federal government.

The Chief Information Officers Council Web site at www.cio.gov/library_category2.cfm/structure/Enterprise%20Architecture/category/Enterprise%20Architecture has more information about FEAF, including guidelines and tools.

Gartner Enterprise Architecture Framework

Gartner Research, a well-known IT research and consulting organization, developed the *Gartner Enterprise Architecture Framework* to work with both commercial and open source environments. The framework provides a model for examination of business, information, and technology requirements and concerns in the overlapping context of both enterprise architecture and business. While it may not have as many reference guides as some other frameworks, it's supported by a large body of ongoing research. More information about this framework is at www.gartner.com.

Gartner provides research and advising as a commercial, fee-based service. In my experience, it has proven to be an excellent resource for medium to large enterprises.

Project management

Project management involves breaking projects into planned stages, each with its own specific activities and requirements, identifying roles, and budgeting costs. General project management elements include

- Initiation
- Planning
- Implementation
- Monitoring
- Completion

General project management approaches may, in some cases, have greater benefit than a formal project management methodology that's highly focused on a specific area such as quality control or constraints.

Project management methodology

The chief architect (and the lead architect, if that role exists) needs experience with some type of formal project management methodology or at least needs to be comfortable with project management concepts. The size of the enterprise and the level of complexity of the project determines the level of management used. For example, small changes may not need a comprehensive risk analysis or approval by the change advisory board.

Some organizations, particularly larger ones, have a Project Management Office (PMO). The PMO primarily provides guidelines, standards, and documentation on the organization's project management processes, and metrics for measuring project success. The PMO may work as consultants with unit-level project managers, providing guidance and training, or may directly manage projects throughout the organization.

Project management across the enterprise involves development of a portfolio of all resources, constraints, service level agreements (SLAs), and other factors that may constrain or facilitate the successful completion of individual enterprise architectural projects. The PMO acts to develop metrics for measuring success, developing scoping constraints and completion criteria, and establishing milestones and project terminus to avoid the "never-ending project." The portfolio can act to consolidate similar projects and identify opportunities where new technology implementation may prove more cost-effective than continuing support for legacy systems, and other similar functions to improve the effectiveness of your efforts.

Project management methodologies

There are several types of formal project management methodologies, the most comprehensive of which include the Project Management Institute's (PMI) Project Management Body of Knowledge (PMBOK) and the United Kingdom's Office of Government Commerce's (OGC) PRINCE2. Many organizations choose to develop their own methodology that's a combination of elements tailored to their particular environment.

You can also supplement project management methodologies with techniques and tools such as these:

- Capability Maturity Model Integrated (CMMI): Process improvement

- Six Sigma: Quality control

- Critical Path Analysis: Planning and scheduling

- Program Evaluation and Review Technique (PERT): Task analysis

The Chief Architect must have a thorough grounding in project management practices. In any environment lacking a dedicated project portfolio manager or PM Office, the Chief Architect must support this function directly or through his immediate staff. Project management can't be buried deeply in the organization structure if reporting of project criteria for success and completion is to be accomplished successfully. It is very difficult for a lower-level functionary to effectively report the failure of a project lead by someone higher up the organizational food-chain.

Project or program?

Is enterprise architecture a project or a program? Programs and projects are similar, but they differ in the following ways:

- A program is continuous, whereas a project has a specific end.

- A program is made up of integrated projects.

- A program focuses on improving business processes, whereas a project focuses on individual deliverables.

Because the process of enterprise architecture is complex, continuous, and comprised of many integrated projects, it can be considered a program and is referred to as such throughout the rest of this book.

Multiple projects that are related are also referred to as *portfolios,* and other sources may use the term *portfolio management* instead of portfolios.

Chapter 3

Pondering Platform Pros and Cons

. . . .

In This Chapter

▶ Understanding the benefits and drawbacks of platform standardization

▶ Solving problems with standardization

▶ Comparing open source and closed source standards

▶ Seeing beyond standards to business requirements

. . . .

*B*efore you can build or restructure an enterprise network, you must lay down detailed plans to ensure that the necessary resources are present, technologies are both compatible and useful, and the proper infrastructure is in place to support the enterprise.

This chapter introduces the concept of platform architecture, its benefits, and the obstacles that lie in the way of standardization. We also discuss open source versus closed source software and issues with each that you need to understand when you consider these options.

Standardizing Your Platform — or Not

An enterprise architecture plan is much like a construction blueprint. Just as the foundation of a building determines whether you will build a shack or a skyscraper, choice of platform architecture helps you determine what computing environment and administrative methods may work best.

A common first step of architectural planning is to establish suitable standards for the body of technologies used by the enterprise. These *platform architecture standards* can include the following:

✔ Approved hardware platforms

✔ Operating systems

✔ Programming environments (languages and development tools)

✔ Database management systems

✔ Desktop and server configurations

✔ Mobile technology solutions

✔ Information worker software suites

Your choice of platform architecture lays the foundation for the construction of your enterprise and is critical because it both provides opportunities and places restrictions on the solutions that you may employ. In making your decision, you need to consider the benefits and challenges of various standards.

Recognizing the benefits of standardization

Some platform architects choose to go with a single vendor's product *stack*, which includes server and workstation technologies, user productivity suite, and vendor-specific communication protocols. Others choose to implement a set of standards upon which they then base purchases. Regardless, standardizing platform architecture provides several direct benefits that you can communicate to stakeholders:

✔ **Economy of scale:** Buying in bulk is often cheaper, as evidenced by the popularity of warehouse shopping clubs. Platform standardization allows your organization to take advantage of bulk discounts when purchasing both hardware and software licenses. Each vendor has its own volume licensing program, but it's not unusual to see substantial discounts when the number of licenses purchased becomes large enough. Alternatively, some vendors offer per-processor, per-seat, or concurrent-use-limit licenses, which may save a medium to large organization a tremendous amount of money compared to per-user licensing.

✔ **Ease of integration:** Standardization also allows applications to be integrated more easily due to the commonality provided through specification. Greater commonality means greater ease of both initial implementation and later upgrade. Whatever platform or standards you select, ensure that enough compatible vendor or third-party solutions are available to allow your organization to implement emergent technologies easily.

✔ **Improved efficiency:** Users and technical staff can obtain greater knowledge and proficiency with a smaller number of solutions, thereby increasing efficiency. Improved efficiency can reduce both training and staffing needs.

✔ **Greater support options:** Selecting commonly used platforms provides your organization with a greater level of community support than selecting little-used ones. This type of support is valuable when troubleshooting technical or user issues. Support resources include community, vendor and developer Web sites, user forums, and customer support options.

✔ **Simplification of future control:** Initially, a great deal of effort goes into the platform selection process as you research and evaluate various platforms for use in your enterprise. After you set your standards, however, future selections are much easier because you only need to evaluate solutions available within the standard platform. Remember to include potential future needs when selecting a standard platform in order to ensure a variety of choices for future purchases.

Platform standardization is almost always beneficial, and we discuss standardization in more detail in Chapter 4. The next section explores a few situations where exceptions to platform standardization are necessary.

Overcoming challenges in standardization

Although platform standardization has obvious benefits, as detailed in the preceding section, you are likely to encounter some hurdles during the selection process:

✔ **Cost:** Replacing existing, working systems is often difficult to justify and may also be prohibitively expensive for some organizations. So make sure that your plans allow for evolutionary change to the new platform as you make new purchases.

✔ **Opposition to change:** Opposition to standardization can arise throughout your organization, whether from business units or key stakeholders. For whatever reasons, some people may refuse to accept the new specification, and opposition is more likely to occur when the new specification differs greatly from the platform currently in use. (See Chapter 4 for suggestions on how to deal with opposition to standardization.)

✔ **Reliance on existing technology:** Your organization may have critical business solutions that depend on a particular set of technologies:

• Applications may rely on a specific operating system or database management system.

- Business functionality may rely on legacy hardware, such as older fax or video processing cards that only work with specific computing hardware.

- Automation and equipment control systems may rely on embedded technology.

Attempting to impose new standards on these types of systems can be difficult, requiring time and effort, and may also be expensive. In some cases, standard alternatives may not exist.

✔ **Risk of falling behind the change curve:** Changes in both hardware and software technology come quickly, and new options are always being offered. By the time the specifications for the new standard have been approved, new versions of your identified platform may be available. Alternatively, if an organization transitions to the new technology in an evolutionary manner, it may find that it is falling behind. Your planning process must remain flexible to avoid standardizing on what is soon to be legacy technology.

Educational systems, governmental agencies and other entities with complex bureaucracy are particularly vulnerable to this hurdle, due to complex procurement regulations. The time between specification and purchase can stretch out to months or longer. Even smaller organizations may need to wait until the next fiscal year for funds to become available. The "best" selection at the time of specification may no longer be the best at the time of purchase.

✔ **Differing partner standards:** When partner organizations don't follow the same standards, difficulties in interoperation between the organizations can arise. Difficulties may also occur even if similar platforms are used, but with a different upgrade cycle. A poor platform selection may have a long-term impact on business opportunities.

The problem of differing standards may also arise during mergers and acquisitions when the organizations involved use different platforms. Integration of noncompatible platforms has the potential to cause disruptions in service as well as incur significant expense in trying to remedy the problem. Don't immediately assume that the solution currently in use is the best one. Instead, examine the technology used in each organization and select the best and most appropriate one.

✔ **Differing scales of need:** The scale of need may vary widely within an organization, and a one-size-fits-all platform specification may not be appropriate for the needs of some business units. For example, a small business unit may find that a personal or workgroup database management solution (such as Microsoft Access or Microsoft FoxPro) is most appropriate because its database needs are limited and enterprise-level features are unnecessary. Upgrading this unit to a larger, enterprise-level relational database management solution such as Oracle, Microsoft

SQL, or Sybase requires creation of a user interface in addition to migration of the data. Conversely, allowing the smaller unit to continue to use workgroup solutions requires additional administrative overhead in supporting both solutions.

Forced standardization within an enterprise can be expensive when existing nonstandard technologies are already in place. A good example is in the case of mobile technologies, where users may already have smartphones and other mobile devices according to personal preference. The elimination of functional technologies that don't fit the mandatory standard entails loss of user preference and additional cost to the organization. However, extending support skills and synchronization services necessary to include all possible devices can prove even more costly. In addition, if a standard you select isn't based on the most common or most familiar technology option, user opposition may present new challenges to the enterprise architectural effort.

Making the Hard Software Choice: Open Source or Closed Source

The open source versus closed source debate is a hot one that has been going on for many years and shows no signs of cooling down. Proponents of each side often argue with religious fervor, citing issues with security, flexibility, and even ethics. What the debate all boils down to, though, is which is "better":

- ✔ Commercial open-source (like SUSE Linux) or free open-source software (FOSS), in which the source code is available for review and modification.

- ✔ Commercial-off-the-Shelf (CotS) software, in which the source code is not provided by the vendor and generally is not easily modified in its most basic functions.

Source code refers to the actual instructions used to control the actions performed by the computer. The instructions are written in a programming language, such as C, Java, Visual Basic, or dozens of others. By having access to the source code, an organization's developers can customize it based on business needs, creating a unique version of the software for the enterprise.

While a full examination of the pros and cons of each side is outside the scope of this book, I do discuss both open and closed source software as they relate to platform architecture standardization.

Open source

Open source software is distributed under a licensing agreement in which you can view and modify source code. In addition, many FOSS solutions are developed outside the corporate environment. This approach allows for fairly rapid application development and modification, creating new or updated versions of software. For example, hundreds of distributions of the Linux operating system are available.

Many businesses that produce FOSS code generate their income by providing support, updates, and more robust versions of their free products. When considering open source products, take into account the shift in costs from product to support in order to predict the long-term financial impact of open source platforms.

Not all open source software is free. Commercial versions of Linux are available, while some open source vendors charge for upgrades or professional editions of their free software. For example, the popular Groundwork Monitor software (www.groundworkopensource.com) used in many enterprises has a community-supported free version and a for-pay enhanced version available as an upgrade.

Open source enthusiasts often point to LAMP as a case study of a successful open source Web application platform. *LAMP* stands for *Linux* (operating system), *Apache* (Web server), *mySQL* (database application), and *Perl/PHP/ Python* (programming languages). LAMP has been around since the late 1990s and has spawned open source platforms such as MAMP for Apple's Mac OS X and WAMP for Microsoft Windows.

The upside of open source

Open source solutions have many benefits:

- ✔ Many FOSS packages have no licensing fees or have low up-front costs.
- ✔ Many useful tools and utilities have been released into the open source community, particularly in the areas of security, server management, and application development.
- ✔ Your organization may want to shift software-related costs from capital expenses to operational expenses, and paying for support as opposed to licenses accomplishes this goal.

You may find that one of the best uses of FOSS is to test new technologies. Because FOSS is generally community-created, it often implements new technologies much earlier than final versions of commercial software are available. You can use FOSS to test the usefulness of the new technology without significant investment.

In addition, you can find many widely used FOSS security utilities, such as the network instruction detection software (IDS) Snort (www.snort.org) and the network mapper Nmap (nmap.org). When evaluating FOSS security utilities, consider the reputation of the development team and whether the utility has been reviewed by a trusted third party, such as a government agency, a university's computer engineering program, or a respected security organization.

The downside of open source

Open source also has some drawbacks:

- The benefit of cost reduction comes with a price in the form of technical expertise. It is generally considered to be more difficult to manage an open source platform than a closed source platform.

- Because multiple developers or groups may work on different parts of an application, the user interface may lack a consistent look and feel. This inconsistency may cause the application to seem overly complex and inaccessible, which can impact productivity and user morale. However, you can minimize that impact with user training and by considering usability when implementing standards.

- Users of accessibility technologies such as screen readers or Braille displays may not find some FOSS solutions accessible, and you should consider accessibility in standards development if it is an issue in your organization.

- Global organizations may find that some FOSS software isn't fully compatible with the international character sets in use in their organization.

- FOSS solutions may suffer sudden and unexpected end of life when a primary developer is lost or the development team moves on to other projects.

- Because products in use by an open source enterprise may be developed by many (if not hundreds) of different developers, there may be a great deal of effort and cost required to integrate the products.

- Malicious material injected into community-created code may also play a role in long-term softening of enterprise security.

 This concern is addressed in the Institute of Electrical and Electronics Engineers (IEEE) paper "Poisoning the software supply chain," which you can find at doi.ieeecomputersociety.org/10.1109/MSECP.2003.1203227.

- Some organizations, whether by legal, regulatory, or operational mandate, are required to identify all intellectual property in use. The use of FOSS solutions may require additional effort to identify the authors of the application code.

Generally, organizations that don't have (or don't want to acquire) considerable technical and help desk resources should not adopt an open source platform architecture for the following reasons:

- Although FOSS has a lower upfront cost, it's typically more difficult and costly to support.

- Integration and unexpected end-of-life issues may be addressed by modifying the source code in-house and maintaining the result as a custom application. You can even recode and recompile the base operating system if sufficient manpower, time, and technical expertise are available.

- Even when sharing common labels, the lack of standardization extends throughout the open-source space. More than 700 variants of the Linux operating system exist, and even the more common applications fork into different product lines. The OpenOffice Linux user suite, for example, has forked into separate development lines maintained at `http://openoffice.org` and `http://go-oo.org`.

Closed source

Closed source software is proprietary and is licensed to be used by the customer, not modified. The source code is typically not available for review. Although restrictive compared to open source, this type of commercial software is popular because it tends to integrate well with other commercial products, and those products by the same vendor will generally integrate seamlessly.

Open source equivalents are available for almost all commercial software, but they're often cited by commercial software champions as having fewer features or more performance problems than their commercial counterparts. Even open source developers admit this issue, as is evidenced by the 2006 LinuxWord presentation in which a Novell developer stated the need for improvement in OpenOffice's Calc after it took three hours to perform calculations that took Microsoft Excel 30 seconds to complete.

The upside of closed source

Some of the benefits of closed source solutions include the following:

- Commercial technologies generally follow accessibility guidelines, making them more compatible with assistive devices.

- In the event of a disaster, recovery and equipment replacement may be easier for large enterprises that can buy computers with well-supported and documented device drivers.

✔ The interface for user and administrative applications is more likely to be standardized by product than by customer, which makes it easier to train new hires with previous experience in that technology.

✔ Because organizations can't modify the source code to customize commercial software, many commercial software solutions are highly configurable, allowing users to add custom fields, logos, and content from within the application's configuration module.

✔ Large commercial software vendors typically try to provide a clear upgrade path for their customers. Easy upgrades encourage organizations to move to the latest versions of software, which allows them to take advantage of new features and increased compatibility with new hardware.

✔ Commercial software may have more robust user manuals and easier access to vendor support services.

 Consider selecting commercial closed source software if your organization has no need for code-level customization. Additionally, if you desire a turnkey solution supporting common business functions, commercial closed source software lets your organization implement applications with minimal configuration and installation effort. The widespread success of these products in enterprises of all scales is due at least in part to this simplicity of installation.

The downside of closed source

Like open source, closed source also has a few drawbacks:

✔ Organizations may get locked into a particular vendor's products and find it so difficult or costly to migrate to another solution that they stay with the original vendor.

✔ Customizing commercial software may require more effort or may involve hiring the vendor or the vendor's partner to perform the customization. In many cases, closed source applications are consumed as-is without change, although well-document application programming interfaces (APIs) and vendor-provided software development kits (SDKs) provide opportunities for in-house customization.

✔ Unlike open source applications, when a closed source product is no longer supported, organizations typically can't continue internal development. Security vulnerabilities may go unpatched, and business functionality may be curtailed due to a lack of new software features after a commercial product has reached end of life. Software licensing agreements may include provisions that the source code be held in escrow to ensure that the customer can continue its use for a set period of time even if the vendor goes out of business. Other vendors may later choose to make their previously CotS/closed-source software available as an open-source or customer-available legacy product.

If your organization requires long-term (15+ years) electronic records retention, consider solutions using open standards instead of those using proprietary formats. Upgrades in commercial software may render older file formats unreadable, and if products are discontinued, they may not run on future operating systems. Traditionally, FOSS solutions have been more likely to use open standards, due to efforts of the open source community to promote their products as more viable long term than commercial software. This movement has seen enough success that even commercial software vendors are implementing open standards for document storage, such as the Office Open XML (OOXML) format used in Microsoft Office 2007 and later.

Working with Open Standards

Open standards is a variation on the open source–versus–closed source debate. The term *open standard* has been characterized in various ways by governments and industries around the world, but it's generally defined as being approved in some fashion by one or more standards organizations (for example, ISO), published in sufficient detail to support interoperability and portability, and available to the general public. Examples of open standards include

- Hypertext Markup Language (HTML)
- Portable Network Graphics (PNG)
- Transmission Control Protocol/Internet Protocol (TCP/IP)

Anyone can use these standards to develop solutions that are interoperable with others of the same type. You can view HTML documents that conform to the standard, for example, in any Web browser that also conforms to the standard.

As you can imagine, open standards are crucial to the Internet and therefore are crucial to organizations that conduct business over the Internet, whether it be directly through retail Web sites or indirectly by exchanging information via e-mail and other communication mechanisms.

Open standards also allow modern software to be backward-compatible with older versions and allow for competing software to have a common file format that can be shared. For example, most, if not all, word-processing applications can read and save documents as plain text files, and nearly all spreadsheet and database applications have the capability to import data formatted as comma separated text.

Before adopting an open standards platform architecture, consider how widely the standards are being used currently and are projected to be used in the future in order to remain agile, flexible, and able to communicate with partners.

Not all proprietary standards present problems for the enterprise, as they may be patent-protected but commonly available for use. As an example, the file allocation table (FAT) file system is patented but widely adopted. Although you should consider open standards for interoperability purposes, it should not be the sole driver for product selection.

Lock-in to open standards is just as possible as lock-in to a vendor's product stack. Without a well-defined, long-term update plan, either situation can prove difficult for your enterprise's evolution.

Looking Past Specifications to Business Needs

The pros and cons of various platforms, as discussed in this chapter, demonstrate why enterprise architecture isn't solely about platform specification. You must also consider the requirements for many constraints of an enterprise network and its business environment, including the following:

- Business functionality
- Technology integration
- Specific applications
- Communications
- Reporting requirements
- Support requirements
- Scale and scope
- Regulatory and legal mandates

By failing to consider these constraints in both their current and future states, you run the risk of making short-term decisions that don't hold up long term. Beyond just reducing long-term efficiency, poor choices can create long-term financial burdens.

Keep the following guidelines in mind when considering platform selection:

- ✔ Platform standards must align with strategic business goals.
- ✔ Specifications should be based on user and business requirements.
- ✔ Negative effects on end users should be minimized.

Part II
Defining the Role of IT Architecture

The 5th Wave   By Rich Tennant

"It worked, honey! I'm connected to the network!"

In this part . . .

Enterprise architecture is all about identifying challenges and advantages for enterprise coordination and planning endeavors, all while demonstrating value. This part takes a look at those challenges, along with a variation of the 80/20 rule that is useful for enterprise planning.

In addition, we talk about why you must know the importance of the information you're working with in order to best determine how to organize and protect it. We also highlight any legal mandates or industry regulations, such as Sarbanes-Oxley or Payment Card Industry Data Security Standards, that apply to your organization, as well as look at managing risk and compliance in your enterprise.

Chapter 4

Reducing Complexity through Standardization and Consolidation

In This Chapter

▶ Identifying sources of complexity

▶ Finding value in standardization and consolidation

▶ Applying the 80/20 rule

▶ Understanding opposition to standardization

▶ Planning for data-center consolidation

George Earle Buckle, a British author and newspaper editor, once said, "To simplify complications is the first essential of success." Although he was referring to the written word, his assertion also applies to enterprise architecture, particularly in the early stages of a consolidation project. A common rule is that "It's cheaper to buy one hundred of one item than to buy one each of a hundred different items." In reducing enterprise complexity, this advice applies to selection of software, hardware, and services as much as the consolidation of authentication silos and physical machine rooms.

Like entropy, complexity requires effort to control because even the simple replacement cycle of equipment will create undesirable variation in any sizable enterprise. Proper planning and change controls are the only tools capable of drawing order as the enterprise grows and evolves to meet change in business and technology. This chapter explores simplifying your enterprise through consolidation and standardization, with a focus on the enterprise's data center.

Recognizing Complexity in the Enterprise

The complexity of the technological environment increases both costs and support requirements. A useful rule is that cost and support increases can be generally said to be the square of the number of equivalent solutions in use. For example, two different workstation operating systems will require roughly four times (2×2) the level of effort and cost to support. Three different workstation operating systems will require approximately nine times (3×3) the resources to maintain, update, configure, support, and secure than if only a single operating system were in use. This assertion also applies to applications, programming languages, and even hardware.

Common sources of complexity

You can find complexity throughout your enterprise, and it can result from events such as mergers and acquisitions or from a business model that allows technology planning or purchasing at the business unit level. Examples of common sources of complexity follow.

Application stack

Application stack refers to the operating system, applications, services, user applications, and other solutions that together form the operating environment for a computer. Application stack may also refer to the *technology stack,* particularly in reference to suites of integrated products by a single vendor or partner vendors.

Both commercial and open-source stacks — including IBM's WebSphere environment; Microsoft's technology stack; and LAMP (Linux Apache, mySQL, Perl/PHP/Python) — are popular in enterprises. In organizations without standardization, multiple stacks may be in use, which leads to support complexities as well as difficulties when users move from one part of the organization to another.

Hardware

Multiple equivalent hardware solutions create as much, if not more, complexity than multiple equivalent software solutions. Here are some examples of the additional work created when you use multiple hardware configurations:

✔ Keeping track of multiple vendors, warranties, and contracts increases administrative overhead and makes procurement more difficult.

✔ The time between software update/patch release and implementation increases due to requirements for testing on multiple hardware configurations. Testing before deployment avoids interruption of service should it fail on a particular hardware build. Unfortunately, it isn't unusual for software updates to be incompatible with drivers for individual components.

✔ The more types of hardware you have, the more complex and costly disaster recovery efforts become.

Some diversity in hardware may be necessary to support legacy or mission-critical functions. For example, accessibility devices, such as foot mice, ergonomic keyboards, and Braille keyboards, are unlikely to be standardized, as each employee may require a unique solution. Alternately, buying all equipment from the same production run can have negative consequences if a bad batch of components causes multiple simultaneous failures, but this occurrence is very rare.

Identity management

Identity management, including directory services, is the core of an enterprise network. It handles user identification, authentication, and authorization as well as other functions discussed in detail in Chapter 7. Complexity arises when multiple directory services or identity management solutions exist in resource silos throughout your enterprise; integration must occur across different directory services; or multiple vendors' products are in use, even though the organization has the option to use only a single standard or product if mandated by a particular business function or application.

Realignment initiatives of all types can benefit from some type of centralized or federated identity management solution — Novell Identity Manager, Microsoft Identity Lifecycle Management, or IBM Tivoli, for example — that facilitates authentication as well as access control across the enterprise. Reducing complexity in identity management also enhances security by decreasing the number of logons a user needs to conduct business. This lessens the tendency to use the same password everywhere or write logon/password credentials on sticky notes stuck to monitors or "hidden" under keyboards.

Application development

Programming style and languages are the foundation of your organization's application development and customization efforts. The programming model (object-oriented or nonstructured, for example) determines the way in which data will be accessed and manipulated. Complexity most often occurs in application development when multiple programming languages are in use. Although some development platforms, such as Microsoft's .NET, support compatibility among different languages, that compatibility does not exist between all languages. As a result, you may have problems with application integration, and you may wind up with equivalent custom code libraries for multiple languages. (You may be able to solve these problems by applying service-oriented architecture development practices — see Chapter 11.)

Another problem with lack of standardization and use of multiple languages is finding developers who are familiar with all programming languages in use. As a result, some programmers may recode applications in their preferred languages in an ad-hoc manner.

In addition, development costs can be increased by the number of computing platforms in use, due to more complex design and testing requirements.

Legislative and regulatory mandates

Several laws and regulations — such as the Health Insurance Portability and Accountability Act of 1996 (HIPAA) and Payment Card Industry Data Security Standards — require specific security measures for particular data types. These security measures can include

- ✔ Encryption
- ✔ Segregation of data
- ✔ Mandated protocols
- ✔ Data classification systems that support mandatory access controls

These measures alone may increase complexity, and if they conflict or otherwise interact negatively, difficulty may increase even more. Chapter 6 tackles legal and regulatory compliance in more detail.

Connectivity

It is a rare organization that does not need communication among different technologies. Modern networks may require connectivity for various types of mobile devices (such as cellphones and laptops), internal and external users, and applications.

Complexity arises not just from connectivity requirements, but also from underlying requirements for security such as encryption and authentication. You must ensure that a reduction in complexity does not result in a reduction in connectivity.

Complications of complexity

Having multiple equivalent solutions can create a variety of problems:

- ✔ **Higher personnel costs:** Your organization can employ a smaller number of individuals with knowledge of multiple solutions or a larger number of individuals with more specialized knowledge. The costs for either solution are similar because those individuals with knowledge of multiple solutions generally command higher salaries. Relative costs may vary slightly between industries, where the cost of benefits, such as health insurance, may impact the relative cost per employee.

✔ **Increased costs for business continuity and disaster recovery:** Recovering from a disaster is difficult in the best of circumstances and is made more so if planning has to include requirements such as restoration of customization and integration between multiple vendors' products. Cost is also increased, particularly in the case of hot and warm recovery sites, if multiple hardware types must be maintained.

✔ **Higher software costs:** Multiple equivalent solutions often require multiple tools and utilities, including anti-malware software and management tools, to secure and maintain each solution according to its own requirements. In a large enterprise requiring license control, splitting licensing among multiple products may result in the organization missing out on volume discounts.

✔ **Redundancy:** In addition to complexities in technology, you must consider the number of resource silos and other types of inappropriate or undesirable redundancy in place in the existing enterprise configuration.

Some types of redundancy are beneficial, however (See the "Implementing desirable redundancy" section, later in the chapter.)

Planning for Consolidation

In almost all enterprise realignments, a conflict exists between the investment in the existing environment and the cost of a rip-and-replace clean start. It's imperative that you take a complete accounting of skills, technologies, facilities, service agreements, licensing contracts, and existing strategic plans to identify elements that can be used in the new architecture.

The most important thing to remember during this analysis is very simple: *Sunk costs should never be the sole deciding factor for staying with an existing solution.*

Additionally, while you don't want to throw good money after bad by allowing sunk costs — that is, money already spent on an existing solution — to be the deciding factor for future purchases, you can conserve value by reallocating or reusing existing technological and human resources when possible.

Even when efforts require rip-and-replace changes, you can often reuse components and technologies for salvage and transfer to the new architectural format. Don't overlook existing skill sets and detailed knowledge of localized network and system issues when planning for major change.

Levels of planning

Planning is the process for making decisions about the future. In business, it involves identifying goals and objectives, determining the steps necessary to achieve them, arranging for necessary resources, and developing a process for implementation and monitoring.

Planning has three fundamental levels:

✔ **Strategic planning,** which is long term (at least 3 to 5 years out), encompasses the entire organization, and occurs at the executive level.

✔ **Tactical planning,** which is medium-term planning (1 to 2 years) and occurs at the middle-management level. Tactical plans are developed from strategic plans.

✔ **Operational planning,** which is short term, occurs at the business unit or workgroup level and is concerned with day-to-day operations. Operational plans are developed from tactical plans.

Applying the 80/20 rule

You may have heard of the 80/20 rule, also known as the *Pareto Principle*. In essence, the 80/20 rule states that 80 percent of consequences come from 20 percent of possible causes. In technology, applying a similar 80/20 split aids in understanding the impact of application development, resource allocation, user productivity suite selection, and a variety of other broadly applied strategies.

You can apply a variation of the 80/20 rule when selecting standard technologies for use across your enterprise. First, identify the technologies that make up the bulk (approximately 80 percent) of the current environment. Identification of the majority of affected technologies may be as simple as looking at workstation operating systems, or as complex as weighing particular pieces of hardware or software based on their importance to critical business processes. These become the standard technologies. Next, look at the remaining 20 percent and determine whether they can be converted to the standard technologies you identified. Aiming for 80 percent rather than 100 percent compliance ensures that projects can move forward to address the majority of cases, without stalling until you have a perfect 100-percent capability for compliance with project directives and policies.

When making this decision, keep in mind that no technology fulfilling a role in the existing architecture is wholly without value. Otherwise, it would likely not be in place, and not all business processes may be supported by standard technologies. This decision isn't simply a case of majority rules. Instead, it is recognizing the value of using established solutions wherever possible.

Keep the 80/20 rule in mind whenever you're confronted by the full expanse of an enterprise network. It isn't always possible to impose 100 percent solutions, such as a completely standardized workstation hardware and software package used by every person in the enterprise. Enterprise architectural projects become nearly impossible when aiming for unattainable goals, so consider the strategies presented when aiming for the first 80 percent of the desired solution. After that goal has been attained, you can begin planning for 80 percent of what remains.

Finding value

Standardization and modernization initiatives offer distributed and complex organizations opportunities to decrease both support complexity and acquisition cost by taking advantage of economies of scale. Managing 1,000 of one item is cheaper than managing one each of 1,000 similar-but-different items. Vendors often agree to better per-item costs when you contract to purchase large quantities. And when you employ a standard across the extended enterprise, support requirements are greatly simplified.

Workstation hardware and software are often the first elements identified for bulk management, but the selection of a standard server virtualization solution, e-mail service, document imaging system, or authentication mechanism can provide a significant cost savings in terms of support, hardware, software, and facilities management.

Planning for technology end of life

Before beginning an architectural realignment, you must work through all aspects of the process from the high-level strategic vision down to the specifications necessary for evaluation and implementation of each element. This planning doesn't stop at a completed solution, however, because the end of the technology life cycle doesn't always provide a clean expiration.

Planned obsolescence

You must introduce the concept of planned obsolescence into technology-related business processes. For example, you must make decisions regarding lease agreements versus outright purchase before procurement can occur, identify retirement strategies for solutions being phased out, and make sure that media and hardware disposal strategies encompass all solutions eventually.

At times, you may find it necessary to maintain legacy equipment because an alternative doesn't exist or has been deemed too costly to acquire. The worst-case scenario here is that a large segment of the enterprise (all the legacy equipment) may be rendered obsolete or unusable.

Long-term enterprise planning should include cyclic modernization of hardware, software, and media throughout the enterprise to ensure that obsolescence is managed in a planned manner.

Hidden obsolescence

The emergence of service-oriented architectural programming methods has given new viability to legacy systems near the end of their life cycle. By providing a Web service wrapper and securing these systems behind more modern technologies, the lifespan of legacy technologies and old big iron systems may be stretched out almost forever. Prolonging the technology life cycle in such a manner affords time to transfer services to more modern alternatives, but should not be regarded as a permanent long-term strategy.

Hardware replacement, service patch and update, maintenance skills, and even data center facilities requirements can become risks to continued operation when legacy systems are maintained beyond obsolescence. An enterprise architect must identify these systems and plan for their retirement in a controlled fashion or one day they will retire themselves through lack of suitable replacement parts or other similar unplanned events.

Cyclic replacement

The rate of change in both hardware and software means that modern technology is not designed to be used indefinitely, or even simply until it fails. Using outdated hardware places limits on your organization's performance and its ability to implement modern software.

Replacing resources in an improvised manner, such as when they fail or when funds become available, may appear to be cost-effective in the short term, but your organization suffers for it long term. That approach keeps technology as a tactical issue when it should be a strategic issue. You must update and modernize systems on a cyclic basis so that you can effectively create long-term technology strategies and budgets. (For more information on this process, see the sidebar "Levels of planning.")

Cyclic replacement, in which a percentage of resources is replaced yearly, also allows for better resource management so that you can plan and schedule a fixed number of upgrades. In addition, cyclic replacement all but eliminates the possibility of having to replace every system at once due to evolutions in critical business technology that suddenly render legacy computing equipment into expensive paperweights.

Maintaining the help desk

Centralization of IT governance and management is often used to gain access to enterprise-wide efficiencies of scale, standardization of technologies and policies, together with support cost reductions. Consolidation of IT operations and services, storage, data centers, and other functions provide additional low-hanging fruit for early enterprise architectural realignment — providing a stable, standard base for future projects.

You must ensure that you have proper help desk functionality during and after consolidation. Employees used to local IT support may become concerned that a centralized help desk won't be as available or responsive, or that nonlocal support personnel won't have knowledge of specialized IT solutions. In addition, cached user credentials, hard-coded hosts, and other issues can create technical difficulties for users during consolidation projects.

Considerations for consolidated help desk functions include

- ✔ Help desk staff must have the necessary administrative privileges or access to tools that proxy those privileges in order to troubleshoot issues in a timely manner.

- ✔ Help desk staff must also have access to all technologies in use throughout the enterprise, including multiple versions, if applicable.

- ✔ Planning should include that today's mobile and geographically diverse workforce is likely to require 24 × 7 help desk support.

While a business unit's IT staff can track problems in a spreadsheet or workgroup-level database, a centralized help desk requires a more robust tracking solution. Both commercial off-the-shelf and free open source help desk solutions are available, and organizations with unique needs may find it more effective to develop their own applications.

An efficient and effective help desk can be of great assistance with user acceptance of centralized services. A slow and incompetent help desk (or even just one that appears that way), on the other hand, can sabotage future projects by alienating users.

Consolidating skills

Consolidation and reorganization initiatives provide you with an opportunity to improve the maturity level of your enterprise by creating focus support groups, such as workstation support, database administration, or application development. Many home-grown or decentralized enterprise settings include support staff members best described as jacks of all trades (and masters of none or very few). This inevitable result is created by the ad-hoc addition of technologies and solutions, rearrangement of personnel due to bureaucratic reorganization, or realignment of support tasks to meet changes in personnel and environment. These actions may also result in support personnel performing duties outside their skill sets, leading to inefficiencies and increased training costs.

The greatest impediments to skill concentration efforts include the funding source for each position and concerns over job loss in the more condensed areas. Take care to identify the source of funding for each position and negotiate with the responsible authority to ensure that value received meets requirements for value funded from each. Work with HR to address concerns over job loss as well as support staff satisfaction with focused skill alignment before making staff changes.

In distributed enterprises with remote or satellite locations, resource consolidation also includes personnel and skills. Keeping a full complement of IT professionals with advanced skills in each satellite location is impractical. It is more efficient to have those personnel with advanced skills in a central location, able to address issues that arise in any location. Not every site needs experts in security, authentication, database administration, or networking on premises. Local (or regional) support personnel may still be necessary to handle hardware and end-user issues. Consolidation of personnel and skills also allows organizations to reduce the number of jack-of-all-trades support personnel commonly found in business units or small remote offices.

Consolidating personnel into focused groups enables each member to develop greater depth of skill and to take advantage of discounted group training opportunities. Consolidation not only allows for more efficient administration and troubleshooting, but also may lead to improved or greater utilization of existing solutions. Advanced software features are often not used simply because the technical staff doesn't have the knowledge to support them adequately.

Grouping personnel also permits adequate support coverage in the event of employee vacation or personnel turnover. This consolidation has the added benefit of improving the morale of technical staffers by allowing them to take desired vacations. Technical personnel may also enjoy more opportunities for advancement than when siloed together with independent enterprise elements, reducing turnover and retention issues.

The process of reorganizing to assign duties based on skills is referred to as *support skill alignment*. The first step in the process is conducting a skills assessment of all support personnel. The second is to identify existing roles and technologies. You can then align personnel with roles and technologies based on skill. This process also allows you to identify any deficient skill areas fairly quickly. The longer it has been since the last support skill realignment was performed, the greater the opportunity for value.

Addressing Concerns about Standardization

Some scholars note that the U.S. Civil War may well have been won due to the Northern states enjoying a standard rail gauge — distance between the rails — allowing the Union to move materials anywhere in the North on the same trains. In the Southern states, rail systems lacked standardization in gauge and rail size, requiring materials to be moved from train to train at each interchange.

Although beneficial in many ways, standardization does impose limitations on user preference, flexibility, and customization, and opposition to standardization can occur at various levels of an organization. Executives and upper management may balk at the cost involved in replacing nonstandard technology. Users may express concern over a perceived loss of functionality or having to learn unfamiliar software. Technical personnel with a strong preference between free open source and commercial off-the-shelf products may fight to retain their preferred technologies. They may even be concerned for their jobs if their skill sets become unnecessary.

Even if an individual's opposition appears to be unfounded or irrational, you should treat those concerns as valid until proven otherwise. Be sure to follow up with the appropriate research and communication.

The following sections address the more common standardization issues you may encounter, along with possible solutions.

Reduced functionality

The biggest issue, and potentially the most valid one, is likely to be the concern over loss of functionality. What if functionality available in the current solution is not present in the new one? Although standard business productivity software, such as word processors, e-mail clients, or spreadsheet applications, tend to have similar performance, it becomes more of a concern if the software has been customized through the use of templates, macros, or workflows.

You can address this concern by communicating with key personnel in business units in order to identify functionality that is crucial to critical business processes, including customizations. If this functionality is not present in the new solution, you will need to have technical staff work with business personnel to develop an alternative solution. Some changes, such as loss of local administrative rights necessary to install personal software, can improve enteprise-wide system stability and facilitate a central registry of installed software.

You shouldn't expect to achieve 100 percent standardization in computing platforms and software overnight (or perhaps ever), and you may need to allow some variation, but it should be the exception rather than the rule. For example, if your organization uses internal Web design personnel, it may demonstrate a need for multiple computing platforms to ensure that the site will display correctly for users of multiple common computing platforms and browsers.

Although some variation is likely to occur, remember that allowing too much variation defeats the purpose of standardization. Where possible, variation should be based on business value instead of political reasons or personal preference.

Decreased productivity

Standardization opponents often point to the disruption and decreased productivity that occur when technologies change as a reason to maintain the status quo. While these issues do occur, they're temporary, and you can handle them with change management and training.

You should identify the solutions being used by the majority of users and determine whether they are suitable for use as the standard in order to reduce the level of disruption to the majority of users and reduce opposition in the user base.

Incompatibility with existing applications

Opponents may also raise concerns about compatibility with existing applications. For example, one of the more common elements to standardize is an enterprise's database management system. Some applications require a specific database back end, such as Oracle or Microsoft SQL, and if that database isn't selected as the standard, these applications will no longer function.

Compatibility issues can arise with file stores as well, particularly with regard to case sensitivity. Moving from a case-sensitive operating system such as Linux to a case-insensitive one such as Microsoft Windows requires greater effort to ensure that filenames that differ only by case are not overwritten.

You should consider these concerns when selecting standard technologies to avoid rendering archive documents unreadable or isolating a mission-critical application. Older legacy solutions may require interface solutions in the form of customized software in order to function properly in a standardized environment.

Risk of technology monoculture

The old adage "Don't put all your eggs in one basket" can be a warning against homogenous technology solutions, also referred to as *technology monocultures*. An example of a technology monoculture is a network of computers running the same operating system or application suites from a single vendor.

Opponents of standardization, particularly standardization involving commercial software, often warn against technology monocultures because of the potential for increased risk due to the rapid proliferation of malware (such as viruses or worms) throughout similar systems, and similar vulnerabilities in multiple products by the same vendor, which may compromise the entire application stack.

Although this concern is valid, keep in mind that diversity alone doesn't automatically improve security. Diversity is just one layer of defense, the advantages of which you can explore in Chapter 17. You must weigh the potential security benefits of diversity against the definite complications caused in disaster recovery planning and patch management.

Preparing for opposition

You will encounter opposition to consolidation for a variety of reasons. In addition to concerns over disruption of business, loss of functionality, and other issues, you'll encounter more personal concerns, such as loss of authority, administrative access, and direct access to hardware. These types of personal concerns usually come up when past decisions on access were based on wants and desires instead of roles and responsibilities. As well, management at all levels of the organization may express concerns over the transfer of strategic budgeting and personnel costs associated with consolidation.

As is to be expected, one of the key factors in a successful centralization or consolidation project is funding. When resources are centralized, funding should be managed as a budgeted expense for the organization, not as a per-item cost (per user, per system, or per network connection). Opponents of consolidation may state that those business units with lower per-item costs would not benefit from consolidation. By focusing on parts instead of the whole, these objections may overshadow the projected reduction in cost or increase in capability for the entire organization. In some cases, the use of a consumption-based chargeback model can address widely variant consumption of noncore IT services, allowing departments to be billed only for the products and services they consume. Network infrastructure, identity management, and a central collaboration platform are typically best managed as capital expenses to ensure uniform availability and use enterprise-wide.

Inevitably, someone will suggest that the consolidation project begin with a voluntary initiative in which those business units in favor of consolidation or with the greatest need can take advantage of consolidation on a cost-recovery basis. Although this idea may appear sound on the surface, it can lead to the following problems:

✔ Well-funded business units choose not to opt in and instead retain their resource silos.

✔ Other business units are forced to pool their limited resources, despite being barely able to fulfill basic requirements.

✔ Opponents point to the "failure" of the consolidated data center to generate antagonism toward the project.

Communication is critical to alleviating any concerns that may be raised. In addition, it's important to convey the benefits of extending resource availability to nontechnology stakeholders involved in paying for the human or tech resources in question. This approach ensures that value received is fully recognized in comparison to value invested.

Consolidating the Data Center

Enterprise architecture projects may involve efforts to consolidate separate information technology silos into a centralized data center, to consolidate technology resources already within the data center, or both. Each of these situations offers opportunities for "low-hanging fruit" projects that result in resource availability for future projects; administrative, procurement, and licensing cost reductions; and an overall decrease in complexity.

The most effective solution for dealing with separate information resource silos (including technology, personnel, and skills) is consolidation into a centralized data center. In addition to restructuring resources, this type of consolidation requires changes to administrative procedures, such as planning, budgeting, procurement, and acquisition. These procedures, if currently taking place within business units, will need to take place at a higher level.

Data center consolidation solutions affect the entire organization, including internal and external users, interconnectivity with partners via data transfer and extranets, and internal communications.

Even though users are affected, information technology implementers and data owners are the most likely employees to be concerned with changes to the data center. As such, you must ensure that their concerns are addressed before, during, and after changes occur.

Although you can perform many functions faster and more efficiently through a centralized data center, you may be able to isolate remote sites from access to critical services through issues with authentication and network connectivity. You must have a clear understanding of your enterprise's remote sites and the needs of remote users prior to consolidation.

You must also be aware of internal and external threats to the data center and include disaster recovery and continuity of operations at every step during consolidation and normal operations. Even concerns over the potential of particular threats, such as the recent H1N1 outbreak, may lead to a significant reduction in operational staff or isolation of facilities. Proper data center planning, such as including the ability to manage servers remotely, can improve continuity of operations.

Identifying the benefits

Data center consolidation has many benefits, both near and long term, although direct cost savings isn't always the end result. Often, the undesirable redundant resources are retasked elsewhere within the organization to improve functionality or desirable redundancy. If reallocation of resources to more appropriate tasks is part of your consolidation project, you must ensure that the value of that decision is communicated and explained to executives.

The following sections cover some common benefits of data center consolidation.

Improved resource use

In general, resource use is improved by consolidating services running on multiple servers onto a fewer larger, more capable systems with the same or less administrative overhead. Consolidation also eliminates resource silos, which often included redundant technologies. Silo-elimination results in greater availability of existing specialty resources across the organization, more extensive pooled resources such as storage grids and high-performance computing, and greater return on investment for new technology initiatives.

For example, some solutions, such as the popular Blackberry Enterprise Server (BES), may be too costly for each business sub-unit in a siloed enterprise but become very affordable as a central service made available enterprise-wide. Sharing of resources is perhaps the most fundamental and long-term advantage that exists in distributed enterprise networks.

Other benefits to resource sharing include the following:

- ✔ More universal resource access for the entire user base, provided that licensing and resource capacity planning are adequate for extended availability.

- ✔ Elimination or reduction of political maneuvering for the best/newest/ best-looking systems by ensuring that all business elements are regularly updated with technologies adequate to meet the needs and be the same across the user base.

- ✔ Ensured access to shared resources for all business units, reducing the "have or have-not" effect that often plagues business sub-units that are lower in the organization's hierarchy.

- ✔ Enhancement of technology agility by allowing newly implemented solutions to become available across the enterprise.

Improved document recovery

Consolidation and integration initiatives also provide an opportunity to improve document management capabilities. You can enhance storage use and user access capability by moving shared file storage to a content management, wiki, or portal solution that supports document versioning and user self-recovery potential. Automatically tracking major and minor revisions allows users to rollback to earlier document versions on their own without requiring more resource-intensive efforts, such as restoring from backup tape. Automatic caching of deleted files is another time-saving feature.

Versioning, self-serve recovery, and caching deleted files can all speed user recovery time, reduce support overhead, and improve transparency in business process. However, these features require greater storage capacity for multiple copies of data and may impact legal mandates for discovery. Communication with the organization's legal counsel and planning for adequate storage should be conducted before beginning document recovery initiatives.

Improved security

Consolidation creates opportunities for improved security in the following ways:

- ✔ The area of exposure is reduced by minimizing the transmission of data.

- ✔ The risk of accidental exposure of sensitive data is reduced by storing it in a secured central location instead of having an uncontrolled number of copies throughout the organization.

✔ It is easier to apply security updates and secure configurations to a smaller number of similarly configured systems than to systems with a wide variation in hardware, software, and system settings.

✔ Justification for purchasing security products is simpler, as both the cost and number of the products are reduced through a lower system count.

Additional benefits

In addition to the preceding advantages, your organization may also realize any or all of the following benefits, depending on the success of the consolidation effort:

✔ File storage and backup solutions can take advantage of economy of scale, providing a lower cost to store and back up data in a centralized fashion.

✔ Service delivery improves as resources become more well-connected, reducing the chances of some elements of a critical process being unavailable due to network issues or overly complex methods of connectivity.

✔ Increased data availability to executives (via consolidation of database and other information resources) results in improved strategic decision-making capabilities.

Reducing complexity through virtualization

Virtualization of servers reduces complexity by decreasing the number of physical servers that must be maintained. The physical servers that host virtual systems must be robust; however, one robust server can host as many virtual systems as its processing power, memory, and storage will allow. The physical system can host virtual systems with the same or different operating systems, depending upon the virtualization technology in use.

Because a virtual server is, in essence, a file on the host server, it can be moved from one physical host to another very quickly and, in some cases, automatically. This ability allows critical services to be restored rapidly in the event of a hardware failure. Finding a server with the same hardware configuration is not necessary, as it would be with a traditional server.

There are many other benefits to virtualization, as well as issues that must be considered, and these are discussed in detail in Chapter 13.

Implementing desirable redundancy

The primary focus of consolidation is reducing undesirable redundancy, but not all redundancy is undesirable. Redundancy in systems, services, storage, and capability can make an organization more resilient against disruptions in business due to disasters or technology-related issues. Consolidation allows organizations to take the resultant cost savings and reinvest it in desirable redundancy supporting key business functions.

Be diligent when identifying redundancies for elimination so that desirable redundancy is not eliminated. Examples of desirable redundancy include

✔ **Data storage solutions:** Redundant data storage solutions, specifically those that make use of RAID (Redundant Array of Independent Disks), are both efficient and fault tolerant. You can find additional information on storage solutions in Chapter 10.

✔ **Failover solutions:** Multiple departmental servers performing the same function is an undesirable redundancy. More desirable is a centralized high-availability cluster in which fewer servers are used but those that are in use provide failover capability to the remaining servers in the event of a hardware failure.

✔ **Load balancing:** Load balancing allows high-demand solutions to spread the workload over multiple servers in order to avoid disruptions in service. In this case, the cost of the extra servers can be justified by reducing disruptions in work during times of peak use.

✔ **Technology personnel:** Having backup personnel is at least as desirable as having backup hardware — more so, when you consider that it is easier to buy a server with the proper specifications than to hire an employee with the proper skill set. Ensuring the multiple members of a support team or workgroup have key skills reduces the impact to the organization when team members are unavailable.

✔ **Alternative sites:** Although expensive, an alternative data center location for disaster recovery purposes may be considered mission critical to your organization. Should a wide-scale disaster occur, rendering your organization's primary data center unusable, having a pre-arranged alternative site outside the affected area means that you can get critical services back up and running more quickly than if you had to scramble for a location after the fact. Chapter 18 has more information on the different types of alternative sites and their appropriate uses.

✔ **Caching:** Caching or proxy servers hold read-only copies of data that changes infrequently, such as name resolution (DNS) and static Web pages. Caching reduces the load on these services, as well as on the network itself.

Planning the centralized facility

While a department or business unit may get away with having a server room, a centralized data center is naturally more robust. Servers require a great deal of power and generate a significant amount of heat. As such, a data center requires greater power capacity than the average server room and more robust environmental controls.

You need to consider capacity planning in the consolidation project and determine power and cooling requirements both short and long term. Failure to do so may result in a data center that reaches capacity halfway through the project, as there may be limits to how much power can be run to the room in an existing structure.

Your planning should include the following elements:

- ✔ Various methods of cooling, such as rack fans, water-cooled cabinets, and blanking panels
- ✔ Organization of rows and racks to minimize hot spots
- ✔ Recovery from natural and human-caused disasters
- ✔ Physical security

When you plan cooling requirements, be sure to consider the hottest months of the year in your geographical location. It will take more cooling capacity to keep a facility at optimum temperature (approximately 70°F) when the outside temperature is 100°F than when it is 75°F.

Standard building fire suppression is rarely suitable for data centers. When renovating existing space for use as a data structure, be sure to budget for overhaul of the fire suppression system as well. Activation of a sprinkler system in a data center can easily cause more damage than a contained fire.

Organizations with existing or planned medium to large data centers may find it helpful to consult professionals in the fields of building design, data center design, fire suppression, and physical security to reduce risk and improve performance.

Automating the Data Center

Use automated solutions wherever possible, particularly in the areas of update/patch management, deployment, and backup solutions. Configuring an automation solution may take significant time initially, but after it is configured properly, it requires very little effort to maintain. In general, automation provides the following benefits:

✔ Allows IT support staff to concentrate on problems instead of maintenance

✔ Improves support staff morale by reducing the number of repetitive and menial tasks they must perform

✔ Provides management consoles that allow support personnel to monitor many systems at once instead of checking each one individually

Standardization is key to benefitting from automation. Implementing automation without reducing complexity in system configuration beforehand just adds complexity and produces more work for support staff.

Patches and updates

In 2009, 5,733 software vulnerabilities were in the National Vulnerability Database, which pulls data from a number of sources. Many of these vulnerabilities are commonly used operating systems and applications. Why these vulnerabilities exist is a topic of discussion for another book. However, the cause of the vulnerabilities is not as important as how to protect your enterprise from exploits. To correct the flaws, vendors release software updates on a set schedule or as needed depending on the severity of the flaw.

Patch management can become overwhelming over a large distributed enterprise without some type of automated patch management solution. Many application solutions have automated update functionality, but without centralized management, IT personnel have difficulty determining whether individual systems are up to date.

Managing antivirus updates can be just as complex, particularly if multiple defensive applications are in use. These updates are also more time-critical, with updates sometimes being released multiple times in a single day, and require automated, centralized solutions in order to protect enterprise resources effectively.

Image-based deployment

A common solution for mass system deployment is to use image-based deployment. This type of deployment utilizes snapshots of configured computers that can be copied to others. An individual system is first configured, patched, and loaded with standard applications and then copied. This image can then be copied to target systems, either over the network or through the use of removable media (USB drives, portable hard drives, etc.), allowing a computer to be loaded to a ready state in minutes without requiring significant human interaction. Standardization is required for this process to be efficient because major changes in computing hardware and any changes in software require a different image.

Supporting both systems and staff

Automated systems still require operational staff. Although some of the following monitoring tasks can be partially automated, human interaction is still necessary:

✔ Logs must be reviewed to look for problems with backups or software updates. Automated alerts may be able to cut the time spent reviewing logs; however, operational staff must still review alerts and prioritize issues.

✔ Operational staff must perform initial configurations and periodic updates.

✔ Backups must be tested to ensure recoverability and backup media must be retired when damaged or as per the established schedule.

You can expect both support and criticism from IT personnel when soliciting input on automation solutions. Some of them may be relieved that they will no longer have to perform the technological equivalent of drudgery, while others may be concerned that their positions will be eliminated.

To help alleviate concerns, stress that the purpose of automation is to make operations more effective, not to replace personnel. Operational staff will always be necessary and some personnel may be reassigned to more useful tasks. Chances are that if your organization's IT staff is performing manual deployments and software updates, either those tasks are not being performed in a timely manner or other work is being left undone.

Backup solutions

Backup solutions can be automated to copy data stores, files, and configuration information weekly, nightly, hourly, or even in real-time, depending on the required recovery point objective (the amount of data that can be lost in the event of a failure). Automation of backup and recovery solutions protects data assets and improves business continuity. You can also obtain efficiency by selecting solutions that don't require physical handling of media on a daily basis, although these solutions may carry increased costs. Even with an automated backup system, technical personnel still need to spend time ensuring that backup media are properly secured, both physically and logically, to protect against any unauthorized release of data. Regular testing of restoration procedures and backup media are also necessary to ensure successful recovery.

You can use imaging solutions for backup and recovery as well as deployment. You can image computers on a regular basis outside of normal business hours for quick recovery in the event of a malware infection, configuration mishap, or software update failure. This type of solution is useful when desktops supporting critical processes have complex, nonstandard software installations.

Chapter 5

Planning Enterprise Information Security

In This Chapter

▶ Understanding the risk of data breaches

▶ Planning to protect information assets

▶ Devising a security policy

▶ Employing security technology

*1*nformation has value. It's an asset that can be worth much more than the hardware on which it is stored. Consider how costly the following events might be to a business:

- ✔ An Internet-based retailer experiences problems with Web services, preventing customers from placing orders.

- ✔ A file is copied to the wrong server, resulting in proprietary information being available on a company's public Web site.

- ✔ A programming team is tasked with making critical changes to a legacy production application, but the source code was lost months ago.

- ✔ A company loses several weeks' worth of billing data after a server crash. Although the data was scheduled to be backed up, the error messages in the backup log files were missed, or the backup was untested and failed during recovery.

- ✔ Network connectivity issues prevent call center customer service personnel from accessing customer data.

Without proper planning and organization, your organization risks not only data loss, but also the capability to use data as required. This chapter gives you an overview of layered strategies for enterprise data protection, strategies for extending data access beyond the enterprise, and security policies. (Later chapters provide more detailed coverage of specific defensive strategies.)

Protecting Enterprise Data

Just as an organization secures its facilities, it must secure its information. All businesses have to be concerned about *data breaches* — the inadvertent release of sensitive or protected data — because no industry is exempt. Common ways in which data is revealed include, but are certainly not limited to, the following:

- ✔ Theft of equipment (particularly laptops) containing unencrypted information
- ✔ Equipment discovered missing during periodic inventory checks
- ✔ Confidential data posted to a company's public Web site or inadequately secured accessible location
- ✔ Improper disposal of data processing equipment
- ✔ Accidental exposure through e-mail

The source of the breach may be internal or external and either accidental or malicious. In the case of theft of hardware, the data may not even be the target. Many breaches are small, fortunately, but the larger the organization, the greater the risk of a large breach. Common targets for data theft include universities, banks, credit-card companies, and information clearinghouses, and that information can be used for identity theft and credit-card fraud. Table 5-1 illustrates how common these data breaches are.

Table 5-1	Recent Large Data Breaches	
Date Announced	*Organization*	*Number of Records Involved*
Jan. 1, 2009	Heartland Payment Systems	130 million
Jan. 17, 2009	TJX Cos., Inc.	94 million
Oct. 5, 2009	National Archives and Records Administration	76 million
Oct. 6, 2008	T-Mobile	17 million

Source: Open Security Foundation's DataLossDB (http://datalossdb.org)

Due to the prevalence of breaches and the amount of damage they can cause, many states have enacted data breach notification laws that force organizations to notify customers or employees if their personal information has been released. In addition, data breaches can result in an organization being fined or being required to pay for credit monitoring services for those whose information was released. Beyond the initial monetary costs, a breach can also damage a company's reputation, causing loss of customer trust and reduced sales.

 Some federal laws also require notification. The recent expansion of the Health Insurance Portability and Accountability Act (HIPAA) by the Health Information Technology for Economic and Clinical Health (HITECH) Act, for example, requires both patients and the government to be notified of any breach that involves the records of more than 500 patients.

Because of the risks, you must make information security a priority. The following sections give you a look at security from a planning perspective. Chapter 17 delves into security measures in detail.

Creating a Security Plan

You must identify and include security requirements in all stages of planning and for all levels of your enterprise architecture. Implementation can't start until the security requirements for all resources have been identified. Physical security requirements need at least as much attention as logical security requirements, as lost or stolen equipment is one of the main causes of data breaches.

Logical security measures other than strong encryption do little more than delay a determined data thief who has access to physical equipment — and with desktop computing power exceeding that of the world's top supercomputer less than a decade ago, even strong encryption can eventually be overcome by raw processing power. Attackers can access sensitive information by using tools intended for use by law enforcement, security personnel, or forensic investigators. In some cases, an attacker doesn't need to have physical possession of the machine, but only needs long enough to boot the system off a bootable USB drive or CD containing forensic tools. Attackers may also search for passwords that will allow them access to sensitive data at a later date.

You must be aware of current and emerging security threats, including both malware and vulnerabilities in technologies currently in use and being considered for future use. You also need to consider user training requirements to protect against social engineering and to ensure that users know, understand, and are capable of following any new security policies.

Use encryption whenever sensitive data is stored, processed, or transmitted, particularly on portable devices and when service-oriented architecture (SOA) is used to integrate legacy systems that are incapable of employing modern security mechanisms, such as secure transport protocols and high-strength encryption algorithms. SOA and SOA wrappers for legacy system protection are discussed in Chapter 11.

Design a workable program

The key to success for any enterprise architecture initiative is having a clear, well-developed security program with identified requirements and attainable goals. Breaking your program into smaller manageable projects ensures that new technology meets your organization's needs before full implementation; establishes clear, distinct goals that can be easily conveyed to the technology implementers; and reduces users' fear of change by taking things one step at a time.

It's also critical to ensure that expectations are reasonable, starting from the top of the organization. Executives must have a firm grasp of project goals to guarantee funding and to communicate those goals to middle management and rank-and-file employees.

Use a layered framework

Security is more than simply the sum of its parts, and it takes more than parts to implement a security framework. Security implemented in an unplanned manner may be effective, but adding elements ad-hoc increases complexity and support requirements, eventually reducing the effectiveness of each element.

As discussed in Chapter 4, however, some complexity is desirable. Using different security technologies keeps attackers from using the same tools to bypass multiple layers of security. For example, in a network configuration that includes a so-called demilitarized zone to segregate computers that must communicate with both the Internet and the internal network, multiple firewalls are used. The attack strategy used on the first firewall is unlikely to work on the second if they use different technologies.

Basically, an enterprise security strategy must include a layered framework to protect the data. A layered approach involves applying security measures to the following elements:

- Data

- Applications that access the data

- Hosts on which the applications and data reside

- Network on which the hosts reside

- Perimeter separating your organization's network from the public network

- Facility housing the computing equipment

This framework, shown in Figure 5-1, is common to both information security and physical security and may be referred to as *concentric-ring security, layered security,* or *defense in depth.* It's supported by security standards and policies, which we address in later sections in this chapter.

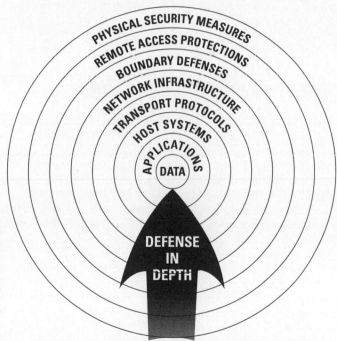

Figure 5-1:
A simple example of the Layered Defense strategy.

Just as a building is only as secure as its least protected entry point, your enterprise is only as secure as its least protected host. One computer with inadequate protections can be compromised even within a protected network and then used to target other systems. Local security compromise is likely to occur in organizations where business units are responsible for maintaining the security of their own systems or where automated patch and update management is not in use.

You may also need to create layers of security around legacy systems or particularly sensitive data to protect them from internal attackers as well as external ones. This may involve the use of technologies such as virtual private networks or shielded subnets, or may simply be a matter of allowing users to access data only through encrypted Web service interfaces. Shielding the way in which data is accessed or arranged prevents exposing information that could be used in an attack.

A simple example is requiring the use of user-friendly error messages in applications. If an application (including a Web page) generates an error, the end user should never see debugging information because it provides information that may be used in an attack, such as application and database server names; database, table, and field names; file locations; and directory structure.

Functions such as service-oriented application wrappers and virtualized servers on a physical host may require the entire set of layered defenses, so this framework can be applied to individual functions as well as to the enterprise as a whole.

Implement security standards

Give strong consideration to conforming to an information security standard. Doing so not only increases the effectiveness of your enterprise's security program but also allows your organization to demonstrate that it follows information security best practices. This standard can reassure customers, partners, and internal users alike that your organization takes information security seriously and is protecting data in an appropriate and approved manner. In addition, if a data breach does occur, it's better to demonstrate that you were being proactive and following a standard when the breach occurred rather than to be found negligent.

Some of the frameworks mentioned in Chapter 3 have information security components, but there are quite a few standards for which information security is the main focus. Following are some of the most commonly used standards:

✔ ISO/IEC 27000 series, published by the International Organization for Standardization (www.iso.org)

✔ Systems Security Engineering Capability Maturity Model (www.sse-cmm.org)

✔ The Standard of Good Practice for Information Security, published by the Information Security Forum (www.isfsecuritystandard.com)

✔ Special Publication 800 standards, published by the U.S. National Institute of Standards and Technology (csrc.nist.gov)

✔ Federal Information Processing Standards (www.itl.nist.gov/fipspubs)

Some states, such as Texas, have their own legislated information security standards, and various industries require specific security practices be put in place. For example, the Payment Card Industry Data Security Standards (PCI DSS) are used by entities that process credit card transactions.

View security as a program, not as a project

Projects have a beginning and an end, but programs are continuous. You must understand — and make sure that executives understand — that the completion of the firewall installation project, for example, does not mean that your organization's network will always be protected. Firewalls and other security appliances and tools require ongoing maintenance and attention to ensure that they remain effective.

Attackers are continuously looking for vulnerabilities and developing methods to exploit them. Thousands of viruses are released every year, along with many other assaults. It isn't much of an exaggeration to say that by the time you say, "The network is now secure," a new virus or other technique for exploitation has been developed or a new vulnerability discovered.

Security is a constant game of cat-and-mouse. The enterprise, as the defender, has a limited set of tools and finite resources for protecting the environment, while there are countless numbers of attackers with access to (almost) limitless attack tools that vary in scope, complexity, and sophistication.

Keep security simple

With security, you can have too much of a good thing. You must find the proper balance between security and usability, or risk having users bypassing controls in order to perform their jobs. For example, password policies that call for frequent expiration of complex passwords may lead to users writing down passwords and storing them in convenient (but insecure) places.

IT security professionals can also suffer the effects of too much complexity. They often want to log and monitor everything, which can be detrimental to the health of the network without the proper tools to filter those logs into usable data. You could compare logs to surveillance footage from security cameras: They're excellent after-the-fact investigation tools, but without the proper detection and alert capabilities they do little to prevent an incident from occurring.

Developing a Security Policy

A comprehensive security policy is necessary so that all network users, both technical and nontechnical, are aware of the enterprise's required security controls. The policy should balance security with usability, and its procedures must work hand in hand with business processes to avoid disruption of normal operations. Requiring an employee who has forgotten his password to report to the IT office and show proper identification, for example, may be secure, but it's also time consuming and cumbersome.

The following sections examine how to create, gain approval for, and maintain a security policy.

Classifying data to be secured

You need to know the type of information that is on your network before you can dictate policies regarding its security. If you've selected an IT governance framework (see Chapter 3), it's likely to have a specific process for data classification. At a minimum, the data storage survey (see Chapter 10) should reveal enough information for you to classify your organization's data by business function, sensitivity, owner, and known security requirements based on legal or contractual mandates.

Addressing basic security elements

A security policy needs to be tailored to the enterprise, but it should address some basic universal elements:

- **Administrative access:** The security policy should contain rules that govern the creation, use, and management of accounts with administrative access.

- **Acceptable use:** The policy should include an acceptable-use policy so that appropriate use of technology is clearly defined.

✔ **Authorized software:** The policy should cover procedures for software installation, including whether end users are allowed to install software on their own.

✔ **Data disposal:** The policy dictates the procedures to follow when disposing of storage media that may contain data. (Chapter 10 discusses data disposal in detail.)

✔ **Encryption:** The security policy should establish the appropriate use of encryption as well as approved mechanisms.

✔ **Firewall:** Rules for how the organization's firewalls will manage network traffic should be incorporated into the policy, including procedures for updating and changing rules.

✔ **Incident management:** The security policy should include clearly defined procedures for security incident handling and reporting.

✔ **Malware:** The policy should indicate anti-malware software requirements, including configuration, definition updates, scanning frequency, and procedures to follow in the event of infection.

✔ **Passwords:** The policy should state the organization's requirements for creating and managing passwords. Remember to include requirements for administrative and service account passwords. You can find password guidelines, such as length and complexity, in Chapter 7.

✔ **Server and workstation hardening:** The policy should provide guidance on necessary security controls for base installations of servers and workstations, appropriate to whatever platforms are in use. This policy can include items such as removal of unnecessary services or changing default passwords.

✔ **Social engineering awareness:** *Social engineering* is a term used to describe a variety of psychological techniques directed against people, such as manipulation, deceit, or impersonation. The security policy should take social engineering into account when addressing relevant policy elements such as passwords, social media, and telephone procedures.

✔ **Social media:** The policy should specify how the organization uses social media and how employees are expected to represent the organization on social networking sites.

✔ **Telephone procedures:** The policy should include what type of information can be provided over the telephone and under what circumstances.

✔ **Waste disposal:** Because attackers can gain valuable information from corporate trash, proper waste disposal must be addressed.

Getting management approval

You must gain executive commitment to the security policy. Getting management approval serves two purposes:

- ✔ It ensures that those who control the finances understand that security is important and must be budgeted for.

- ✔ It lets employees know that security is a valid business concern.

Employees are more likely to follow the lead of top management. If top management has to follow the same security procedures as rank and file employees, those rank and file employees are more likely to take it seriously. Executives need to lead by example. The executive who orders IT to allow him to use his initials as a password while forcing everyone else to use complex passwords sends a message to employees that security is a hindrance and not important.

Risk assessments (see Chapter 6) are critical tools for showing management the value of the procedures outlined in the security policy. Although the average executive is unlikely to understand technical details of vulnerabilities, exploits, and countermeasures, he is going to understand risk when phrased in terms of probability and effect on the business.

Maintaining the policy

Security policies are living documents, and as such, they should be reviewed and updated periodically. The following events may also trigger a review of the security policy:

- ✔ Emerging security threats
- ✔ Changes in business functionality or data classification
- ✔ Implementation of new technology
- ✔ Mergers and acquisitions
- ✔ Security incidents

With the exception of security incidents, these triggers involve possible changes to security policies due to changes in the environment. Security incidents should elicit a review of the security policy because a successful occurrence indicates that something, somewhere, failed. That failure may be technical, procedural, or a combination of both. After the enterprise is restored to a secure state and the incident investigated, the security policy should be reviewed for improvement based on the results of that investigation.

Training employees

After the policies are in place, employees must be educated about the policies and the reasons behind them. They must also have clear instructions for reporting suspicious behavior or events. This training should be conducted regularly, to help keep employees alert and up-to-date on new procedures.

Employee training can be performed electronically using existing information portals, or in person in small units or larger classes. Having properly trained staff leading these events is critical in order to increase the likelihood of employees both understanding the presented material and accepting the training's validity. Larger organizations usually have training staff available through their human resources office. An organization lacking experienced training staff should consider hiring an outside firm to provide this support.

Issues may come up in training sessions that aren't addressed in the security policy. Trainers should note these issues in an after-action review so that the related policies can be reviewed and updated, if necessary.

Using Technology to Support Security Operations

Technology exists to support the business process; the business process doesn't exist to follow selected technology constraints. Business processes are often modified to include new technology, but there should always be a valid business reason behind it, such as improving efficiency or adding value. However, an organization should not be expected to change its operations only because a new application was purchased or developed. Information technology is simply a logistical component that supports operational functions.

In short, technology must be aligned with business goals, not the other way around. One way this can be accomplished is through the application of clear governance principles, as discussed in Chapter 3. Other ways follow.

HITECH Act

An example of regulatory mandates affecting partner organizations involves the HITECH Act, mentioned earlier in this chapter. This Act did not just specify requirements for data breach notification; it also formally required business associates of entities covered by HIPAA to comply with the standards and implementation specifications in HIPAA security rule where formerly they were required only to "appropriately safeguard" the information. Examples of business associates include partner entities that perform functions such as claims processing, billing, transcription services, or others that require access to protected health information.

Use collaborative technologies

Collaborative technologies can be of tremendous assistance during any project, from something as simple as a server upgrade to a complete migration of technology from one platform to another. These technologies include, but are not limited to

- E-mail and messaging
- Discussion boards and wikis
- Scheduling and task management
- Conferencing (Web, voice, and video)

The architect must ensure that these solutions are in place before beginning a security project so as to promote open communication among all stakeholders. Collaboration tools can serve to

- Communicate new security policies
- Announce potential threats
- Detail how to address, report, or respond to these risks
- Remind users of their responsibilities with regards to security
- Provide a mechanism for security incident reporting

You'll explore collaboration solutions and communication technologies in more depth in Chapters 8 and 9.

Remain flexible

Making changes to production architecture is difficult, at best, particularly with regard to mission critical architecture. In a production environment, you should expect that there have been changes to the resources involved since the initial review was conducted, and plans must be updated accordingly in order to avoid disruption of services.

Flexibility is just as necessary for long-term planning, but remaining adaptable becomes more complex as the environment fluctuates from year to year due to changes in technology, operations, business focus, and regulatory or legislative mandates. It is not unusual for organizational priority to shift from one topic of technology to another, and sometimes these shifts cause plans to change rapidly. For example, if your organization decides that the project to switch from regular telephone lines to Voice over Internet Protocol (VoIP) is to be given priority, it also means that any projects having to do with network infrastructure upgrades also need increased priority.

Inclusion of entirely new vistas of computational capability can require significant changes to existing strategies and policies. The emergence of cloud computing has introduced difficulties for organizations using strict ITIL service management practices due to the black-box nature of cloud service host details. Other organizations concerned over the protection of confidential or proprietary information may find data stored in public clouds to be available for disclosure requests under different legal systems, depending on where the cloud storage hosts are located. Until cloud computing has matured and its processes become more transparent, many organizations have been forced to adopt only private cloud services or avoid cloud computing altogether to retain alignment with existing service and security management strategies.

Plan for partner relationships

Increasingly, organizations are entering into partner relationships with other businesses, customers, vendors, and others that all require some type of integrated external connectivity and information sharing. Examples include vendor-managed inventory systems, joint ventures, automated shipping management, and clearinghouse functions (such as billing and account management).

You must be aware of partner relationships and how they may affect your enterprise, particularly with regard to connectivity and security. Enterprises cannot afford to be blindsided by unforeseen IT requirements due to new regulatory mandates or other requirements imposed on the business due to a partner relationship.

When is outsourcing security a good idea?

Although you can't transfer liability, it may be cost-effective for some organizations to consider outsourcing individual security functions that are laborious or that require specific skills not available within the organization. Surprisingly, some security functions, particularly those that are time consuming, lend themselves well to outsourcing. Organizations considering outsourcing security functions can choose among several models, two examples of which are

✔ **Security as a service:** In this model, economy of scale is used to offer services and products to organizations at substantially lower costs than if the organization had to make the purchase itself. The products and services are owned by the provider and delivered and managed remotely on a pay for use or subscription basis. Antivirus products, managed e-mail products, and

log management services fit into this model. Log management, especially in large organizations with extensive logging capabilities, may be a candidate for outsourcing in order to have access to more robust log management software and 24x7 monitoring.

✔ **Managed security services:** In this model, the hardware or software involved may be owned by either the organization or the provider, but are managed remotely by the provider. These services are more likely to be customizable, and include offerings such as vulnerability scanning, virtual private networking, and firewall management. Smaller organizations may find firewall management to be exceptionally cost effective due to the significant amount of technical expertise that is required to implement and maintain the system.

Outsource only when necessary

Executives often find it tempting to outsource IT services, particularly those in which hardware purchases are required, in order to reduce costs. Technology may become obsolete before it's fully amortized and a company may want to move the costs from the capital budget to the operating budget for accounting purposes. Due to the dynamic nature of information technology, this year's state-of-the-art firewall could be next year's state-of-the-art doorstop.

Data processing and software development are also commonly outsourced functions, but that has the potential to carry significant risk. It should be done only when necessary and then only after carefully reviewing the laws and rules that apply to the data involved in those functions.

The decision to outsource should not be taken lightly or made quickly because it is often easier to streamline local operations than to return operations in-house after an outsourcing failure. Recommend outsourcing only when it's truly necessary to avoid adding complexity or excessive cost to your operating environment. As an alternative to outsourcing, you may want to explore insourcing, in which contract personnel are hired to supplement company personnel.

If you're considering outsourcing to a foreign company (offshoring), it is also necessary to review the applicable laws in that country since information protection and privacy laws may vary. Differing laws may make prosecution or civil lawsuits difficult if the provider violates its contract or engages in illegal activity such as data theft. In addition, even when there are appropriate laws in place, they may rarely be enforced. There may even be issues with laws in countries through which data is transmitted.

Outsourcing security functions may help reduce your organization's liability by reducing the number of incidents, but it's impossible to outsource liability.

Chapter 6

Complying with Mandates and Managing Risk

In This Chapter

▶ Recognizing the importance of compliance

▶ Reviewing the risk management process

▶ Developing risk management strategies

Inexpensive, powerful computing systems have transformed business operations and levied expanding interconnectivity provided by the Internet to extend services to customers and consumers around the world. As connectivity expands, businesses face ever-expanding regulations and controls over data expression, service availability, and service use. In many industries, specific legislation identifies minimum levels of compliance with risk management and security guidelines; other industries impose specific requirements on their own customers as a mandate for service availability.

You need to be familiar with any regulations, legal mandates, and industry directives that may affect enterprise planning and compliance reporting for your organization. Also, you must create a risk management strategy, both to meet regulatory mandates and to ensure the availability and integrity of data and services necessary for everyday operations.

This chapter presents some issues you may encounter if your organization is subject to some of the more common legal mandates, as well as an introduction to the basics of risk management as it applies to IT Architecture.

Keeping Your Company Compliant

Many laws and industry requirements require detailed documentation and certification of compliance in order to avoid fines, fees, or other negative effects. Any efforts made to develop or realign an enterprise must take into account existing and emerging legal requirements from the very start. For example, logging must be in place before an application is moved into production because without this logging, it may be impossible to comply with privacy or regulatory mandates that require audit trails for viewing or changing data. It's difficult, if not impossible, to review past actions without the proper controls (logging, for example) in place beforehand.

Legal mandates that affect the organization

Legislative responses to issues such as data loss, privacy violations, and fiscal accountability generate an ever-growing number of "alphabet soup" legal requirements that you must incorporate in enterprise planning. These include

- ✔ Sarbanes-Oxley Act (SOX)
- ✔ Gramm-Leach-Bliley Act (GLBA)
- ✔ Health Insurance Portability and Accountability Act (HIPAA)
- ✔ Federal Educational Rights Protection Act (FERPA)
- ✔ Children's Online Privacy Protection Act (COPPA)

Each of these carries its own potential pitfalls when applied to the enterprise, although not every organization will be subject to all, if any, of these requirements. SOX, for example, applies only to publicly traded U.S. companies, and HIPAA applies only to organizations that handle protected health information.

HIPAA requirements for segregation of electronic personal health information from other organizational data, for example, may complicate data storage, backup, and archival planning. Also, mandates for truthful disclosure of intellectual-property ownership under SOX may complicate the use of free open-source software, for which individual package IP ownership may be difficult to document.

You may also find that the mandates themselves are driving your organization's enterprise realignment. Simplification of organizational data storage complexity (see Chapter 10) can provide the basis for realignment in an industry subject to reporting mandates. The emergence of a large body of privacy mandates may drive the reorganization of data access, authentication, logging, and backup strategies.

Many of these laws have common themes, which makes it easier to integrate specific requirements for compliance into more general planning steps. For example, privacy and protection of personally identifying information (PII) are required by privacy laws (such as COPPA, HIPAA, and GLBA) and industry regulations such as the Payment Card Industry Data Security Standards (PCI DSS).

Discovery and retention

Because so many legal investigations and compliance reviews require access to electronic records, you should include provisions for information archival and reporting in your long-term planning. Subpoena-management practices should be firmly in place before requests for data are received to ensure continuity of operations and minimal impact on operations.

An enterprise architect can provide great value to your organization by including data archival, storage, and handling options in your long-term enterprise strategy. Mapping data resources together with details on backup and archival practices for each can act to identify data held beyond a desirable discovery window. This map also provides a ready reference for organizations presented with a subpoena to avoid accidental destruction of data due to normal backup media and archival procedures.

Additional requirements

Beyond information technology–specific directives, legal requirements can include generalized mandates. You must consider accessibility requirements under Section 508 of the Rehabilitation Act of 1973 (amended), for example, in authentication and data access planning. Complex multi-factor or biometric authentication systems may prove difficult to operate for individuals with physically disabling conditions. Public-facing applications that don't support assistive screen reading technologies such as JAWS and Window-Eyes may be unusable by some consumers. You explore the application-design accessibility implications of Section 508 later in this book.

You also need to consider legal requirements that are likely to be enacted in the near future. Following recent large-scale accidental data exposure events, particularly in the retail and financial industries, it is likely that new laws will deal with backup media and other responsibilities in the management of PII. In addition, legislation under consideration could impose mandatory data retention for Internet service providers and other agencies responsible for the storage, processing, and transmission of information that could be useful in law enforcement investigations.

In the United States, multiple states recently passed privacy laws that require encryption in storage and use whenever personally identifying data is collected on citizens living in that location. Many of these laws require not only protective measures, but also a mechanism for registration of the data storage with affected citizens' home state and mandates for reporting security breaches of databases containing personal information. These laws can suddenly affect an organization merely because a person living in one of these states becomes a client, member, or consumer of services that involves entering data classified by their home state's legislature as protected.

Planning to Manage Risk

Risk is based on the probability and impact of events or threats. For information technology, these threats may include theft or loss of computing hardware, unauthorized access to data, denial of service, and identity theft. Much of the "alphabet soup" legislation discussed earlier in this chapter requires formal risk management for certain industries and settings. You must identify risks faced by the enterprise network's configuration, organization, and use. Once identified, you can engineer controls to reduce overall risk and achieve compliance with regulatory mandates.

Regular review of risks and strategies for dealing with each are required because this is a process, not a goal to be achieved once and for all. Emerging regulations and threats present a perpetually moving target. Risk management also provides value to the enterprise by reducing vulnerability and enhancing operational capabilities.

Risk control and management start with the lowest levels of operational readiness such as power, telecom, and network availability. Planning includes technical considerations such as data center management solutions and technology replacement agreements, as well as physical security and data center planning measures (see Chapter 5).

A formal risk management process is necessary for every technology, service, or data deemed critical to your organizational operations. In this process, you identify threats and vulnerabilities, assess risk, and then address the risk. The following sections detail these steps.

Identifying threats

You need to consider all threats that have the potential to cause harm to or interfere with your enterprise information technology resources. After you identify a threat, you must also document any vulnerabilities associated with that threat.

Threats typically fall into three categories: natural or environmental, electronic, or human.

Natural or environmental threats

Natural threats include weather events such as floods, storms, tornadoes, and hurricanes. *Environmental threats* include events such as fire, extended power failures, and water leaks. Natural threats can cause a significant amount of direct physical damage, as well as a general disruption of business. Environmental threats have similar impact. Unlike natural threats, however, they may be caused by human elements with various motivations. You can read more about these motivations in "Human threats," later in this chapter.

Electronic threats

Organizations increasingly depend on the availability of electronic resources as electronic records and digital services permeate aspects of operations from time clock and human resources functions through accounts payable and receivable. This technology dependence creates a target for attackers who may insert malicious code into seemingly innocuous documents, or who may hide attacks in the normal flood of electronic operations and requests for services.

Electronic threats include

- ✔ Malware such as viruses, Trojan horses, and spyware
- ✔ Bugs and weaknesses in software applications and operating systems
- ✔ *Bots* and *botnets,* which are computers infected by malware and controlled by malicious individuals
- ✔ Phishing e-mails, which attempt to trick individuals into providing passwords, bank account numbers, credit card numbers, or other sensitive data to fraudulent Web sites

These threats may be directed at the organization by malicious persons for reasons discussed in the following section or the organization may simply fall victim to them. You can find more detailed information on these and other electronic threats in Chapters 16 and 17.

Exploitation of vulnerabilities associated with these threats can cause disruption of business and the unauthorized release of information. There is also the possibility that workstations and servers within the enterprise could become compromised and be used to attack other organizations.

Human threats

Human threats can be deliberate attacks by malicious individuals for purposes such as causing damage to an organization's assets, data, or reputation, or stealing its physical or electronic assets. These individuals can be criminals, disgruntled employees, or your organization's competition. Industrial espionage — the theft of trade secrets — is a growing problem in many industries.

Not all attempts to circumvent security controls involve malicious intent. Examples of such benign events include propping open a secure door while moving equipment, software developers leaving "back doors" in applications for testing or administrative purposes, or employees sharing login credentials instead of waiting for access requests to be approved.

Human threats aren't limited only to physical actions taken by individuals. The electronic threats discussed in the prior section often originate with or perpetuate because of a human element.

Consider motivation when people are involved because it can help determine the methods they'll use. If industrial espionage is the motivation, attackers may be likely to use social engineering techniques to trick employees into giving them access. Alternatively, a disgruntled employee with revenge in mind may destroy or corrupt data or provide his or her login credentials to unauthorized persons. Other motivations include curiosity, monetary gain, blackmail, and destruction, and other methods include hacking, theft, bribery, denial of service attacks, and system intrusion.

Identifying vulnerabilities

You will continually spend time reviewing emerging and returning vulnerabilities, exploits, and threats that must be dealt with through updates, patches, or changes to protocol and service settings. There's no such thing as "secure forever" — attack and vulnerability options are always evolving into new forms and mechanisms that must be included in enterprise defensive planning. Some online sources for review include

- ✔ The SANS Institute's Top Cyber Security Risks (www.sans.org/top-cyber-security-risks/?ref=top20)
- ✔ United States Computer Emergency Readiness Team (www.us-cert.gov)
- ✔ National Vulnerability Database (http://nvd.nist.gov)
- ✔ SecurityFocus (www.securityfocus.com)
- ✔ Vendor Web sites for software in use in the enterprise

Fixing what you find

Here's a real-life example of how risk assessment can assist with both compliance and security:

I (Kirk) was brought in as a consultant for enterprise and security architecture in a large healthcare organization. One of the vulnerabilities I identified early in my review was the need to allow physicians throughout the area the ability to remotely access medical records stored in the hospital imaging systems. The text-only logon/password combination accessed through an encrypted external connection (not visible to the network-based Intrusion Detection System) without lockouts for multiple failed logons presented an opportunity for unauthorized access. This situation was a significant security issue because the information was both HIPAA-controlled (so it required more secure authentication controls) and a valuable asset for the hospital.

I implemented a host-based Intrusion Detection System to facilitate identification of appropriate access, established Internet Protocol Security policies to allow access only from IP addresses registered to doctors joining the access program, configured automatic logon lockout after three failed attempts within a 15-minute window, and added multi-factor authentication requirements (SecureID tags) to mitigate the risk of unauthorized access to a level gauged acceptable by the organization's risk assessment metrics.

In addition, you need to identify the vulnerabilities specific to your enterprise, based on factors such as your organization's industry, facilities, personnel, and data. You can identify these vulnerabilities by considering scenarios based on threats and motivations identified earlier in your risk assessment process.

Assessing risk

In assessing risk, each threat is analyzed to determine its probability and impact. *Probability* is the likelihood that the threat will materialize into an actual event, and *impact* refers to the loss that would occur from a successful threat event. This loss can be tangible, such as loss of funds, equipment, or personnel, or intangible, such as a loss of reputation.

Insurance companies conduct *quantitative analysis* when determining risk, because they have a significant amount of actuarial data to work with. For example, a comprehensive automobile insurance policy's premiums are based on the cost of the vehicle (the loss the insurance company would suffer if the vehicle was stolen or destroyed) and the probability of that loss occurring. Probability is determined by factors such as how often that particular make and model of vehicle is stolen and where the vehicle is stored and driven. A numerical risk rating is then determined by multiplying probability and impact.

This type of actuarial data is generally not available for information technology. Rapid changes in technology lead to rapid changes in threats, making trend analysis extremely difficult. As such, IT risk assessment typically involves *qualitative analysis*. Instead of numbers, values such as Low, Medium, or High are assigned to probability and impact, and a risk matrix determines the level of risk. You define Low, Medium, and High based on what is appropriate to your organization's business.

You may find that ratings of Low, Medium, and High aren't adequate for your organization. If you require more granularity, you can add ratings such as Very Low or Negligible on the low end or Very High, Severe, or Critical on the high end.

The following sections delve into all three parts of this process — determining probability, determining impact, and calculating a risk rating.

Determining probability

Probability can be determined by looking at how often threat events (both successful and unsuccessful) occur in your organization and in general and also by whether or not there are appropriate countermeasures in place to protect against exploitation of vulnerabilities. For example, if your organization's antivirus software is blocking hundreds of viruses per day, then a probability rating of High could be assigned for any threats involving malware.

For countermeasures, a rating of High might be assigned if no countermeasures are in place, Medium if inadequate countermeasures exist, and Low if the countermeasures in place are sufficient. For example, if a confidential data file is stored in an open file share, the probability of unauthorized access to it would be High; if it's stored in a file share with appropriate access control but weak passwords, it'd be Medium; and if it's stored on an encrypted file share with appropriate access control and strong passwords, it would be Low.

Determining impact

Impact can be determined by the nature and severity of the consequences of a successful threat event. In some cases the impact is simple to establish, such as the cost of repairing or replacing stolen or damaged equipment, the cost of penalties or credit monitoring service in the event of unauthorized access to customer personally identifiable information, or sales lost due to a denial of service attack on your organization's Web site. Deciding the impact rating for loss of reputation or other intangible consequences may be more difficult. However, in a qualitative assessment there is quite a bit of wiggle room.

In all cases, the impact rating depends upon the organization. One company may consider $10,000 in lost sales deserving of a High impact rating, while another might consider that Low. Regardless, these ratings must be defined and used consistently to accurately compare risk between threats.

In circumstances where threat events could lead to loss of life, the impact should always be considered High and may need to be rated even at Very High or Critical, depending upon the potential for harm. Examples of this include threats against network-enabled medical equipment, control software for industrial facilities, or traffic control systems.

Using a risk matrix to determine risk rating

After you assign ratings to probability and impact, you use a risk matrix to determine the risk rating. Figure 6-1 shows a simple risk matrix using ratings of Low, Medium, and High. Note that if probability and impact are both rated as High, the matrix lists the risk rating as Critical. You can also use more granular ratings, which results in a more complex matrix.

		Probability		
		Low	Medium	High
Impact	Low	Low	Low	Medium
	Medium	Low	Medium	High
	High	Medium	High	Critical

Figure 6-1: A simple risk matrix.

Addressing Risk

After you have established the level of risk for the identified threats and vulnerabilities, you should determine the best way to address it. The following sections can help you make this decision.

Prioritizing threats

Generally, risks are addressed in order of priority, highest to lowest. There are four possible strategies that may be used to address an identified threat:

- ✓ **Acceptance:** The risk may be identified, examined, and accepted, provided that the impact is fully understood and recognized.

- ✓ **Avoidance:** The risk may be avoided by selecting an alternative option that does not include the same level of risk or by simply not engaging in the risky behavior.

- ✓ **Mitigation:** The risk may be reduced to an acceptable level by including additional protections or by altering the parameters producing the risk.

- ✓ **Transference:** The risk may be transferred to another responsible party, often through outsourcing or insurance protections.

You can't always avoid or transfer risks completely, and you can't accept many risks simply due to regulatory or legal mandate, as discussed earlier in the section "Keeping Your Company Compliant." Additionally, these strategies are typically applied at the strategic level, such as making the decision to outsource a function, getting insurance policies, or dropping a line of business.

As an enterprise architect, you are likely to select mitigation as the most appropriate strategy to reduce risk to elements of the enterprise, including both physical components and data. Risk mitigation involves taking steps to reduce probability, impact, or both.

Reducing probability

Reducing the probability of a threat event involves employing countermeasures appropriate to the vulnerabilities associated with the threat. Table 6-1 lists some common threats and associated countermeasures, which are discussed in detail in Chapters 16 and 17.

Table 6-1	Common Threats and Countermeasures
Threat	*Countermeasures*
Data exposure from lost or stolen backup media	Encrypt backups and implement greater physical security controls on backup media.
Theft of user credentials from keylogging software	Install anti-malware software and include information about malware in end-user security awareness training.
Data exposure from lost or stolen portable computing or storage devices, such as laptop computers and external hard drives	Encrypt data on laptop computers. Consider prohibiting users from storing high-risk data on portable devices.
Data loss or interruption of business due to exploits of known software security vulnerabilities	Test and apply vendor security patches and updates in a timely manner and apply vendor-recommended workarounds when patches or updates cannot be applied.
Unauthorized access to the corporate network	Install a firewall that blocks unauthorized incoming network traffic.
Employee theft of confidential or proprietary data files	Disable USB ports on computers to prevent users from saving files to flash drives. Implement Data Loss Prevention software to monitor the movement of files across the network.

Threat	Countermeasures
Unauthorized access to data through compromised user login information	Implement multi-factor authentication, such as a combination of passwords and tokens or passwords and biometrics.

Reducing impact

The most effective strategy for reducing impact is to have a comprehensive contingency plan. Contingency plans include actions to take in the event of a specific occurrence. They are closely related to business continuity and disaster recovery plans, which are discussed in Chapter 18. Contingency plans may involve the use of marketing, communications, or public relations personnel to mitigate the loss of reputation that might be encountered from an event such as exposure of custom financial information.

Other strategies include

✓ Implementing redundant solutions such as clusters, load balancing, and alternative sites (discussed in Chapter 4).

✓ Ensuring that copies of critical data are stored in a secure, off-site facility for use in the event that on-site data is corrupted or deleted.

✓ Training users to report suspected security incidents to appropriate personnel as quickly as possible.

✓ Configuring intrusion detection applications, integrity verification solutions, data loss prevention software, and other security solutions to notify appropriate personnel of threat events such as denial of service, attempted theft of data, or unauthorized altering of system files so that the threat may be contained in a timely manner.

Watching out for risk homeostasis

Sometimes a change made to reduce risk can cause people to act in a more risky manner, which offsets the intended reduction. This is known as *risk homeostasis* and can be illustrated by a German case study involving taxicabs equipped with antilock braking systems. Because drivers felt safer, they engaged in riskier behavior and ended up involved in more accidents than prior to the introduction of the "safer" braking systems. Clear and regular reminders of the purpose of security measures can offset this effect somewhat, but the tendency remains. For example, users may be more likely to open unexpected e-mail attachments if they know antivirus software is installed on their workstations.

Choosing appropriate mitigations

The goal of risk mitigation is, quite simply, to reduce risk. You may find that the same amount of overall risk reduction can occur by mitigating a small amount of significant risks across a large number of systems. Because all risk mitigation requires expenditure of resources, be it in the form of money, personnel, or equipment, your organization must obtain the best value out of those resources. A cost benefit analysis may assist with decision making, particularly in the following scenarios:

✔ If the cost of a mitigation strategy exceeds the expected loss, you should investigate other less-expensive strategies.

✔ A mitigation strategy that isn't cost effective for one asset may become so when spread across multiple assets.

✔ The cost of a mitigation strategy may be minimal, but can significantly impact business productivity due to an increase in the time it takes to perform certain tasks.

✔ A mitigation strategy that calls for security measures that are so burdensome to users that they actively try to circumvent it, is a clear waste of resources.

✔ If no mitigation strategies are cost effective and acceptance isn't possible due to regulatory or legal mandates, evaluate the possibility of transferring the risk through outsourcing. Many risk management practices require significant changes in policy or environment, or initial investment. Buy-in from key stakeholders is required in order to obtain these requirements and to effectively mandate organizational alignment with policies and operational practices developed as an outgrowth of enterprise planning. Risk management provides an opportunity to clearly demonstrate the value of enterprise strategies, by providing metrics for measuring relative risk before and after change implementation as well as by illustrating concrete direct-cost-per-instance penalties for failures in data access control or unauthorized exposure.

When enterprise changes can be directly tied to legal or regulatory mandates, funding is much easier to obtain because cost to comply can be directly compared to cost of failure or noncompliance.

Part III
Creating an Enterprise Culture

The 5th Wave
By Rich Tennant

"We're outsourcing everything but our core competency. Once we find out what that is, we'll begin the outsourcing process."

In this part . . .

An effective enterprise is more than just technology; it's also about culture. It's about using the technology to foster communication and collaboration in an effective manner. In this part, we tell you what you need to know to create a successful enterprise culture.

Chapter 7

Developing Identity and Access Management Strategies

In This Chapter
▶ Authorizing access to the enterprise
▶ Planning a strategy for identity management
▶ Putting an identity-management solution in place

A network enterprise includes all components, services, software, equipment, and interconnectivity elements in use by an organization. User identification is fundamental to resource access and control and a central standardized mechanism for access control is the element that bridges components of the enterprise, consolidating siloed users and resources into a cohesive whole. Also, without unique user identification, functions such as accountability and resource availability control are unavailable.

This chapter introduces the concepts of Identity and Access Management (IAM), with a particular focus on the process of identity management, which underlies the topics covered in all later chapters.

Introducing Identity and Access Management (IAM)

Identity and Access Management (IAM) combines identity management and access controls in order to facilitate resource availability and to prevent undesirable exposure of your organization's data. The three steps to IAM are

1. **Identify the user.**

   Credentials are presented that identify the requesting user or service to the enterprise authentication service. Examples of these credentials include a username and password or an access token (such as a smart card) and a personal identification number.

2. **Authenticate the user.**

   The authentication service must determine whether the credentials and the requested resource are valid. Authentication is limited to determining whether the requester and requested resource exist within the authentication boundary (domain or directory, for example).

3. **Authorize access.**

   After successful authentication, access controls (that is, permissions) determine whether the requester is allowed to access the requested resource and within what limits. For example, a user may be allowed database access with read-only permissions, or members of the chief financial officer's staff may have access to sensitive financial documents, while marketing staff would be denied access.

The following sections discuss these steps in detail.

Identifying Users

Identification systems operate based on four general categories of credentials:

- Something users know
- Something users have
- Something users are
- Something users do

The following sections detail these categories.

Custom mechanisms for authentication in high-security environments may also include restrictions for access at specific locations or via specific access terminals. This level of access control is not common in business environments, but the growing integration of Global Positioning Systems (GPS–enabled mobile devices) may make this type of control more attractive to businesses.

Something users know: Password

Perhaps the most widely used type of identification is the alphanumeric user logon and password combination. It easily integrates with standard user interface devices, such as keyboards, mouse-driven on-screen keypress entry, and various assistive technologies.

Password-based identification systems, however, are susceptible to several types of attacks, such as *brute-force attacks,* which sequentially test all possible combinations of numbers, characters, and symbols; *dictionary attacks,* which manipulate common words by replacing letters with numbers (as in passw0rd); and *social-engineering techniques,* which manipulate users into revealing their login credentials.

Password strength

The relative strength of a password is affected by the following factors:

- ✔ **Obscurity:** Identification credentials built on commonly known criteria such as first name/last name logons (john.doe or john-doe, for example) or passwords composed of pet names, birthdays, or personal interests are more easily guessed than those derived from random or unrelated data. Passphrases in the local language are also easily broken by dictionary-based, brute-force attacks.

  Note: Passwords are typically short (6 to14 characters), whereas passphrases are longer (20 to 30-plus characters) phrases or sentences.

- ✔ **Complexity:** Passwords and phrases comprised of simple alphabetic characters are easily broken by dictionary, brute-force, and sequential testing attacks. Password strength can be greatly increased by including mixed-case (upper- and lowercase alphabetic characters), numeric, and symbolic characters. Where supported, passwords developed from two-byte character sets, such as international character sets, extend sequential testing by several orders of magnitude.

- ✔ **Length:** Length is one of the most important elements of password strength. The longer the password, the more complicated sequential brute-force attacks become. A four-character, alphabetic-only password requires more than 450,000 tests, while an eight-character password of the same type requires more than 400 billion tests to try every possible combination.

- ✔ **Expiration date:** Passwords that are never changed are vulnerable to brute-force testing in which only a small number of tests are conducted over an extended period of time, which may avoid detection. With enough time, any fixed password will eventually be compromised by automated guessing. By forcing password changes through regular expiration, maintaining password history tracking, and imposing minimum time between changes, extended brute-force attacks are compelled to start over after each expiration. A minimum time between password changes without administrative override prevents users changing passwords repeatedly to bypass password history requirements and reset to the same password as used before.

Something users have: Access token

The most common form of "something users have" is an *access token* — an electronic device that provides information to the requesting user or directly to the authentication service. Access tokens come in two types:

✓ **Directly applied:** Tokens that are read directly by the access control system include radio-frequency identification (RFID) proximity cards and circuitry-embedded keys, such as those found in high-end cars. These tokens provide information through a specialized access portal using radio-frequency transfer, direct electrical contact, or magnetic signature.

✓ **Informational:** Informational tokens provide time-synchronized codes or one-time-use passwords to the user, adding a "something users have" requirement to the usual "something users know" single factor logon/ password combination. Figure 7-1 includes an example of an informational access token, which displays a new code every few minutes based on a mathematical key generation process that is synchronized with the access control service.

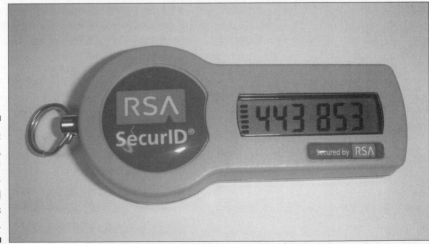

Figure 7-1:
An RSA
SecureID
informa-
tional
access
token.

Minimum password standards

The minimum standards for username/password combinations vary from one organization to another but should include the following elements:

✔ **Length:** In many enterprise authentication schemes, eight characters are considered to be the minimum.

✔ **Complexity:** Passwords should include characters from at least three of the following categories: uppercase (A-Z), lowercase (a-z), numeric (0-9), and special characters (~, !, >, and others).

✔ **History:** At least five prior passwords should be remembered to limit re-use. Some industries mandate a "never reuse" policy that extends history to the entire lifetime of an account.

✔ **Time between changes:** The minimum amount of time between password changes should be at least 1 day.

✔ **Expiration:** User password expiration should be based on the sensitivity of the protected data. Frequent expiration of passwords tends to cause users to write down passwords, weakening security, or to use only minor variations of the same password (MyNewPass1, MyNewPass2, MyNewPass3,…), requiring very minimal additional effort to crack.

A common non-IT example of "something users have" can be found in almost everyone's pocket: the key ring. Keys provide unique access control to many different resources from your office to the family car, which means that it's necessary to carry a large number of unique items. This level of complexity is undesirable in most enterprises, where each additional key further separates resources and consumers into disparate silos.

Mere possession of a physical key is sufficient to obtain access to a lock-secured resource. Single-factor authentication tokens such as proximity detection of RFID tags or smart-card readers are vulnerable to theft or duplication. Multi-factor authentication such as a combination of token and personal identification number strengthen defense by mixing "something users have" with "something users know" mechanisms of identification.

Something users are: Biometric identification

One of the most personal mechanisms for identification involves tests for "something users are." The most detailed test would be the review of individual DNA, but even that has the potential to be confounded by identical twins.

More effective biometric tests rely on traits that are different even in twins, such as the following:

✔ **Fingerprint:** Fingerprint characteristics such as arch, whorl, loop, and ridge detail vary from one individual to the next. Figure 7-2 provides an example of a USB fingerprint reader suitable to low-security biometric identification. Because copies of fingerprints can be obtained easily and duplicates made, this type of biometric identification remains unreliable. Dirt and even minor nuisance injuries such as paper cuts can reduce the effectiveness of this type of identification, although more advanced systems are more resistant to spoofing and may include blood flow, blood oxygenation, and thermal sensors to ensure that the finger is still attached to a living and conscious person.

✔ **Palm print:** Similar to the fingerprint biometric identification, palm sensors examine the patterns of lines and creases across the entire hand. Their functionality is reduced by injury to the hand, and some users are resistant to touch the reader for hygienic reasons.

✔ **Hand geometry:** Hand geometry identification relies on the underlying bone or blood vessel structure in an individual's hand. Accident, injury, aging, and growth can all impair effectiveness by altering the geometric measurements between bones, joints, and other internal relationships.

Figure 7-2:
An example of a USB fingerprint biometric reader provided by Engineersoft through the Wikimedia Commons.

✔ **Facial geometry:** Facial recognition uses a noncontact form of identification that makes it more easily accepted by users concerned with potential exposure to pathogens through contact. Some users, however, find the potential for remote identification and tracking to be invasive to their privacy and attempts to implement facial identification systems continue to experience legal challenges based on privacy laws. Because facial recognition systems operate at a distance, changes in lighting and angled perspective can often yield false identification results.

✔ **Iris:** This noncontact form of biometric identification uses an imaging system capable of identifying the unique patterns and hues in the iris (colored portion of the eye). Iris readers are prone to false negatives due to pupil dilation, which is affected strongly by changes in lighting conditions, illness, medication, and even mood. The volume of detail in iris identification mechanisms also tends to require much larger data sets for identification than other types of biometric measurement.

✔ **Retina:** Similar to the iris identification mechanism, retinal detection relies on unique characteristics present in an individual's eye. These systems identify the unique pattern of blood vessels in the back of the eye and require close proximity to the identification scanner. As a result, even though this form of identification enjoys the lowest false identification rate, user acceptance is very low due to concerns over hygiene, contagion, and potential for injury. Medical conditions such as cataracts can also render this form of identification useless for some individuals.

 Because the biological variations being measured are subject to change due to injury, age, and general health, they must be regularly updated to remain effective. Biometric forms of identification may also prove problematic for users with disabling conditions that prevent easy access to the "bio" being "metered" or who simply lack that body part outright.

Something users do: Behavioral identification

The least mature form of identification involves using behavioral characteristics to identify people, because these characteristics are easy to counterfeit through mimicry. Following are a few common behavioral identification measures:

✔ **Gait:** Analysis of patterns of movement, weight transfer, and body posture allow identification of an individual who is walking or running. This mechanism's usefulness is limited by its need for unobscured observation of the subject.

✔ **Signature:** The rate, stroke pattern, pressure variances, and geometric characteristics of handwriting can be used to identify an individual. Variances due to mood, attention, environmental conditions (if the user is shivering, for instance), or injury can all compromise the usefulness of this form of identification.

✔ **Voice:** Voice analysis is one of the most readily accepted forms of identification. It identifies unique patterns in timbre, pitch, and tonal qualities in a spoken pass phrase. Because background noise, changes in vocalization due to illness or growth, and sound reflection from the local environment can affect the analysis, this form of identification is susceptible to false negatives. High-resolution sound recording devices can also provide for noncontact counterfeiting of access credentials.

Authenticating Users

After an access request and identifying credentials have been submitted, the enterprise access control system must determine whether the credentials are valid. This process involves examination of the credentials provided and verification that the credentials match a known entity within the authentication boundary.

If the format, time stamp, or other details present in the provided credentials are incorrect, the authentication service returns a failure. If the credentials are acceptable to the authentication service, they must then be compared to a known registry of users and resources.

Authentication standards

Numerous network authentication solutions exist, with common directory projects implementing one or more authentication standards as well as various homegrown or proprietary mechanisms found in specialized network environments. Security systems, payment tracking, medical records and imaging, and similar environments often have mandatory requirements for security that determine which authentication mechanisms fulfill regulatory access control and auditing requirements.

Following are a few common standards:

✔ **X.500 suite:** A suite of standards that facilitates large-scale authentication solutions, including Directory Access Protocol and Directory Systems Protocol. The X.509 framework in particular provides standards for public-key certificates that underlie various types of Public Key Infrastructure (PKI–based enterprise authentication). Chapter 16 has additional details on public-key encryption.

- ✔ **Lightweight Directory Access Protocol (LDAP):** A very popular light-weight authentication protocol derived from the X.500 standards. This is perhaps the most widely used protocol in environments up to a half-million identities per database.

- ✔ **Extensible Authentication Protocol (EAP):** A protocol developed for point-to-point connections between remote systems, widely used by modern wireless solutions. The Wi-Fi Protected Access (WPA) standard implements this protocol to facilitate cross-manufacturer secured interconnectivity.

- ✔ **Internet Protocol Security (IPSec):** A suite of standards for transactions based on Transmission Control Protocol/Internet Protocol (TCP/IP), capable of encrypting and authenticating all data packets transmitted between endpoints. This standard includes protocols for transaction integrity, authentication, and confidentiality.

- ✔ **Kerberos:** A time-synchronized protocol that authenticates endpoints against a trusted third source. Its name is taken from the triple-headed dog that guarded Hades' realm in Greek mythology, due to the three functions of the Kerberos service (authentication, authorization, and auditing). Because this protocol underlies the authentication mechanism in Microsoft and many Linux networks, it is widely used in modern enterprise environments.

Although LDAP, X.500, and other protocols facilitate authentication, they validate identity but provide no built-in mechanism for access control. Solutions like Microsoft's Active Directory combine both authentication and authorization functions and can't be directly replaced by authentication-only services during enterprise planning.

Directory

The database of valid identities, services, and registered resources is often referred to as a *directory*. Most modern directory services include support for common authentication protocols, such as the X.500, LDAP, and Kerberos standards. Common directory implementations include Microsoft's Active Directory, Novell's eDirectory, IBM's Tivoli, and the open source OpenLDAP.

Central authentication

Central authentication services can exist apart from the network infrastructure, including solutions implementing Central Authentication Service (CAS) or Shibboleth standards. (Both are open source options for authentication). You can use these services to form an application access bridge between silos in ad-hoc, independently controlled network enterprises. CAS can aid during early stages of consolidation projects, such as those following business acquisition and merger events. Note that the effort necessary to implement a CAS service may be difficult to justify if one of the entities already employs an integrated technology base that can simply be extended to the other.

Federated authentication

Federated authentication systems also aid in providing authentication pass-through between siloed network segments by caching user credentials when first entered and later providing them to various resources on behalf of the user. Sometimes referred to as *metadirectories,* these services provide a database for storing user credentials needed to access different resources; they also provide alternative credentials on behalf of a user who previously provided authenticated credentials to the service.

This is a common solution employed in portal-based aggregate information access. In these situations, a user might authenticate to the portal's service directly but then the federated authentication service provides the user's secondary logon details to separate systems like payroll and sales tracking. This automation allows the user to experience seamless access.

Federated services have several weaknesses, however:

- ✔ They may tend to be tied to a particular vendor or technology.
- ✔ Passwords may expire, without an easy method of updating them automatically.
- ✔ A compromise of the metadirectory has the potential to expose a large number of credentials.

Single sign-on

Single sign-on (SSO) refers to the user experience of providing credentials only once, which allows authorized access to any resource anywhere in the enterprise. Although SSO may seem similar to federated services on the surface, federated services consolidate individual logon credentials for each resource, while SSO provides a single logon for multiple resources.

SSO is the holy grail of enterprise resource management. While it can exist if the technology base is homogeneous and integrated with a directory providing both access control and authentication services, almost any real-world enterprise will include technologies from third parties that simply do not always play well with others. Any SSO project should be considered under a variation of the 80/20 rule (see Chapter 4), aiming for the best-fit access solution that can be achieved in a reasonable time frame. Attempting a perfect solution is often in the "impossible to never" realm, beyond a very simple single-technology enterprise network.

A number of products facilitate cross-platform SSO solutions, including Novell's Identity Manager, Microsoft's ForeFront Identity Manager, and Hitachi's Identity Management Suite. However, not all applications will function identically when a native logon is used compared to a cross-platform logon — in particular, administrative permissions and component integration within portals are often pain points for SSO implementation. Many SSO solutions function by creating a database of credentials associated between authentication realms, meaning that a compromise of the SSO host system can potentially expose resources from any integrated realm and weaken security enterprise-wide.

Cross-platform SSO services are often presented as an alternative to consolidation and centralization by restructuring opponents, by allowing existing information silos to be retained indefinitely. Because services such as application virtualization and data de-duplication generally can't function well across authentication realms even when an SSO service is in place, use of an SSO service should be considered a short-term solution during consolidation projects and not a mechanism for long-term retention of inefficient and complex siloed resource pools.

Cross-realm authentication

Suppose that you're charged with implementing an authentication scheme that will allow users to continue using the same logon on legacy key business solutions as well as the new Microsoft Exchange e-mail system. The Exchange collaboration service operates within the company's Microsoft Active Directory domain, while the legacy systems are supported by a Kerberos-based authentication solution that will not be migrated to Active Directory until next year. Continuity of operation is the key driving factor, with a mandate from key stakeholders that users be able to access both resources with the minimum number of remembered logon/password credentials possible.

You decide to create a realm trust between the Kerberos realm and the Active Directory forest, provision (create) user accounts in the AD for each Kerberos identity, and associate the respective Kerberos identity with each individual AD account. Users can then log on to the legacy systems as well as the new Exchange service using the same Kerberos identity because the realm trust extends authentication between the two silos. Access controls over the legacy line-of-business applications and over the Exchange service are still managed independently, but the authentication of user identity is performed automatically across the independent systems.

Because access tokens generated by Kerberos pass-through logons differ slightly from those using native Active Directory, administrative actions may not function properly or as expected. For admin logons, native mode operation will ensure that proper tokens are generated based on group membership and security constraints imposed natively within the Active Directory infrastructure. Common Kerberos cross-domain logons that do not need elevated privileges generally do not suffer this problem.

Authorizing Access

After authentication is completed successfully, authorization provides access to resources based on access rights assigned to or inherited by the requesting identity. It involves comparing state conditions (time of day, day of the week, computer originating the request, and so on) and the requestor's identity against defined security and access rights. Controls over specific grant or denial of access may be applied to an individual entity directly or to an individual's group or role. Specific rights are determined by the type of resource being protected as you'll see in the following sections.

Access control systems must negotiate a complex combination of rights, particularly when membership in multiple groups or roles creates conflicting access results. Each access control solution will have a mechanism for resolving conflicts that must be well-understood before planning for rights assignment and resource organization begins.

File and database rights

File and database rights control what actions users can perform on individual or grouped elements of the data itself. Simple file and database user access rights include read, write, edit/change, and delete, while more complicated access rights include the capability to view or change permissions or take ownership of a file. Database rights may extend to the table or even record attribute level, allowing very fine grain control at the cost of access management complexity.

Service rights

A service, also called a *daemon* on UNIX or Linux-based systems, is an application that runs in the background and performs functions that are designed to work without direct user interaction. These applications range from basic, such as file and print, to complex, such as e-mail and database. User accounts, including administrative user accounts, may have permissions such as

- ✔ **Logon:** This permission determines whether the user can log on to the service, typically in administrative mode, either directly from the console or from a remote computer.

- ✔ **Startup/shutdown:** Typically, services start automatically on server boot, but they may need to be shut down or restarted in order to troubleshoot or perform maintenance. These permissions allow technical staff to perform these actions without restarting the server itself.

- ✔ **Administrative management:** Administrative management permissions are specific to each individual service and include abilities such as setting configuration parameters, assigning user permissions, and determining data storage locations.

- ✔ **New object creation:** This specific administrative permission determines whether a user can create a uniquely identifiable object such as a mailbox, a Web site, a user account, or a database. It is common to restrict this permission, even within technical support staff, to avoid the proliferation of unnecessary objects.

Application rights

Application rights are those that determine what a user is allowed to do in a specific application, and those rights may vary widely from application to application. An organization employing a content management system to control publication of information to its Web site may allow many users to create content, but restrict the actual publishing right to certain communications staff. Applications supporting human resources operations may allow individual employees to update their own contact information. However, updates to salary and benefits would be restricted to appropriate human resources personnel only.

Creating an Identity Management Strategy

Identity management, authentication, and authorization solutions will vary from one enterprise environment to another. There are a number of strategies that should be employed in enterprise planning, regardless of the particular solution selected.

Reviewing technologies

A thorough review of employed, required, and desired technologies will help to define the authentication and access control mechanisms best suited to a particular enterprise. Before you can add any resources to an enterprise structure, you must make provisions to identify each resource and to establish access controls based on strategies aligned with business process and best practices. This may involve modification of current access controls.

Assigning aggregate rights

Access rights tend to accumulate as accounts change role or position across an enterprise. Assigning rights and permissions by account can become impossible to manage properly, creating barriers to access or accidental disclosure from misconfigured access rights. Roles should be mapped out carefully, rights assigned to each role, and accounts assigned to roles in order to manage inheritance of authorization characteristics.

Rights assignment strategies should apply the principle of least privilege, where an identity is granted only the most minimal level of access required to perform job function. This prevents inadvertent disclosure of information, as well as strengthening the security posture of your enterprise. For example, separating administrative functions through business utility applications and ensuring that administrative logons are not used for common business purposes reduces the severity risk of malware incursion and propagation.

Meeting legal requirements

Compliance mandates for many laws include specific requirements for identity management. Penalties range from financial to regulatory and provide strong business motivation to adopt proper practices under the guidelines for each.

Accountability for unauthorized access, system misuse, unauthorized modifications, or discovered data of evidentiary value becomes very difficult, if not outright impossible, to determine when shared accounts are used. If multiple users log on using a shared Administrator account, it is impossible to associate privileged actions with a specific operator. Enterprise access should only be permitted through unique account access, with both successful and unsuccessful access attempts logged and reviewed.

Keeping it simple

Authentication boundaries define separation between enterprise elements, which creates undesirable redundancies and added support complexity. They also create barriers to future efficiencies if resources can't be shared. Elimination of authentication and authorization silos must be a primary strategy in enterprise reconfiguration. Enterprise total cost of ownership, support requirements, change management complexity, and business agility are all improved by centralizing identity provisioning, authentication, and access rights management.

Finding benefits

Identity management has benefits beyond compliance mandates. Organizations may employ identity management strategies to enhance operations or maximize enterprise value, particularly in the areas of cost, security, and complexity:

- **Cost savings:** User provisioning and deprovisioning applications tied to personnel databases can greatly reduce administrative overhead by ensuring that access rights are automatically managed as part of standard human resources processes. Elimination of access control silos allows sharing of key resources, which reduces redundancy and improves operational efficiency.

- **Improving security:** Identity management solutions offer enhanced boundary management, asset inventory, and data access logging across the entire enterprise. This helps identify fraud, misuse, and internal access violations and provides for nonrepudiation of logged events by uniquely identifying the accessing entity and thereby ensuring validity.

- **Reducing complexity:** Eliminating boundaries between business elements improves resource sharing and reduces the number of credentials needed to access resources from multiple sources. This is key to SOA application development and data consolidation solutions.

Implementing an Identity Management Solution

Whenever your enterprise environment allows, solutions that include both authentication and authorization functions are desirable over independent services for each. These solutions have a greater rate of convergence (the speed at which changes are propagated to all systems throughout the enterprise) and are more easily supported when standardized with the technology of access and resource services.

Examples of available packages for identity management include Novell's eDirectory, Oracle's COREid, Microsoft's Identity Lifecycle Management (ILM), and IBM's Tivoli. Typically, the selection of a particular product depends on the deployed technology base, such as Tivoli in WebSphere integrated networks or Microsoft ILM for Active Directory environments. By implementing similar-technology interfaces in existing enterprises, management and adoption are simplified.

Identification

Before you attempt an enterprise realignment, conduct a review of all users and services that will need to be uniquely identified. You may find exceptions that will require additional strategies, such as service accounts that run more than one application or kiosks allowing anonymous access. Only after conducting this review should the process of implementing the identification solution be performed.

Authentication

A centralized authentication solution is critical to connecting enterprise consumers with resources distributed throughout the extended network. Without a central service, collections of resources and consumers are unable to be configured, shared, and maintained efficiently. Such silos stand in the way of acquisition, support, and operational efficiencies.

It is necessary to identify all services and support functions throughout the enterprise, including mobile technologies, which may only support a limited set of authentication mechanisms. Some solutions may employ proprietary mechanisms for authentication or may require additional data values to be added to be able to function, such as in a custom LDAP schema. You must take these solutions into account when planning the authentication mechanism and response.

Customization of schema attributes is available in many authentication systems that use an object-oriented model, where additional attributes can be added to "extend" the *schema* (a database of objects, with multiple attributes available for each object). As an example, an extra BILLING attribute may be added to the user-type object so that applications can automatically access the proper account to bill a department for CPU time, printing consumables, and other per-access usage. It is critical to document all modifications to the schema and to include these additions when testing new applications that may extend the schema for their own operational needs.

As the new authentication solution is being tested, you need to review what occurs as data is passed between applications or storage segments to watch for compatibility problems that negatively impact any of the applications in use. Common compatibility problems include timing issues that may affect the order of operations or applications with conflicting password requirements.

Even legacy applications unable to directly interact with the directory can be included in a central authentication scheme by "wrapping" them using service-oriented architecture design utilities. Authentication and access control operate from the consumer to the wrapper and legacy mechanisms of access operate between the wrapper and the application itself. In this way, greater value can be drawn from existing application services, and migration projects can be performed with minimized disruption. Using service-oriented architecture (SOA) wrappers for support of legacy systems is discussed in Chapter 11.

If you simply cannot make technologies work, you may need a different authentication solution, or you may need to replace the noncompliant system.

Authorization

When implementing authorization schema, create and align lists of access and resource categories in order to facilitate a coordinated strategy without accidentally elevating access permissions. This inventory may also present opportunities to reduce complexity enterprise-wide by identifying applications of similar function currently in use.

Additional functions

Identity management utilities offer additional functionality besides identification, authentication, and authorization. Some of these functions are explored in the following sections:

✔ **User account provisioning:** User account provisioning is the most commonly used identity management function and can be performed by a standard identity management application or by a homegrown application. In high-turnover enterprise environments with a revolving user base, such as educational or health-care settings, automated account management can translate into immense savings in administrative cost. Automation of account creation, update, and retirement allows organizations to provide timely access to enterprise resources and deactivate accounts immediately upon termination or separation.

✔ **Password management:** Identity management utilities aid in controlling password strength, history and reuse constraints, PKI certificate association, and other details necessary for security and viability of access control strategies.

✔ **Self-service:** Another commonly used identity management utility is a self-service mechanism for password resets. These solutions allow users to reset forgotten, expired, or locked logon authentication settings without involving the technical or help desk staff.

✔ **Workflow:** A few identity management utilities extend self-service to account creation or access change requests, whether from the individual user or by management, supervisors, or other program coordinators. Automation of this process can reduce administrative effort and aid in operational transparency.

✔ **Auditing:** Formal identity management systems facilitate compliance audit, logging, and reporting mandated by many alphabet-soup legal requirements. The use of standardized mechanisms for audit and reporting also improves the quality of change-over-time measurements by ensuring the metrics measured remain constant from one reporting cycle to the next.

Chapter 8

Developing a Network Culture through Collaboration Solutions

● ●

In This Chapter

▶ Examining the value of communications networks

▶ Identifying uses for social networking in an enterprise

▶ Understanding collective intelligence

▶ Exploring collaboration solutions

● ●

*O*rganizations today can leverage the global Internet to develop increasingly sophisticated pools of customers, suppliers, and other consumers. These together form unique societies built on communication streams that bypass geological, political, and linguistic boundaries.

Communication extends to a larger scale than ever, with friends and business elements communicating at near real-time between any two points around the world. The complex social hierarchies that arise in a culture now reach beyond geographical location, presenting new opportunities and challenges for the modern enterprise.

This chapter discusses the value of communication and the uses of collaboration solutions such as groupware and portals. Details of specific methods of communication (e-mail, instant messaging, wiki, and others) are covered in Chapter 9.

Establishing Networks of Trust

Each of us has personal networks of trust, starting out with family and friends and extending outward. We use these networks on a regular basis to do things, such as the following:

- Find someone to perform a service, such as babysitting, home repair, or catering
- Locate people who have knowledge or items we need
- Expand our social circles

We do this because we are naturally more comfortable dealing with people whose trustworthiness has been vouched for by someone we ourselves trust. This is referred to as an extension of trust.

We also have professional networks of trust that we use to

- Give and receive references
- Acquire new professional contacts
- Increase awareness of business opportunities

Employees develop networks of trust within an organization for essentially the same reasons. An enterprise that provides an efficient mechanism for employees to build up meaningful and diverse networks of trust has the potential to improve performance and productivity through improved collaboration.

Creating a team from a mob

Working alone, individual ants are limited and yet ant colonies exhibit complex problem-solving and construction capabilities. Communication between individuals is the key to coordinated effort in examples of swarm intelligence, where individuals fuse to perform significant tasks.

Ants use chemical signals to coordinate their actions and when these chemicals are masked, the ants' normal coordinated team collapses into a mob of individuals. Although human behavior is much more complex, diverse interests and talents can be fused to perform significant tasks when effective communication transforms a mass of people into groups driving toward common goals.

Technologies like those examined in this chapter interconnect people in modern enterprise environments by creating lines of communication from the strategic level down to the individual to ensure that each person's efforts are directed toward common goals. Similarly, these technologies provide a means for each individual to express a unique perspective on the evolution of guiding policies.

Developing strong lines of communication

Groupware, portals, and other technologies supporting coordinated enterprises facilitate the transformation from mobs to teams. Communications must be efficient, transparent, and continuous in order to coordinate people into teams.

Ants can exist with only tiny chemical markers, but humans enjoy the use of e-mail, portals, text messaging, and other means to coordinate action. Human interaction also includes qualitative assessments not necessary in the ant's world, where established networks of trust can add to the perceived value of communicated information based on its origin.

An effectively connected enterprise presents a tremendous opportunity for alignment of business goals and technological tools — the value of which is limited only by the ease of use and availability of communications mechanisms.

Calculating the value of networks with Metcalfe's Law

Metcalfe's Law states that a communication network's value increases exponentially with its size — specifically, value = n^2, where n is the number of users. According to Metcalfe's Law, the value of the network may quadruple as the number of users doubles.

Figure 8-1 compares the number of connections in three-person and six-person networks. Each line in the figure represents two-way communication, so in this example, three lines (left) are six individual connections and 15 lines (right) means 30 individual connections. Each user in the figure can be an individual employee, a business unit, a division, a geographical location, or any entity that is part of your enterprise or associated with it (such as partners, vendors, or clients). The communications network can encompass any type of collaborative solution, including groupware, social networks, portals, intranets, and extranets.

Figure 8-1: Comparing the number of connections in a three-person network and in a six-person network.

Applying the formula of Metcalfe's Law to this figure, you see that

✔ The value of a three-user network is $3 \times 3 = 9$.

✔ The value of a six-user network is $6 \times 6 = 36$.

Whether value = n^2 is correct is a matter for debate by mathematicians and engineers. There is no denying, however, that increasing the number of users increases the number of connections and, therefore, the network's potential to be useful.

Developing Network Culture through Social Media

Today's network-enabled culture brings people into well-connected groups unrelated to physical proximity. This assists individuals seeking others who share similar beliefs, and offers access to resources such as specialized materials and crafts not available locally. We are no longer limited to our neighborhood for social interaction, our community for customers, or our region for goods and services.

The same expansion of scope creates new challenges for organizations that must compete against similar organizations around the world. Organizations must embrace the emerging social networking and group decision-making solutions to better meet the expectations and demands of an increasingly well-connected global population.

Don't assume that all employees are familiar with social networks, online communities, or any other online collaboration mechanism. Be prepared to create training materials suitable for employees with a wide range of experience. The first-time user will need practical training on general use and the veteran user may need reminding that content suitable for Twitter may not be suitable for the corporate social network.

Using social networking

Social networking Web sites provide an online means for creating trust networks across traditional boundaries, including geographic, socioeconomic, and cultural. They allow members to communicate with each other synchronously through online chatting or instant messaging and asynchronously through mechanisms such as e-mail, message boards, forums, and games. They also provide multiple ways to connect, such as through Web browsers on personal computers or mobile phone applications and custom applications are available that allow members to update multiple sites at once.

Here are some examples of popular social networking sites, both general and specialized:

- CafeMom — Mothers (www.cafemom.com)
- Classmates — School/college (www.classmates.com)
- Facebook — General (www.facebook.com)
- Flickr — Photography (www.flickr.com)
- LinkedIn — Professional/Business (www.linkedin.com)
- MySpace — General (www.myspace.com)
- Twitter — General (www.twitter.com)

Implementing social networking in an organization

Enterprises can implement social networking internally through an intranet, portal, or other collaborative solutions. These networks can be of varying scope, from a project team to an entire distributed corporation. When considering scope, remember Metcalfe's Law. The more users in the network, the greater the potential for value and usefulness. Value is found in the increased ability for employees to share information, locate resources, and get help solving problems. (For more information, see "Calculating the value of networks with Metcalfe's Law," earlier in this chapter.)

Some companies choose to block employees from accessing social networking sites through the company's network. However, some business units such as marketing, sales, and human resources can benefit from using these sites to communicate with customers, solicit new customers, and research job applicants. Therefore, consideration should be given to allowing some business units or individuals access to these sites through the corporate firewall.

Addressing management concerns

When researching collaboration tools that involve any type of social networking, you should be prepared for the following management concerns:

- ✔ Control over the flow of information will be lost.

- ✔ Employees will spend too much time "playing" online and become less productive.

- ✔ An open exchange of information may cause employees to question management decisions.

- ✔ Information that should be kept private, such as discussions on cutbacks or layoffs, may accidentally be published.

You should be able to reassure management by selecting solutions with adequate security controls and planning for user training. It may also help to implement features slowly in order to allow enough time for the corporate culture to change. Management concerns may also be alleviated by backing up your selections with citations from well-known technology research and consulting companies such as Gartner (www.gartner.com) and Forrester (www.forrester.com). Although some of these resources are available only at a cost, many are provided as public press releases, such as this Gartner report on the 2010 and later expectations for social networking: www.gartner.com/it/page.jsp?id=1293114.

Employing collective intelligence

Collective intelligence arises when groups of individuals, through collaboration and cooperation, are able to create a body of knowledge that is greater than the sum of each individual's knowledge. It's seen frequently in nature, most often in social insects or herd animals, but it also exists in human society in forms such as political parties, juries, and crowds.

In recent years, technological advances in communication methods, particularly the Internet and the World Wide Web, have created new arenas for collective intelligence to flourish. Collective intelligence is at work in the following:

- ✔ Community-maintained knowledge bases such as Wikipedia, which in 2009 had more than 85,000 active contributors

- ✔ The open source community

- ✔ Social networking sites

- ✔ Online communities focusing on topics such as information technology, medical conditions, consumer advocacy, information security, and parenting

Collective intelligence is valuable in an organization. The more individuals who are able to collaborate on a project, the greater the range of skills, knowledge, and experience that can be brought to bear. The communications media used by millions of people over the Internet can be used on a smaller scale within an enterprise, facilitated by solutions such as groupware and enterprise portals.

Be careful when you attempt to apply collective intelligence to all settings because the loudest (or most persuasive) participant can drown out facts, while the weight of a collective status quo can crush innovative ideas.

Setting social-media policies

Companies that encourage their employees to make use of social media sites for business purposes, such as sales and marketing, participating as company representatives in forums or on wikis, or blogging on industry-related topics, should strongly consider instituting policies and guidelines that govern that use. This serves to protect the company's confidential or sensitive information, intellectual property or trade secrets, and reputation.

Disallowing anonymous communication over enterprise social networks helps keep people professional.

Following are some very general statements that may be appropriate for adoption into an official policy:

- ✔ Don't speak on behalf of the company unless you're authorized to do so, and use disclaimers where appropriate.

- ✔ Follow all applicable confidentiality policies.

- ✔ When speaking of the company, its customers, or its clients, be respectful.

- ✔ Follow all applicable copyright laws.

✔ Ensure that online actions, comments, and activities don't embarrass the company.

✔ Ensure that online activity doesn't interfere with primary job duties.

Employing Groupware

Groupware is loosely defined as a class of software that allows groups of people (workgroups or teams) to work together regardless of location by using integrated tools that facilitate communication, conferencing, and collaborative management. Tools that facilitate communication include e-mail, contact lists, mailing lists, and discussion boards. Other communication tools, such as videoconferencing, Web conferencing, and chat specifically facilitate virtual face-to-face meetings. These and other communication and conferencing tools are covered in Chapter 9.

Groupware also facilitates collaborative management, particularly through the use of shared group calendars and task lists. Groupware can also be used to develop workflow systems that include components such as automatic routing of e-mail or notifying managers of task completion. It may also integrate with and support project management software.

Although groupware is excellent in supporting project management, it should not take the place of actual project management solutions.

Considering the benefits of groupware

Enterprise-wide groupware has distinct benefits, including the following:

✔ Real-time collaboration that goes beyond telephone calls between users in different geographic locations

✔ The ability to archive communications in an easily accessible format

✔ Improved communication among the organization's locations (headquarters, satellite offices, sales offices, retail locations, distribution centers, and so forth)

✔ Improved connectivity for employees who travel frequently, telecommute, or don't always access network resources from the same computer

✔ Multiple means of storing and accessing data, which allows users to use the method that is most appropriate for them

✔ IT-related cost savings, such as the following:

- Server consolidation through the integration of standalone application servers

- Reduction in administrative overhead

- More efficient backup and restoration operations than separate variant local systems maintained departmentally

✔ Non-IT–related cost savings, such as these:

- Reduction in physical mail due to expanded use of electronic mail and electronic document sharing

- Reduction in the need for travel and long-distance telephone calls through the use of real-time communications such as instant messaging and Web conferencing

Selecting a groupware solution

To select the proper groupware solution, you need to understand the business needs of the users and make sure that the solution is both beneficial to the users and aligned with the enterprise plan.

Clarifying your needs

Not all groupware solutions are created equally and it is important to select a solution that meets both your current and future needs. Examples of groupware solutions include Microsoft's Office suite (Exchange, SharePoint, and so on), IBM's LotusLive Suite, or the open source pgpGroupware and eGroupware applications. Answers to the following questions may help you determine your organization's needs:

✔ How do groups or people need to communicate with other groups or people?

✔ What are the goals of the users and the organization?

✔ Are competing solutions already in place?

✔ Does the solution need to integrate with other applications?

✔ What type of workflows does the solution need to support?

Many organizations have personnel who don't regularly use computers and would gain little benefit from having access to the groupware solution. Depending on their job duties, their productivity might actually decrease over the long term if they were required to use the system due to the additional duties and the ongoing training.

Deciding where to host the solution

Another consideration is whether the solution should be hosted locally or by a vendor, such as in a Software as a Service (SaaS) model. This decision involves several factors:

- ✔ **Sustained connectivity:** Relying on an Internet-based solution carries a certain level of risk, mainly due to network connectivity issues. This risk may be more or less depending on the stability and capacity of your organization's Internet connection.

- ✔ **Cost:** After you figure in the cost of hardware, software, and administrative overhead, SaaS solutions are generally cheaper than locally hosted solutions, at least for the first year. This initial savings leads some organizations to choose SaaS solutions and then migrate to the same solution in a locally hosted setting. This approach allows the organization time to hire and train technical staff, procure hardware, and take advantage of vendor expertise during design and implementation.

- ✔ **Security:** Your confidential, sensitive, and proprietary data must be protected. When you research SaaS providers, be sure to inquire about the protections they offer customer data. To be considered as a vendor, a provider should be able to make proper assurances, in writing, that it will be able to secure your data in accordance with your security standards as well as with applicable legal and regulatory mandates. You may also wish to look for providers with privacy-related certifications, such as those conferred by TRUSTe (www.truste.com) and the United States Department of Commerce (www.export.gov/safeharbor/).

Planning the implementation

For your comprehensive groupware solution, it may be beneficial to consider a phased implementation that begins with a limited version of the solution hosted by the vendor and ends with a fully implemented, self-hosted solution. The benefits to this type of implementation include the following:

- ✔ Your organization gains the benefits of using elements of the solution while planning, designing, and implementing a self-hosted solution.

- ✔ Your organization may spread the purchase of expensive hardware over a period of time.

- ✔ The vendor is responsible for all system maintenance, allowing the organization time to train its IT staff in these processes or hire new personnel.

Working with Enterprise Portals

In architecture, a *portal* is an entrance, a door, or a gateway. In enterprise architecture, a portal is a virtual entrance into an organization's information resources. It aggregates content from multiple sources, bringing it all into one place for easy access and creating a single point of contact. Many portals use a Web-based interface, which allows the portal to be platform independent and accessible from a variety of equipment, from desktop computers to mobile devices.

Provided compatible solutions are selected, portals can integrate with groupware, which enables users to access e-mail, calendars, tasks, and other groupware tools from within the portal. Conversely, some solutions may allow users to access portal content from complementary groupware software.

Popular portal solutions include

- DotNetNuke (www.dotnetnuke.com)
- IBM WebSphere (www.ibm.com/websphere)
- Microsoft Office SharePoint Server (sharepoint.microsoft.com)
- Open Text Corporation's Vignette Portal (www.vignette.com/us/ Solutions/Intranet)
- Oracle Portal (www.oracle.com/appserver/portal_home.html)

The following section highlights some common portal features.

Activating common features of portals

Many of the features in the following sections are made possible through the use of *portlets* — software components that can be plugged into portal pages and used to display dynamic content. Many portal solutions use the vendor-neutral Java Portlet Specification standard (JSR 168), whereas others use proprietary components.

Authentication and access control

Enterprise portals contain built-in authentication and access control systems, which have three essential benefits:

✔ You can develop applications that use a portal's integrated authentication and access control system, which simplifies coding and reduces the number of logon credentials users must provide when compared to a standalone solution with its own internal authentication and access control service.

✔ Permissions may be assigned at many levels within the portal, from entire portal sites down to individual list items. This allows portal administrators and content owners to assign appropriate access to content and features.

✔ Single Sign-On (SSO) functionality, if present, can provide authentication details to other information resources, such as databases, documents, and spreadsheets, which allows that information to be aggregated within the portal.

When researching portal solutions, remember to consider compatibility with identity management solutions, as discussed in Chapter 7.

Collaboration and communication technologies

Enterprise portals may include a variety of tools such as blogs, wikis, forums, polls, and various messaging components. These components, particularly when combined with the following features, help an organization collaborate and communicate efficiently on projects and tasks. We discuss these tools in Chapter 9.

Content aggregation

Content is aggregated from various sources and presented in a Web-based format through the use of Web components. Information feeds can be created from this content and targeted to appropriate groups of users using mechanisms such as e-mail alerts and news feeds.

Content management

Content can be customized based on audience, date, time of day, or other factors. In addition, some portals contain true Content Management System (CMS) functionality, which includes information creation, approval, and versioning. This functionality allows for efficient and timely updating of portal content, particularly by nontechnical users.

Document management

Many portals include document management features such as sharing, version control, and approval mechanisms. Users can check out documents, which locks them for editing by anyone other than the user who has checked them out. If versioning is activated, documents may be rolled back to a previous version. This type of self-service restoration is much more efficient and cost-effective than having IT staff restore earlier versions of documents from backup.

Depending on the size of the document repository, enabling version control may require a significant amount of disk space. Careful consideration should be given to the number of versions retained and how long versions are retained after the document has been marked as final.

Enterprise search

Even a small corporate portal may contain hundreds of sites and thousands of documents, necessitating the capability to search the entire portal. All content on the portal, including user profiles, may be indexed and searchable but will only be displayed to authorized users based on access restrictions. This allows users to find content across multiple file formats and search for users who may have the skills or knowledge to assist them with a problem.

Personalization

An enterprise portal may offer several personalization features, including these:

- ✔ **Profiles:** Users can create a profile that contains the standard information that would be in an employee directory such as name, title, and contact information. The profile can also contain nonstandard, but highly useful information, such as background, education, skills, experience, and interests. These profiles are easier to keep up-to-date than published employee directories and can aid in team building by allowing team members to come to the table with some basic knowledge of each other's skills and experience.

- ✔ **Personal sites:** Users can have personal sites within the portal that can include personal information, links to other portal sites, documents, and information about current projects. These personal sites may have public and private sides in which different information is shown to co-workers and to the user. This allows the user to present useful information to co-workers, but also use the site as a desktop or workspace.

- ✔ **Personalized interfaces:** The enterprise portal interface can be customized, allowing users to arrange content to suit their preferences.

Before investing in a commercial portal product, consider creating a test portal, using open-source solutions or free/demo versions of commercial solutions. This will allow both test users and IT staff to experiment with portal technology and determine the content, features, and organization that would best benefit your organization.

Developing network culture with portals

Portals are excellent for helping an organization develop and support its network culture. In addition to providing a single point of contact for users to communicate and collaborate with others, portals also allow executives to have greater contact with their employees. Executive staff can take advantage of features such as blogs, information feeds, Web pages, and shared documents to connect with employees and keep them up-to-date on your organization's strategic plan.

Portals can also be used to conduct surveys or take quick polls on any number of subjects, allowing Human Resources to obtain opinions or information from employees in a swift and efficient manner. Blogs or discussion boards can be used for similar purposes and are particularly useful for getting feedback on ideas and soliciting suggestions from employees.

Integrating business intelligence tools

Enterprise portals can also facilitate decision-making through the integration of business intelligence tools such as dashboards, decision support systems, spreadsheets, and reporting. These tools filter through tremendous amounts of data and display it in a usable format that allows executives to see the status of the organization at a glance in a visually appealing format. Key performance indicators and thresholds must be properly configured, which requires collaboration among executives, the business architect, and IT personnel.

Chapter 9

Reviewing Communication Methods

*T*he days when using e-mail provided a business advantage are long gone; it is simply an expected element of business communication. Similarly, new forms of communication emerge regularly, and the enterprise architect must contend with an ever-increasing selection of communication services and technologies. These technologies may provide a business advantage to your enterprise if appropriately integrated and properly managed. Both asynchronous and synchronous forms of communication may benefit your organization, its employees, and its clients. As such, you should consider their appropriate use when planning, paying attention to factors such as availability, security, and convenience.

This chapter looks at appropriate uses of various communication mechanisms, many of which can be integrated into groupware solutions or enterprise portals as discussed in Chapter 8.

Identifying Classes of Communication

There are two main classifications of communication: asynchronous and synchronous. In *asynchronous* communications, people can communicate over a period of time without worrying about schedules or meeting attendance because real-time interaction is not required. Like older physical means of information exchange, modern electronic systems allow parties to transmit or post information in threaded and community discussion forums whenever opportunity allows. Asynchronous communication mechanisms aid in the development of online communities, moving beyond simple back-and-forth conversation by allowing participants to conduct research and use forethought before posting their comments.

In *synchronous* communications, both parties are connected and have the ability to communicate at the same time. This type of real-time online communication can replace or supplement face-to-face meetings or telephone calls and is particularly useful when the individuals involved are in different geographic locations. Instant messaging (IM) clients presenting real-time status indicators can save time compared with traditional "walk down the hall and see whether Joe is available" ad-hoc meetings.

Synchronous communication allows participants to clarify information or attempt to correct misunderstandings in a timely manner and offers the capability to solicit and receive feedback immediately, resulting in fewer project delays.

The rest of this chapter explores the most common asynchronous and synchronous communication mechanisms and their appropriate uses within the enterprise.

Messaging

Messaging technologies extend the function of conversation enterprise-wide. These solutions allow individuals and groups to rapidly communicate and coordinate when those involved are widely distributed. Synchronous forms of messaging allow real-time exchanges, whereas asynchronous forms facilitate the "when I have time" exchange of information that is vital when participants don't share the same work schedule.

Chat, electronic mail, instant messaging, and text messaging are some common types of messaging.

Chat

Chat systems allow multiple people to interact in real-time, usually utilizing a Web browser but also specialized client software. Most chat systems are text-based, although some may have media components or interact with peripherals, such as webcams. This method of synchronous communication is commonly found on social networking and distance education classroom Web sites, and commercial sites may use a simple form of chat to allow customers to communicate with customer service or sales representatives.

Internet Relay Chat (IRC) is the most widely used form of chat, and you can access it through client software or through Web browsers with a built-in client. IRC has many security issues, such as malware, denial of service attacks, and back doors in clients. IRC is also the primary command and control mechanism for *botnets* (also known as zombies), which are groups of malware-infected computers under the control of a bot herder. A *bot herder* is a malicious individual that accumulates large numbers of machines and then leases or sells access to them to the highest bidder for use in illicit activities, such as denial of service attacks and spam.

Even with its flaws, IRC is used in some organizations, particularly by IT help desk personnel to assist with problem management. In addition, IM systems (see the next section) sometimes serve as chat systems when more than two people are involved. You can use chat services to provide clients a mechanism for synchronous communication with first-level technical support for simple problem resolution. You can use more direct interaction via a one-to-one IM session for the next level of service escalation.

Chat functionality is particularly useful for employees who multitask. They can use chat to carry on multiple conversations at the same time from their desks. Some services may be included in groupware solutions or integrated into enterprise portals. You should determine which solution is best for your organization, based on business needs.

Electronic mail (e-mail)

Electronic mail is perhaps the most well-known and widely used form of electronic communication. E-mail is a simple, cost-effective means of asynchronous communication for individuals and organizations and can be used to contact large numbers of people with very little effort.

Planning e-mail use in the enterprise

As an enterprise architect, you need to plan your organization's e-mail system with the following concerns in mind:

- Integration with other communication methods
- Storage capacity
- Spam management
- Compliance with the organization's records-retention policies
- Methods of access
- Protocol to be used
- Security

Any e-mail that is routed over a public network should not be considered private. It may be intercepted, stored, or modified at any number of steps along its route. Therefore, sensitive or confidential information should never be sent via e-mail unless it is encrypted, and digital signatures should be used to verify the integrity of the message.

Choosing an e-mail protocol

E-mail uses several communication protocols to send and receive mail. Simple Mail Transfer Protocol (SMTP) is the standard protocol used to deliver messages between services, and you should consider it a fundamental component of system-to-system communication on the enterprise's internal network and on the public Internet.

You can receive mail, however, using several different client protocols, including

- ✔ **Post Office Protocol (POP):** Mail clients using the POP protocol connect to the server only long enough to download the messages. Messages are typically deleted from the server after download, but you can leave the mail on the server. POP is an older protocol with some limitations. Although POP supports encryption for authentication, it's not the default, and you can configure the client/server to transmit passwords in clear text. As well, if a user checks mail from multiple computers, e-mail messages may be spread out over different computers and not easily accessible.

- ✔ **Internet Messaging Access Protocol (IMAP):** This client/server protocol allows clients to access and manipulate e-mail stored on a mail server without downloading them to the local device. IMAP is more robust than POP3 and allows additional functionality, such as allowing multiple users to access a single mailbox at once and storing message state information (such as read, unread, forwarded, or replied) on the server.

- ✔ **Hypertext Transfer Protocol (HTTP):** Although HTTP is a Web protocol, it's relevant to e-mail due to the popularity of Web-based e-mail clients. Microsoft Windows Live Hotmail and Google's Gmail are examples of popular Internet Web-based e-mail (often called webmail) systems. In addition, most, if not all, major e-mail applications support some type of Web client.

- ✔ **Vendor-specific protocols:** Some e-mail applications use proprietary protocols for communication between the mail server and client applications. Microsoft Exchange/Outlook and Novell GroupWise, for example, use their own native protocols although they offer support for the preceding protocols as well.

Choosing a protocol is highly dependent on the e-mail client you select and the devices that will be used to retrieve mail. Use vendor-specific protocols and preferred e-mail clients whenever possible because they may operate more efficiently and offer extended product-specific capabilities.

Getting your messages out in mailing lists

Electronic mailing lists are used to send messages to groups of recipients using a single e-mail address instead of sending separate e-mails to a long list of individual e-mail addresses. Lists serve two primary functions:

✔ Announce-only lists are one-way mailing lists in which only certain individuals have permission to send messages to list subscribers. This type of list is useful for marketing communications, newsletters, or announcing events.

✔ Discussion lists provide a way for large groups of users to discuss various topics in e-mail. In an unmoderated list, any subscriber can send a message to all list subscribers. In a moderated list, designated moderators approve messages before they're sent out on the list.

Depending on list configuration, users can self-subscribe or send a subscription request to the moderator. Organizations that employ this mechanism may also require employees to be subscribed to particular lists. In both types of lists, messages can be archived and some type of search functionality is usually present.

Lists can be useful in your organization, but you must determine how best to implement them. Lists can be implemented as part of the e-mail or groupware solution, as part of the enterprise portal solution, or through a dedicated list application — LISTSERV, Majordomo, or Sympa, for instance.

If native protocols aren't available because your e-mail server doesn't use them or certain devices can't run the client, IMAP is generally the preferred solution for enterprises. Its features are more robust than POP, and because everything is stored on the mail server, it is more appropriate in a centrally managed environment. POP removes e-mail from the server and may increase help desk calls regarding "lost" mail. It's also not appropriate for employees who need to access e-mail from multiple devices.

Using HTTP to support browser-based e-mail retrieval is an excellent choice in an enterprise that supports multiple operating systems because it's platform-independent and does not require a client to be loaded. This solution is also suitable for employees who check e-mail from devices that are not under their control, such as airport kiosks or clients' offices.

Instant messaging

Instant messaging is a synchronous communication mechanism that allows two or more people to communicate in real-time. IM sessions are primarily text-based, but some messaging solutions allow users to transfer files, insert graphics, display a photograph or avatar (graphical representation of a user), or display webcam video.

IM requires a client application and a service provider. Service providers may be Internet-based (AOL, Yahoo!, Microsoft, or Jabber, for example) or internally hosted. Many groupware and enterprise portal solutions offer some type of IM capabilities, such as Novell's Groupwise Instant Messenger or Microsoft's Office Communication Server. Client applications are varied and may have robust features such as an allow/deny list to restrict who can initiate chat sessions, status features (online, busy, away), and logging. Like chat, IM is useful for employees who multitask.

Before implementing instant messaging, it is essential to develop a policy on logging and archival. Some enterprises may be required to log communications due to regulatory or legal mandates and some enterprises may wish to prohibit any form of logging.

Text messaging

Text messaging — technically, Short Message Service (SMS) communication — allows people to send short text messages between mobile phones in order to carry on a conversation asynchronously. In addition to text messaging (also known as *texting*), SMS can also be used to send configuration data, ringtones, and software updates to mobile devices. Outside of the cellular arena, SMS can be used to facilitate machine-to-machine communications, such as device monitoring, and is also used in vehicle tracking solutions.

If your organization utilizes cellphones, SMS can be a useful tool for

✔ Broadcasting alerts to employees, particularly remote employees

✔ Quick "conversations" between employees or employees and clients

✔ Automatically alerting IT staff of problems

Confidential or sensitive information should not be transmitted via SMS, nor should SMS be used for communications that are required to be logged.

Community Sites

Community sites replace the traditional office bulletin board with an electronic equivalent available to hundreds or even thousands of users at once and form the foundation for social networking (see Chapter 8). The asynchronous communication mechanisms discussed in the following sections improve collaboration by allowing mass participation in group efforts, providing point-in-time reference for project evolution, and serving as a repository for information.

Microblogging

Microblogging can be said to be a combination of blogging and texting. Instead of log posts, microbloggers can post short text-based messages to their site from desktop applications, Web browsers, or mobile phones. Popular microblogging services like Twitter and Facebook are used primarily by individuals, but companies are beginning to use these services for advertising and promotions.

Organizations may find microblogging to be usefully internally as well as for marketing purposes, using solutions such as Tumblr, Yammer, or the well-known Twitter. Employees can send status updates to supervisors or project managers, and employees who travel frequently can update the organization and their family of their whereabouts.

Blogs

Blogging is a form of asynchronous online publishing that you can use to post news stories, personal journal entries, or commentary on a variety of topics. Posts typically appear in reverse chronological order, with older items rolling off or being archived. Some blogs also allow readers to comment. Blogs can contain authentication and access controls to limit both reading and commenting capability. Public blogging is popular with individuals and organizations of all types, and some organizations have moved to blog format for their public-facing Web sites.

Organizations can use blogs internally, via enterprise portal or intranet solutions, as another method of communication for workgroups or project teams.

Some organizations encourage senior executives to maintain blogs so that those executives are more visible and accessible to rank-and-file employees.

Discussion boards and forums

Forums provide a mechanism for threaded discussions and are commonly found on community Web sites and customer support sections of company Web sites. Forums are typically organized by topic, and discussions (subtopic or conversation threads) appear in reverse chronological order. They can be moderated to control content or may be left open to all users of that particular forum's community. In addition, they often have search functionality that, when used properly, reduces the number of redundant discussions.

Discussion boards are often used when a group leader wants to publish a question that members of the group can respond to, often limited to participation only by authorized group members. This type of dialogue is exceptionally effective in building interest and buy-in for new opportunities, allowing participants to actively engage in the early phases of identification and planning.

Organizations may find that forums and discussion boards can be useful alternatives to e-mail in situations where the information would be useful beyond those copied on the mail. This information includes clarifications on policies or procedures and general IT support questions. In an enterprise portal or groupware solutions, forums and discussion boards may be created on project sites, allowing project team members to ask questions and share information in the same workspace as the rest of the project documentation. You can also configure extended forums to allow employees to pose questions to a wider audience than just their fellows to obtain input and assistance from people with varied knowledge and skill sets.

Wikis

A *wiki* (from the Hawaiian term "*wiki-wiki*" for *fast* or *hurry*) is a Web site that coordinates information provided by various contributors and provides a single location for each subject. Wikis take advantage of collective intelligence (see Chapter 8) and collaboration, which results in a product that may be more comprehensive than one produced by individuals working alone. Moderation of participant additions and corrections is necessary in some settings to avoid defacement, disinformation, or other misuse.

Wikis are used for projects such as community Web sites, collaborative sites, and knowledge management systems. They can be private or require authentication, but the essence of wiki is open collaboration in which contributors can review, add, and edit content as they find necessary. For example, Wikipedia, perhaps the most well-known wiki site, allows visitors to edit some content without registration and trusts the community to self-police content, although administrators will take action when necessary.

One of the benefits of wikis is built-in change control and versioning, so that changes can be rolled back in case information is lost or erroneous information is added.

Wikis may serve multiple purposes in organizations:

- ✓ Project-based wikis may be implemented as a way to coordinate project deliverables.
- ✓ Marketing, communication, and public relations personnel can use wikis to publish guidelines and standards for print and electronic communications.

- Application developers may find wikis helpful for documenting software development issues and testing results.

- Organizations can use them as frameworks for developing knowledge bases on various topics.

Conferencing

When people need to meet and discuss strategies and policies, the traditional process of filing into the same room is no longer necessary. Conferencing technologies create virtual rooms, allowing synchronous communication among all members, regardless of location.

The primary benefits to all the electronic conferencing mechanisms discussed in the following sections are the reduction or elimination of the expense and time involved with travel and the availability of expertise without the disruption involved in bringing resources to the same physical site.

Videoconferencing

Videoconferencing allows groups or individuals in different locations to participate in two-way (sending and receiving, not only between two end points) audio/video communication in real-time. Individuals may participate in videoconferences from their local computers (including their home computers) with the proper equipment (audio and video input sources) or from specially configured rooms. Videoconferences can also be archived and replayed later for employees who were unable to attend the session.

This technology is widely used in educational environments, primarily for distance education but also for internal administrative functions, and is catching on in the business world both for internal communication and communication with clients or partners.

Videoconferencing can be particularly useful to organizations in the following ways:

- In scenarios such as corporate training or product demonstration, text and audio-only communication may not be adequate to the task.

- People who are adept at reading nonverbal cues, such as facial expressions and body language, may be able to communicate more successfully using videoconferencing. For example, they can alter their communication strategy if people are inattentive and provide additional explanation without needing to wait for questions if people appear to not understand.

Virtual terrorism

In 2007, "virtual terrorists" destroyed the Australian Broadcasting Corporation's virtual island in Second Life. The visual appearance of the island was changed so that it appeared to have been bombed and very little was left untouched. This virtual destruction wound up costing the company real money, as it had to spend resources to restore the island (which cost tens of thousands of dollars to create) to its original condition.

Some employees may be uncomfortable with videoconferencing due to concerns over appearance, especially if the session is being recorded. It is generally felt that this discomfort will fade over time with repeated use. As well, recent research has suggested that allowing the employee to see his or her own image as it is being transmitted assists with easing this discomfort, as it allows the employee to make minor "corrections" in appearance, such as adjusting glasses and smoothing hair.

Virtual reality

Virtual reality allows the expression of real-world environments as well as entirely fantastical ones. Architects and designers can make use of virtual reality to allow virtual walkthroughs and equipment testing without the expensive process of building actual physical models. Participants can engage in training events involving simulated hazardous environments and dangerous circumstances such as emergency response or disaster recovery without risk or consequence.

Interactive environments, such as the well-known Second Life environment by Linden Labs (http://secondlife.com), provide a shared interactive experience to thousands of participants simultaneously. Within this environment, universities, businesses, and governmental entities may all have virtual representations available for interested consumers. Because such an environment is highly interactive, you must think about protection of these virtual resources.

In addition to providing a cutting-edge mechanism for interacting with customers, virtual reality solutions present an opportunity to eliminate bias based on gender, race, and physical condition during communications. It may also allow for testing of new products without having to build them physically, which decreases development costs.

Voice over Internet protocol (VoIP)

Voice communication is no longer limited to conventional telephone service. Voice over Internet protocol (VoIP) technology is capable of replacing traditional telephony with similar functionality. VoIP systems enable users to talk over familiar handsets or headsets using TCP/IP connectivity over data networks.

VoIP is a fairly new technology and although improvements have been made in its ability to access emergency services by dialing 911, it is still inferior to standard telephone service with regard to tying a phone number to an identified physical location for emergency response. In addition, VoIP is subject to the same issues as data communications, including latency and packet loss, and because VoIP and data communications may share bandwidth, both services can suffer performance issues.

Organizations may find VoIP solutions useful for the following reasons:

- ✔ VoIP typically has a lower per-line cost than traditional telephone service and does not carry long-distance fees.

- ✔ In a new or temporary location, you can set up voice and data communications immediately after installation of only data communication lines. Although this solution may not be permanent, it does allow employees to make voice calls while waiting for traditional telephone service to be installed.

- ✔ VoIP eliminates the need for costly private branch exchange (PBX) telephone systems typically by medium to large organizations with many telephone numbers. Some VoIP solutions provide equivalent functionality with software that can run on existing servers.

Organizations considering implementing VoIP should ensure that it's not the sole method of voice communication during an emergency or disaster recovery operation.

Web conferencing

Web conferencing is gaining popularity and is regularly used for meetings, product demonstrations, training, and education. Unlike videoconferencing, Web conferencing may not provide a video link among participants and as such doesn't mandate video equipment for each participant. Participants can attend Web conferences from the privacy of their own offices or can attend as a group through a single computer in a conference room, using only a computer or a computer and telephone.

Features of Web conferencing include

- ✔ Voice communication, through VoIP or telephone service
- ✔ Whiteboards, either shared or controlled by the presenter
- ✔ Desktop sharing, enabling presenters to conduct live demonstrations or software training
- ✔ Text-based chat
- ✔ Event registration
- ✔ Polls that allow the presenter to get feedback from the audience
- ✔ Presentations
- ✔ Archiving for later replay

Webinars are Web conferences that have defined presenters and audience members. The presenter controls the display and audio, and audience members may have limited communication in the form of chat or audio. They're widely used by vendors for product demonstrations and industry-specific organizations for training or continuing professional education.

Web conferencing software can be hosted internally by the organization or by a hosting service. Some solutions require users to download and install a client and some are completely browser-based. For browser-based solutions, meeting invitations can be distributed as URLs in e-mail or other text-based communication mechanisms.

Much like videoconferencing, organizations should take advantage of Web conferencing when data-only or audio-only communications are insufficient. Web conferencing is particularly useful in the following ways:

- ✔ Traveling or telecommuting employees can receive the same level of training as on-site employees through the use of webinars.
- ✔ Desktop sharing can allow software demonstration and testing of new applications without requiring installation of any software components onto users' computers.

Broadcast Communications

Not all communication needs to be two-way. Sometimes an organization simply needs to present information to a variety of audiences, including employees, clients, or partner organizations. You can use the following communication technologies when audience participation isn't necessary.

Podcasting

Named after Apple's iPod media player, podcasting is a relatively new communication mechanism. *Podcasts* are rich media files (audio and/or video) that are episodic in nature and are published through feeds, which is what differentiates them from simple streaming media files. Major corporations, news services, the entertainment industry, educational institutions, and even individuals heavily use podcasting to provide rich content to a mobile audience.

Organizations can use podcasting as a way to present downloadable active-media content to employees when text isn't sufficient. Because podcasts are designed to be downloaded and accessed via a portable device, do not include confidential information or sensitive intellectual property in podcasts. For example:

- ✔ IT staff can use podcasting to supplement the organization's IT security awareness training program.

- ✔ Senior executives can address employees in the "fireside chat" style made popular by President Franklin D. Roosevelt.

- ✔ Human Resources and Employee Development may wish to use podcasting to supplement or replace lecture-style training sessions.

Really Simple Syndication (RSS)

Also known as a news feed or Web feed, Really Simple Syndication (RSS) is an XML-based publication of electronic headlines and articles. Typically, only a snippet of the article is included in the publication in order to streamline the feed and make it easy for individuals to review large quantities of information in a short time and pick out items of interest. Many news and informational Web sites publish RSS feeds, sometimes many, on various topics of interest. For example, a news site may have feeds for local news, health, technology, and world news. Retail and vendor sites also make use of RSS feeds as a way of informing customers and partners of new products or promotions.

An organization can use RSS feeds internally to publish event details, announcements, changes to policy, IT change notices, and even newsletter-type items. Enterprise users can read feeds using Web browsers or e-mail clients that support RSS, collected by RSS readers (also called aggregators) or through the enterprise portal.

An organization employing RSS technology may want to require employees to subscribe to particular feeds such as those involving policy changes or announcements from human resources.

Streaming media

Audio and video data may be transmitted over the network using standard clients such as Web browsers and media players (QuickTime, Windows Media Player, RealPlayer, and so on). Instead of simply being downloaded and played locally, streaming media buffers as it downloads, allowing media to be played as it downloads. Both live and on-demand content may be accessed through streaming media, such as on news or entertainment Web sites.

Organizations can implement streaming media services internally as part of its employee training program or as a way for employees to view live or archived footage of events. Allowing employees to view live events remotely reduces travel expenses and increases employee participation. Streaming feeds may also be used as part of an organization's security system.

Part IV
Developing an Extended Network Enterprise

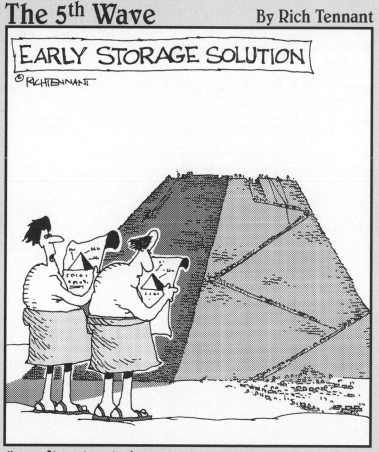

The 5th Wave   By Rich Tennant

EARLY STORAGE SOLUTION

© RICHTENNANT

"Configuring it has been a little tougher than
we thought."

In this part . . .

Beyond consolidation and standardization, enterprise architecture involves strategies for data storage management, application development, and anytime/anywhere enterprise access. In this part, you explore all those strategies and more.

Chapter 10

Managing Data Storage

In This Chapter

▶ Identifying storage requirements

▶ Examining data categories

▶ Developing data storage policies

▶ Protecting stored data

*T*he foundation of networked services and enterprise resource architecture rests squarely on the storage and organization of data. You can find static digital content, compiled application files, and digital media of all types throughout the modern enterprise. Without planning for the acquisition, storage, organization, identification, maintenance, and retirement of enterprise data, organizations will be constantly burdened by cost, resource, and regulatory challenges in trying to manage this flood — a task very similar to attempting to hold back the sea with a whisk broom.

This chapter addresses storage technologies and strategies applicable to enterprise networks of all sizes. While smaller organizations may not need high-speed dedicated storage area networks (SANs), other factors, such as security and availability, affect smaller storage pools as well.

Determining Storage Requirements

Determining an organization's requirements for data storage is critical to the enterprise architecture program. Not only must you determine how much storage is currently being used, but you must figure out whether it's being used effectively and efficiently. In the early stages of a storage restructuring project, it isn't unusual to find personal multimedia files, archived junk and spam e-mails, multiple copies of a file in different locations, and huge log files that are no longer necessary.

Your organization's data storage requirements affect both its storage policies and strategies, ranging from the number of days e-mail is kept before archiving to the type of hardware used. You must also take into consideration how storage requirements will change during enterprise restructuring. Implementing an enterprise portal solution, for example, may increase storage requirements due to file versioning (discussed later in this chapter) and the use of index files in searches, but it may also decrease storage requirements due to a reduction in document redundancy by using shared file storage locations for common items. (For more information on portals, see Chapter 8.)

Conducting a storage survey

A storage survey (or inventory) identifies the size, type, configuration, location, and age of all elements of storage in the enterprise network. It also includes identification of the type of data stored on each storage device and the relevant legal, regulatory, and security requirements. Conducting the survey may involve discussions with data owners or stewards, but the survey isn't a questionnaire or checklist to be run through top to bottom; it's instead an accounting and identification of storage and its use.

If a central systems management utility, such as Novell ZENworks or Microsoft System Center Operations Manager, is in use, its system inventory can serve as a good starting point. However, you can find a significant amount of storage outside of the file server and obvious storage systems. For example, the workstation excess data storage may compose a storage grid opportunity (see Chapter 14) far greater than the storage on all file servers because of the expanding size of basic disk drives installed in workstations by default. There may be unmanaged hardware in various resource silos throughout the organization as well.

The storage survey should also include removable or backup media such as tape storage, removable optical media, and newer moveable storage devices such as thumb drives. It's important to have an accurate inventory of this type of portable storage in order to reduce the risk that loss or theft will go unnoticed. Data may be retained on these devices past established retention periods.

In addition to the storage elements themselves, the survey should identify technical support requirements and any warranties, service contracts, and service level agreements in effect.

This survey ensures that policy decisions take into account the capacity and availability of storage resources. It also allows you to identify resource silos, as well as old or legacy equipment in need of replacement. The survey should reveal any constraints that can affect storage policy planning, such as requirements for encryption or segregation of data, as well.

Interviewing personnel

The initial storage survey provides you with a list of what exists, while interviews allow you to identify how the storage is used throughout all levels of the organization. An added benefit is that this communication assists with proper IT governance, which ensures that IT policy decisions take business requirements into account. (See Chapter 3 for more details.)

You need to interview both technical and nontechnical personnel. Data resource managers, database architects, and application designers can provide valuable information about current usage and the expected rate of growth. Managers in charge of key services can provide insight into mid- to long-term planning and expectations that may influence storage requirements. In addition, interview principal stakeholders to make sure that their projects are taken into account when planning storage requirements. Owners or stewards of unusually large file stores identified in the storage survey may also provide understanding of their unique storage requirements, such as the public relations manager who may receive video clips or the marketing director, who may have to produce poster-size, high-resolution documents.

Identifying Important Data Categories

During your survey, you identify a wide range of data types stored within the enterprise. Although many forms exist, most enterprises contain several standard categories. These categories generally have the greatest impact on storage requirements and policies.

File repositories

A *file repository* is a logical location (as opposed to a physical location) for saving files. For various reasons, not the least of which is that many users feel the need to save every file ever created or received for all eternity, file repositories are particularly prone to bloat. They have a tendency to grow until forcefully restricted, such as by quotas or simply running out of disk space.

Portals and other types of online file repositories store files in databases, which means that bloat caused by long-term or unnecessary retention of files can be mistaken for normal database expansion. In addition, because other information is stored in the database along with the files, backups of database-driven file repositories often require more storage space than backups of traditional file systems.

Regardless of the nature of the file repositories in the organization, you must plan carefully to ensure not only that enough file space is available to users but also that the allocated space is not wasted. A proper data storage policy can assist with this, and that's discussed later in this chapter.

 Unfortunately, it's not unusual for less computer-savvy users to use various parts of the operating system (such as the Recycle Bin and Deleted Items folder in Microsoft Windows) as storage locations. Having these locations purge automatically after a set period helps curb this behavior. Many storage management services and integrated operating systems provide mechanisms for automatic clearing of deleted file areas. One example of this is the storage-related Group Policy settings in the common Microsoft Active Directory environment.

File versioning

File versioning — having multiple versions of the same document available in active file storage areas — can increase storage requirements significantly. However, the benefits of providing users with the ability to roll back to previous versions of documents without administrator intervention are likely to outweigh the cost of additional storage capacity. This functionality is commonly found in portal or content management systems, but is also found in operating systems.

When implementing any type of file versioning, it's critical to ensure that the maximum number of saved versions is appropriate based on the amount of available storage. Maintaining ten versions of a file may become equivalent to maintaining ten files of the same size, or perhaps larger when change logs are added. Some versioning technologies track only changes between versions, while others record each file version uniquely. When planning total storage requirements, file versioning depth (the maximum number of copies to be kept for a particular file) must be included as a multiplier of file storage need.

Databases

Databases have become critical to many different business processes. The databases and their associated indices can become quite large, especially in the case of data warehouses. As well, operational or legal mandates may require that individual transactions be logged and archived. It is common for databases with high utilization to have transaction logs that take up a greater amount of storage space than the actual data, and you must plan for this when designing storage solutions.

Because databases are the back end for many types of applications and services, any plans to consolidate storage areas that host databases must be thoroughly reviewed and tested to avoid any loss of connectivity.

Multimedia

The ease with which document authors can include audio, video, and other rich content into everything from presentations to e-mail to spreadsheets has resulted in an increased need for storage space. Other content types can be included with text in either streaming, embedded, or downloadable formats.

Due to the proliferation of both cheap disk space and broadband Internet connections, users no longer have any incentives to keep file sizes small. You must assume the following:

✔ Digital video and photographs will be saved with the maximum resolution and file size.

✔ Users will bring large high-resolution graphics into word-processing documents and presentation, and then resize them.

✔ Instead of downloading a single image, users may download entire image galleries.

You must also plan for future use of existing multimedia types as well as emerging technology. Expect to continually investigate emerging solutions and test them in your enterprise to identify new solutions and new opportunities. The only constant in the enterprise is change.

E-mail

E-mail is a vital part of business communications. Not only that, it is often an official record that is required for compliance not only with internal operational directives but also with legal mandates. Retention and discovery requirements for e-mail are particularly evident with respect to governmental entities. As such, it's not unusual for organizations to save years' worth of e-mail messages, including legitimate business messages, spam, junk mail, and incidental personal messages.

In determining storage requirements, you must look at the volume of mail being processed in addition to the volume of valid mail. You can then categorize the valid mail as either "working" mail that must be easily accessible to users or archival mail that is accessed infrequently, if at all. Be sure to specifically include e-mail retention in your organization's data storage policy.

E-mail volume — Yale University

Yale University makes its e-mail processing statistics available on its public Web site (www.yale.edu/its/metrics/). From July 2008 to June 2009, the university processed approximately 2.6 million incoming e-mails per day. Of that, approximately 317,500 were actually delivered after making it through spam and antivirus filters. While this type of volume is not typical for most organizations except large ones, it serves to illustrate the ratio of signal to noise. For each valid message received, the organization also processed seven invalid ones.

Logging

These days, it seems that just about every software application logs some type of activity, including but not limited to security events, file access, object access, authentication, and transactions. Depending on the level of activity, these log files have the potential to grow to enormous size.

Each application may have different requirements for access and activity logging as well as log archival.

In addition to auditable information, logging requirements may also include e-mail, instant messaging, or other methods of communication. These requirements affect not only active storage and backup requirements, but also archival storage requirements.

You need to balance requirements from various mandates and directives against the amount of data that is reasonably possible to log. Simply logging everything may be tempting; however, the cost in resources (CPU, storage, bandwidth) may not justify that decision. You should evaluate logging on a case-by-case basis, ensuring that logging is maintained for a period of time that remains ultimately useful to the organization. As an example, retaining SharePoint Unified Logging Service (ULS) logs beyond their useful term for diagnostic evaluation serves no purpose. Some logs generated by default in many applications may never be used for any purpose, and so retention periods can be adjusted accordingly.

When determining the information to be logged, ask the following questions:

✔ What *must* be logged?

✔ What *should* be logged?

✔ What *can* be logged?

Because you can't perform logging after the fact, you need to determine logging requirements sooner rather than later.

Virtual servers

You need to ensure that you have sufficient storage capacity before implementing virtual systems. In its most simplified form, a virtual server is a file containing an operating system, applications, storage, and communications services. Because they're file-based, virtual servers can place an enormous burden on your organization's data storage capabilities.

Examples of virtual server sprawl and impact on storage systems include the following:

- ✔ You can move this file between physical systems or use it as a template when provisioning (creating) other virtual servers.

- ✔ You can archive multiple copies of an individual virtual server for disaster recovery purposes.

- ✔ Virtual servers are easy to provision, which sometimes leads to a large number of single-purpose servers or a sprawling development environment.

- ✔ Virtual disks often expand automatically for internal operations.

Without careful planning, virtual servers can overrun an organization's available storage capacity. In addition, because virtual servers can store any type of data, from staff contact lists to confidential customer financial records, take care to ensure compliance with mandates regarding data protection and segregation.

You can find greater detail on this topic and other aspects of virtual computing in Chapter 13.

Creating a Storage Policy

Initially, you design a storage framework to align business requirements with preliminary broad-stroke storage policies. Then, you design the system and refine policies as you proceed through the process of storage configuration. The final solution should provide the basis for detailed storage policies transmitted to the users. You should review these policies, as with all others within an organization, regularly (at least yearly, if not more often) to engage emerging technologies and changes to storage requirements.

Addressing specific storage topics

Storage policies should address the following topics, at a minimum:

- ✔ Storage quotas, including file and e-mail
- ✔ Long-term or archival storage (retention)
- ✔ Backup and recovery
- ✔ Authorized data storage locations
- ✔ Authorized types of data
- ✔ Security
- ✔ Storage media reuse and disposal

Many times, you can reduce storage requirements by a surprisingly large amount by eliminating temporary files, cleaning out deleted item traps, and purging data accumulated through common application use. For example, mobile multipurpose devices allowed within the enterprise can consume large portions of file storage and backup media when users inadvertently synch personal media files within their enterprise user storage profile, as many media management tools will do by default.

Figure 10-1 illustrates the impact on my (Kirk's) system when I synch up my mobile media devices with my user file storage profile. I use the WinDirStat utility to display an example of the file storage impact created by synching attached media devices to a file server. Relative individual file sizes are reflected by corresponding block sizes in the lower half of the utility's display. The large similar areas in the upper half of the relative file size display are all media of one type or another, with rough percentages by file type presented in the upper-right tree display. The operating system and all applications occupy only 20 percent of the file display on the right side.

You can temporarily reduce storage demands by implementing policies for automatic removal of deleted items, emptying trash cans before logout, and providing user instruction on proper procedures for configuring their multimedia devices. Clearing accumulated application data, such as the browser cache, can also recover a surprisingly large storage volume to ease short-term storage overruns until additional solutions can be acquired and put into operation. Maintenance actions alone can't manage the avalanche of data that is poured into storage systems every day, without a mechanism for control and removal. When you lack policies restricting retention and controlling quotas, storage pools rapidly become virtual dumping grounds for jokes, videos, old holiday memos, and thousands of other types of data lacking value to the organization's ongoing function. Similarly, content management and events management systems may retain articles and event entries from many years ago, further bloating storage requirements without proving organizational value in return for the cost of an ever-expanding storage requirement.

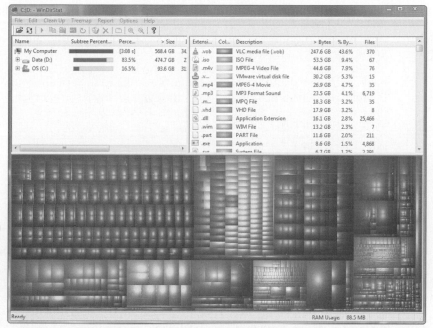

Figure 10-1:
Synched
media files
can balloon
file storage.

Distributing the policy

Storage policies, like other forms of technology, use policies and should be developed and reviewed by a committee comprised of both technical and nontechnical stakeholders. Executive buy-in is critical prior to announcement of policy changes in order to ensure support.

You can write a storage policy as a process policy detailing the sequence of steps for requesting, using, and releasing file storage. You can also write it as a constraint policy, which defines length of data retention, per-user storage limits, and other restrictions based on file type, use, or job roles. Policies may also be a combination of processes and constraints in order to define specific circumstances when appropriate, but should be limited in scope to avoid creating ambiguity.

Ideally, an announcement of new storage opportunities and policies will be made in a monthly or quarterly newsletter with an All Staff distribution and then posted for long-term archive and access on the enterprise intranet. This notification ensures that personnel hired since the initial announcement have access to all policies. Review of this and other policies should be part of new hire in-processing.

Recent studies have found that user compliance with company data storage policies is fairly low, which may be due primarily to lack of employee knowledge of both the storage policies and the consequences of not following them. Employees may not understand the difference between their local hard drive or a mapped network drive and may assume that every network location is backed up on a daily basis. You should coordinate the collaboration between IT staff and human resources to ensure that employees are aware of the new data storage policies and receive adequate training.

Designing a Storage System

After you complete your storage survey and identify areas in need of correction, update, or addition, you can define appropriate storage policies and then design the end-state storage elements of the enterprise network. This design begins as a preliminary plan that includes any existing elements that you can retain or retask and then is refined by identifying new technologies to be acquired as purchasing cycles allow.

You should be familiar with your organization's purchasing contracts, cycles, and any limitations affecting acquisition of new storage technologies. Few storage designs can be immediately implemented, so you may need a phased strategy across multiple purchasing cycles to transition to the final design. Many changes and new technologies may emerge during this time, so you should review the storage design before each purchasing cycle to identify any appropriate changes made necessary by new options.

Selecting appropriate storage configurations

The organization and placement of file storage within the extended enterprise will be affected by the data type and expected use. Your organization's data storage complexity will affect growth and manageability of storage resources in the mid to long term. After discovering what is currently in use, you must then determine short-, medium-, and long-term storage goals in order to guide the organization toward a desirable future state.

You have to become aware of things that will be resource-intensive before they move into common business use and make sure that you have adequate storage before it becomes vital. For example, when you change from a simple file storage solution to a version-controlled file storage solution, such as those often found in portals (see Chapter 9), file storage requirements for the same number of files may skyrocket.

Here are some of the more common storage configurations:

- **Direct attached storage:** *Direct attached storage* (DAS) includes storage devices and arrays (groups of storage devices) attached directly to a computer, either internally or externally. This type of storage provides high availability to the user of individual desktop or portable computers. However, data sharing and disaster recovery planning become problematic. With regard to servers, file services may have to compete with other services, resulting in decreased performance.

- **Network attached storage:** A *network attached storage* (NAS) device is a server that provides only file storage services. It runs on a scaled down operating system (in order to provide a file system) and utilized direct attached storage. Implementation of a NAS solution can improve backup and access audit control. A NAS solution can be an intermediary step to a storage area network (SAN), particularly if SAN implementation isn't possible due to costs.

- **Storage area network:** Unlike a NAS system, a SAN system provides storage but not a file system. It uses specialized protocols and dedicated network connectivity to allow high-speed communications between storage devices and servers. The storage devices that make up a SAN are seen by servers as locally attached devices. SAN solutions allow greater control over resource allocation and management, particularly backup and recovery efforts. They're particularly suited to data centers and to organizations that use high-density servers (blade servers, for example).

Exploring enterprise-level storage strategies

As your enterprise moves beyond by-system storage, you can achieve a more dynamic and cost-effective solution by moving to consolidated storage area network (SAN) alternatives. These solutions allow host servers to access remotely connected data storage blocks (called *logical unit numbers,* or LUNs) as if directly attached to each host. When additional storage is needed, you can expand a LUN (into a metaLUN) as needed by simply changing the SAN configuration, without requiring removal or exchange of in-place storage as with embedded local hard drives.

You can select a particular SAN technology by determining raw throughput requirements, standardization of connectivity (TCP/IP versus Fibre Channel, for example), or prior training and experience available in existing support personnel. The most common types of SAN connectivity include the Fibre Channel, Internet Small Computer System Interface (iSCSI), and ATA over Ethernet (AoE) formats.

Fibre Channel

Due to its high data transfer rate and maximum number of devices, Fibre Channel is considered the standard for enterprise SANs. Characteristics of Fibre Channel include these:

- The maximum number of ports depends upon the topology.
  - *Point to Point:* 2 ports
  - *Arbitrated Loop:* 127 ports
  - *Switched Fabric:* more than 16 million ports
- Fibre Channel can use either optic fiber or copper cable, although the transfer rate is significantly greater over optic fiber (up to 4000MB/sec).
- Each port requires a host bus adapter for communication.
- Specialized SAN-aware software must be used for both resource management and backup/recovery.

Fibre Channel over IP (FCIP) and Internet Fibre Channel Protocol (iFCP) allow for Fibre Channel communication over standard IP networks, allowing data transfer between SANs in different geographic areas.

Fibre Channel carries significant cost due to specialized infrastructure requirements and may not be cost effective for small to medium organizations.

iSCSI

Internet Small Computer System Interface (iSCSI) is a SAN protocol that allows SCSI connectivity over IP networks. You can use iSCSI to link SANs in different geographic areas or to provide SAN access over local area networks, wide area networks, or the Internet. Characteristics of iSCSI include the following:

- iSCSI is slower than both Fibre Channel and direct attached SCSI because it's based on the speed of the network. For example, you can expect a data rate of approximately 120MB/sec over a standard gigabit network. However, 10-gigabit Ethernet devices, although not commonplace, are available, and data transfer rates would scale accordingly.
- iSCSI transmits data in large blocks, providing greater throughput and reduced latency.
- You can use existing network infrastructure.

If the data transfer rate of iSCSI is acceptable, there may be value in migration from direct attached SCSI to iSCSI in lower administrative and maintenance costs.

AoE

ATA over Ethernet (AoE) is a lightweight SAN protocol that operates using an Ethernet connection, but does not utilize the full TCP/IP protocol suite. As such, devices don't have IP addresses, but instead have ID numbers, much like SCSI devices. You can connect AoE devices directly to servers or plug them into network switches.

AoE is an open protocol that you are more likely to find in organizations that employ open source software. However, AoE is also compatible with proprietary operating systems. AoE is a lower-cost alternative to iSCSI or Fibre Channel.

Dealing with expanding storage needs

Moore's Law, published in 1965 by George Moore, then the head of Research & Development at Fairchild, stated that transistor density on integrated circuits doubles every two years. Mark Kryder, a former Seagate Corp. Senior Vice President and current Carnegie Mellon University professor, extended Moore's Law in 2005 to encompass storage density, stating that it doubled on roughly the same cycle.

Increasing Internet bandwidth and broadband access has facilitated a massive explosion of large file transport options. Inexpensive large storage devices in thumb drives, digital cameras, and personal computers eliminate the need to clean out older files to make room for newer ones. These trends combine to create ever-growing digital piles of junk, duplicated and backed up and copied over and over. Particularly in mobile form, the growth of storage capacity has even overrun Kryder's Law at times, and the future enterprise faces challenges in synchronizing, organizing, maintaining, and ultimately eliminating data — or risk being buried under rising mountains of accumulated information.

Although the question of whether the rate of increase is truly following Kryder's Law is outside the scope of this book, storage requirements undoubtedly continue to expand. To meet this unbounded body of data, you have several strategies available.

Additional storage

The most common solution to expanding file stores is to simply buy more storage every year to accommodate doubling within Kryder's threshold. (For more on Kryder's Law, see the preceding section.) The general target measure is a 60-percent storage utilization fraction (meaning that average file storage should not exceed 60 percent of the maximum available space) to avoid overruns during transient peak utilization. This strategy is one of the most common for storage management because it involves the least disruption to end users and can be budgeted as part of a cyclic update scheme.

Regular expansion strategies allow flexibility in the type of data being stored when purchasing is coupled with effective policies directing types of data to appropriate storage locations with adequate bandwidth. For example, you can locate rich media presented as streaming content on larger, slower remote storage with large bandwidth capacity, while you can place critical-use items on high-speed access storage devices located on network segments close to the consuming business unit to reduce latency and minimize potential for interception.

Tiered data storage

Placing the right data on the right storage system is an effective strategy that has been extended to technologies that can automatically shuffle immediate data from ultra high-speed, solid state storage (very high cost per GB of storage, fastest access rates) to 15kbps hard drive storage as the data moves past immediate to current thresholds. The data is later moved to storage for older, never-accessed archival data on low-speed 7kbps storage until eliminated at the end of its data duration lifespan or when recovered to higher-speed storage following use.

Figure 10-2 illustrates a simple tiered storage solution with three layers of storage managed by time since last access. Other options include file type or file size constraints to manage storage efficiently based on the unique needs of a particular organization.

Tiered storage solutions allow older legacy storage technologies to be retained and continue to provide value to the enterprise by forming the base level of archival storage, provided sufficient measures have been taken to ensure fault tolerance. By retaining operational hardware and applying newer, higher-speed storage where it will provide the most bang for the buck, an enterprise can enjoy better performance without the price tag required for a rip-and-replace, edge-to-edge replacement.

Data de-duplication

Another technology gaining popularity in storage management planning involves the use of software agents that scan data stores, identifying files or storage blocks that are absolutely identical. *De-duplication* technologies identify matching items, maintaining one in storage and placing pointers from all other locations that direct access to the single master copy. If a user makes changes to his copy of the file accessed via the link, a new copy unique to his use is created from the master and retains any changes applied by the user.

In any large enterprise, you can have thousands of copies of widely distributed files, such as the flyer for the Halloween costume party or the user handbook. By retaining only a single master copy, but providing links to that master in every location users had previously saved identical copies, end-user consumption remains the same, and changes to the file remain local to individual users while storage requirements are reduced. Block-level technologies apply the same function to parts of files that are identical, but these technologies can present data discovery complexity in regulated industries or where legal motions for discovery are filed.

Automated Storage Tiering

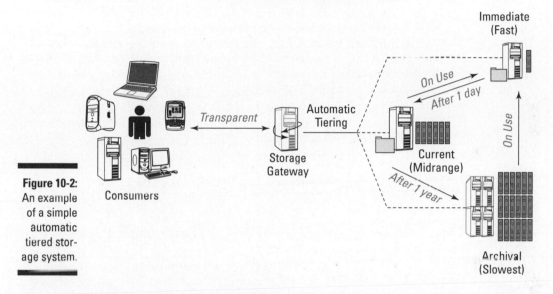

Figure 10-2:
An example of a simple automatic tiered storage system.

Protecting Stored Data

Information in the form of stored data is the lifeblood of modern organizations. It's an asset in need of protection commensurate with its value. Data protection involves more than authorization and access controls; it also entails increasing the likelihood of successful recovery from hardware failures, preventing unauthorized access to data from physical access to backup media, and ensuring that an organization's data isn't exposed during disposal of storage media.

After the appropriate types and levels of protections are determined, they should be included in the storage policy.

Fault tolerance

RAID (redundant array of independent disks) is used when a fault tolerant data storage system is desired. In a *fault tolerant system,* if one hard drive fails, another can immediately take its place with no administrator intervention. RAID comes in many configurations, referred to as *levels.* Combinations of levels are identified using multiple digits (examples: 6+0 or 10).

RAID 1 and RAID 5 are two of the most commonly used configurations when fault tolerance is needed (see Figure 10-3). These levels include

- ✔ **RAID 1:** Also called *disk mirroring,* two or more drives are used, and all drives hold the same data. RAID 1 allows another disk to take over in the event one fails.

- ✔ **RAID 5:** Three or more disks are used, and both data and parity blocks are saved across all disks in such a way that if one disk is lost, the data can be reconstructed and remains available to users, although performance suffers.

Figure 10-3: RAID 1 (mirroring) places identical copies of each data segment on both drives, while RAID 5 (striping with parity) distributes data segments and parity information across several drives.

Examples of Redundant Arrays of Inexpensive Disks (RAID)

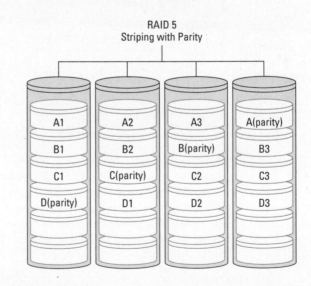

Backup and recovery

The specific backup mechanisms used depends on many factors, most notably the technology involved, the applications in use, and the organization's business continuity and disaster recovery requirements. These requirements are discussed in Chapter 18.

The CIAs of data security

The three core principles of information security are confidentiality, integrity, and availability (CIA), which you must keep in mind during all stages of data storage planning:

✔ **Confidentiality:** Data must be protected from being accessed by unauthorized entities.

✔ **Integrity:** Data must be protected from modification or deletion without authorization.

✔ **Availability:** Data must be available for authorized use when needed.

Regardless, you need to extend the same or greater protection to the backup media as to the original data. Protections are both logical and physical, including

✔ Encryption of confidential, sensitive, or proprietary information, in the event that backup media is lost or stolen

✔ Physical protection of backup media, such as tapes, hard drives, and other portable storage devices

✔ Tracking the movements of backup media within the organization and to/from off-site storage facilities

✔ Appropriate access control permissions for replicated data

Data removal

Deleting files and even formatting media doesn't actually remove data. Instead, it simply removes the pointers and makes it generally inaccessible without the use of data recovery or forensic tools. These tools aren't difficult to acquire (or even to write), with both free and commercial versions easily available. Even if the equipment appears to be nonfunctional, you can still recover data in a laboratory environment. This procedure can be time consuming and costly, but well worth it if the reward is trade secrets.

There are three levels of data removal:

✔ **Clearing:** This method makes data inaccessible to software tools, but not to laboratory recovery processes. Clearing is appropriate when you're reusing media within an organization, such as when you transfer data from one user to another within a business unit. Clearing is typically accomplished by overwriting. The media is overwritten with data, such as 0s and 1s or random characters. Storage clearing is applied on a file storage location, on unassigned storage space, or across an entire storage device or RAID volume.

✔ **Purging:** Purging removes data, making it inaccessible to both software tools and laboratory recovery processes. Purging is appropriate when media is being discarded or when it's being retasked to a purpose that requires different security controls. Methods of purging include

- **Overwriting:** You can use this process for purging, but it requires multiple repeated passes over the entire storage area. However, evidence indicates that you may still be able to recover data through the use of electron microscopy.

- **Degaussing:** This process uses a strong magnetic field to erase data on magnetic media, such as video tapes, hard drives, floppy disks, and magnetic tape. Modern media types are rendered unusable when degaussed, so don't apply this form of data removal to media that you need to reuse.

✔ **Destruction:** This method is the most effective for data removal and involves crushing, shredding, melting, or otherwise rendering the media completely unusable and data unrecoverable. Destruction is appropriate when you can't purge or discard media. Methods of destruction include degaussing, shredding, crushing, and incinerating.

While you may be tempted to use power tools or other unconventional methods to destroy media, remember that many types of computing equipment, including storage media, contain hazardous materials (lead, mercury, cadmium, and various other chemicals). You should dispose of this equipment in accordance with industry and governmental requirements. You may want to consider outsourcing this function to a specialized destruction company.

Creating a destruction policy

Due to the low cost of removable media such as floppy drives, CDs, unencrypted thumb drives, and memory cards, you should consider implementing a destruction policy for this type of media instead of retasking it. Manpower requirements for successfully purging removable media can far outweigh the cost of simple destruction and replacement.

As a matter of course, you may want to implement an across-the-board purging or destruction policy for all media, regardless of the type of information processed. Although this type of policy may result in increased operational costs, it also lowers the risk of significant expenses, such as those arising from data breaches. For example:

✔ Even if the data on the storage media isn't confidential or proprietary, if it contains licensed software, you may be in violation of license agreements if the media is disposed of without proper sanitization.

✔ You can't be absolutely 100-percent sure that confidential information has never been saved to a particular device.

Could your organization's data be won by the highest bidder?

In 2003, MIT purchased 158 used hard drives from online auctions and other sources of used computing equipment. Of those, 29 were found to be inoperable, 12 were properly sanitized, and 117 had recoverable data. Confidential data, such as credit-card numbers, financial records, and medical records, were found, as well as large amounts of personal information.

✔ Some legal mandates, such as HIPAA, require sanitization of any media that may have contained specific classifications of information, even when transferring that media between business units.

✔ Human error can result in the wrong procedure being performed, possibly leading to release of confidential data.

Take nontraditional media into account when developing a data removal policy. Nontraditional media include portable devices, such as cellphones and PDAs, networking devices, such as routers and switches, copy and fax machines, and specialized scientific or manufacturing equipment. Contact the device manufacturer for the proper sanitization procedures, and follow those procedures. Removable media may also provide an avenue for data theft, requiring policies for device use or restrictions on USB port availability.

Leased equipment and warranty replacement

Problems may arise if data storage media has to be returned to the vendor, such as with a lease or warranty replacement. Consult with procurement personnel and if necessary, address these issues in the data storage policy. For example, if your organization makes use of leased equipment, you may want to restrict the type of data that can be stored on equipment not owned by the organization.

Fortunately, hardware vendors are beginning to realize that organizations are uncomfortable with or unable to return hard drives containing confidential or proprietary information for warranty replacement. In response, some allow their customers to pay a small premium to keep their hard drives. This option should be used wherever feasible.

Chapter 11

Managing Application Development

In This Chapter

▶ Defining the software development life cycle

▶ Selecting a software development model

▶ Making use of service-oriented architecture

▶ Remembering accessibility in application development

A tremendous variety of applications are available, ranging from commercial, off-the-shelf turnkey solutions to free open-source applications that you can alter, rebrand, and recompile at will. When extensive customization isn't necessary for alignment with business requirements, turnkey applications are often easier to integrate with other products from the same vendor or through closely aligned vendor partners. Customization in application design can rapidly introduce undesirable complexity at all levels, from protocol interoperability issues and language incompatibility to varying terminology and UI placement of standard functions, such as the Print button.

It is critical to include application development in enterprise architectural planning in order to ensure that clear standards are implemented and maintained to address current and emerging programmatic development styles and technologies. You should conduct a survey of custom, customized, and off-the-shelf applications to ensure that architectural planning includes constraints created by existing applications and identifies corrective actions for trouble spots before problems arise.

In this chapter, we discuss application design from a high-level perspective to provide insight into formal application development methodologies that may be useful in your planning. Very few enterprises follow only a single method of application design for all tasks, so you should focus on identifying standards before addressing specific technologies, languages, or programming styles.

Exploring the Software Development Life Cycle

You need a formal process or methodology for application development, generally referred to as the Software or System Development Life Cycle (SDLC), to ensure that you plan, manage, and control software projects and incorporate quality and security into each phase of development.

Although many different SDLC models exist, they typically include the following phases:

- **Initiation and planning:** In this phase, someone within the organization identifies a need for the application. Management then evaluates the need, usually through a feasibility study and/or cost benefit analysis, and provides funding and resources. Finally, planning documents are created that assist with software project management.

- **Requirements analysis and definition:** Project personnel identify and document requirements for the application specified by users and managers. They should also plan for requirements specified by legal or regulatory mandates (see Chapter 6).

- **Design:** This phase includes design of the user interface, business processes, and database structure, as well as any other design elements that are required before the actual programming starts.

- **Programming:** Developers write code based on design documentation and requirements.

- **Testing:** Code testing through peer review and automation occurs during this phase. Code segments and completed code tests are conducted in many different ways in order to make sure that it works as planned and meets all requirements.

- **Implementation:** Approval team, designated senior application development leads, or members of the data resource management team deploy applications into the production environment during this phase.

- **Maintenance:** Application maintenance staff members regularly update code to fix bugs, add functionality, or incorporate improved or new business requirements.

The following sections explore some of the more popular SDLC models.

Waterfall

The waterfall model was the original SDLC method, and in some organizations, you may find that people still refer to it simply as SDLC. In this model, all development phases are sequential, without overlap or iteration. Distinct deliverables exist, with fixed deadlines, which simplifies scheduling and task management. Figure 11-1 illustrates an example of a waterfall model.

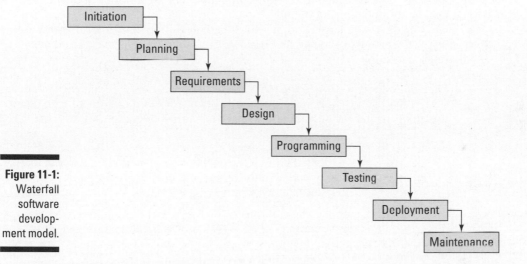

Figure 11-1:
Waterfall
software
development
model.

The waterfall model is the simplest SDLC. However, it's also the most inflexible. Most notably, because no iteration occurs, the waterfall model doesn't allow for the addition of new requirements. Although this approach prevents the uncontrolled addition of features, called *feature creep,* it also prohibits the addition of potentially necessary features that aren't discovered until the project is well underway.

Use the waterfall model when requirements are well known and unlikely to change, such as rewriting an existing application in a new language or developing an application that supports a business process. This model is also a good choice when you're trying to introduce structure to a development team that is used to working in an unstructured fashion, without the guidance of formal software project management.

Prototype

In the prototype iterative model, developers create a basic version of the application based on requirements analysis. Developers and users test the prototype, which they then rework based on user feedback. This cycle continues until the prototype is acceptable and can be used to create a final product. The cyclic nature of this model is evident in Figure 11-2.

The biggest advantage to the prototype model is the amount of user feedback that is obtained during the development process. It allows developers to work closely with users and provides a greater opportunity for understanding requirements than can be obtained by reading requirements and design documentation.

Lack of documentation is the main shortfall of this model. Because each iteration of the prototype results in features being added, removed, and changed, it is not unusual for developers to fall behind with documentation.

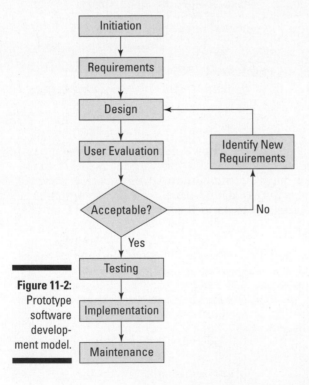

Figure 11-2:
Prototype
software
develop-
ment model.

The prototype model is best used when a set of fully developed requirements or an environment where developers and users can work together closely is unavailable. Prototyping allows geographically dispersed team members an opportunity to try out new code functionality and coordinate between programming operations — a particularly useful capability when programmers hand off to the next team overseas so that continuous development can be maintained throughout the 24-hour day.

Spiral

The spiral software development model, shown in Figure 11-3, is a combination of the waterfall and prototype models (see preceding sections). It includes steps from the waterfall model, such as defining detailed system requirements and creating a preliminary design. It also includes steps from the prototyping model, such as creating multiple prototypes. The first one is a basic prototype created from the preliminary design. This prototype is analyzed, new requirements are defined, risks are identified and resolved, and a second prototype is designed, constructed, and tested. The process is repeated until a final product is developed or the project is aborted.

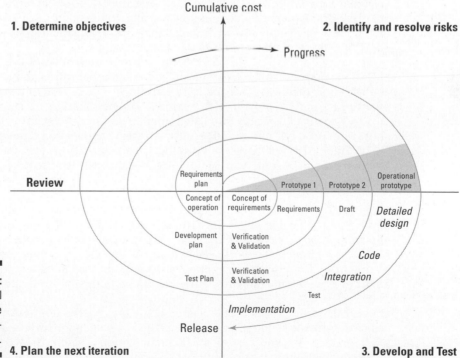

Figure 11-3:
Spiral software development model.

Larger application development tends to follow the waterfall and spiral models because planning and scoping criteria can help protect against feature creep and provide clear measurable deadlines for stakeholders. Companies such as Microsoft and Oracle use these strategies for complex application development by distributed teams.

The spiral model is typically used for large, complicated development projects. Consider the spiral model when requirements are known, but not fully developed enough to create a final product without prototyping. This model is also useful in situations that call for the use of periodic risk assessment.

Rapid Application Development Strategies

Rapid application development (RAD) strategies attempt to reduce the planning "overhead" found in structured strategies, such as the waterfall and spiral models. Rapid application development practices trade planning for short-term cyclic production of small incremental prototypes for integrating project and time management directly into the development process. Frequent face-to-face meetings between sponsors, developers, and consumers drive development focus to timeliness and communication, making these techniques constructive in producing useful programmatic output within short time frames and within rapidly changing scope.

In RAD strategies, feature creep is considered an input rather than an enemy, and the short timetable for each iteration allows a great deal of flexibility over the course of a project. This flexibility can negatively impact larger projects by encouraging forays into programming that may be suitable for the short-term need but not for longer-term strategic application development. Taking only very small steps can produce small projects quickly, but allowing feature creep to become part of the process can easily lead to projects that have no true endpoint or goal.

Many rapid application development methodologies employ common strategies like *pair programming,* where two developers sit at the same terminal and share a single keyboard for input, encouraging quality through observation. This approach can work well in cultures that clearly define social strata so that both developers can operate as equals, but may fall apart when a social or professional disparity encourages one of the pair to be dominant.

Other RAD strategies require a master, who may lack the political clout necessary to provide required resources in the absence of more detailed project planning, to drive group progress. Communication is also critical to RAD programming, where lack of physical proximity or an effective means of rapid communication can produce delays in timetables measured in hours and days rather than months and years.

The never-ending project

Projects without a clearly defined scope and specified go/no-go review milestones can easily turn into the never-ending project. Continuous incremental changes, features added without control by change management practices, alternations of the intended function, consumption of project deliverables, and a lack of attention to project progress all contribute to the undesirable evolution from a defined project to a continuous iteration of updates and changes.

The never-ending project often becomes embedded in the culture and operational landscape, consuming time and resources, increasing operational costs and creating complexity by continuously expanding deliverables to meet requirements outside of the defined scope. Addressing the problem presented by never-ending projects can free up valuable time and resources for use in new projects.

The first step toward developing a cohesive application development strategy involves identifying all current projects and assessing their progress toward defined scope and completion criteria.

Carefully consider the cultural and professional organization of your enterprise before attempting to adopt rapid application development practices as your development standard. Attempts to drive the enterprise into these models can create disruption without adding value.

Following is a look at a few of the more common rapid application development strategies.

Agile programming

Agile programming involves very short timetables applied to incremental programmatic output, with overall goals often measured in weeks and with daily meetings to measure progress. Code tests are typically developed first, followed by the code to suit those tests. Each small code segment is then added to the whole until all pieces have been completed. Agile goals are often constrained to a rigid timebox — if programming output fails to meet goals within the designated time, it's defined as a failure in the process.

Agile techniques can be useful in little, nonmission-critical projects involving small programming teams located in the same physical facility.

Extreme programming

Extreme programming also involves timebox deadlines, iterative code releases, and common practices such as pair programming. It attempts to simplify code to the very basics, preferring operational minimal-feature code over more complex application design that takes longer to provide a useful product.

This methodology is often criticized for producing a lot of small pieces that work well alone, but require continuous re-integration to work together — a process made more difficult due to the lack of an overall plan or detailed documentation.

Extreme programming is useful when development calls for small components, often operating alone or for a short term only.

Scrum programming

Scrum-style development shares many of the standard features of agile programming methodologies including timeboxes and a short iterative release cycle. Scrum programming begins by identifying requirements that are added to the product backlog. These requirements are broken into sprint goals with very short timetables, which are facilitated by the ScrumMaster. A sprint may last 30 days, with meetings every 24 hours to identify progress or barriers that must then be addressed by the master. The end goal of a sprint is to produce a working increment of the final application, which is not necessarily operational by itself like the increments in extreme programming.

Scrum programming may be seen as a direct embodiment of the Pareto principle, (also called the 80/20 rule) where much of the application UI and structure might be reached by the end of the first sprint, with each successive sprint spent developing the functions behind each UI element in finer detail. Here, 80 percent of the final product can be accomplished in the first 20 percent of allotted time, while continued development acts only to refine a portion of the remainder.

One of the criticisms about Scrum programming is the amount of time spent in scrum meetings every day, at the end of each sprint, at the end of a scrum iteration, and in scrum planning and after-action review. Scrum is also fragile because it depends on specific role facilitators like the ScrumMaster and product owner (who represents the stakeholders) — meaning that the scrum cycle can be disrupted by illness of key role holders.

Scrum programming techniques work well with small team-organized development groups enjoying physical proximity or effective teleconferencing capabilities. Because scrum depends on frequent meetings with designated key role holders, widely distributed teams (particularly those in time zones eight or more hours apart) may find scrum to be too cumbersome.

Designing Application Architecture

The development of custom applications within an extended enterprise can take many forms. Traditional application design may utilize a client-server or multi-tiered architecture of deeply integrated application components. An online product-ordering Web site may use a traditional approach by presenting inventory details provided by a middleware component that pulls data from a back-end database linked to the warehouse inventory management system. Modern virtual applications, such as the mashup, can combine services provided by many different technologies into a single interface or within a new service front-end. By employing standards for intercommunication, such as the eXtensible Markup Language (XML) and the XML-based Simple Object Access Protocol (SOAP), various unrelated services can be combined. The same product-ordering Web site may be built by integrating weather patterns in user locations to present items from an inventory management listing to catch user interest by displaying a furnace first for users in colder climates, while an air conditioner is placed at the top of the list when a user is connecting from a warm area.

Multitiered architecture

Client-server application architecture, in which the user interface is separate from processing or data storage, led to the evolution of tiered application architecture. The most common form, *three-tier architecture,* occurs when the client communicates with a middleware application instead of directly with the server on which data is stored. Middleware functionality can also be tiered, such as separating business logic from data access services, leading to modern *n-tier application architecture*. The letter "n" simply refers to the idea that there can be multiple layers between the client and server.

This type of architecture is highly flexible and allows for reconfiguration of individual tiers (or elements within tiers) with minimal disruption of other tiers. For example, multiple clients can be developed for an application without requiring updates to the middleware or data tiers. Additionally, data storage can be scaled up or down without affecting the business logic of the middleware tier or the user interface of the client tier.

N-tier applications exist in distributed application environments in which many systems and services interact. This environment led to the development of standards for application and data identification, use, and, most importantly, integration.

N-tier applications allow programmers to separate service functionality using distributed processing design, coordinating data storage, and retrieval functions on one server with data processing and presentation functions on other systems. Early distributed application environments were tied closely to vendors through proprietary protocols and application programming interfaces (APIs) that often required costly licensing for use. Continued evolution of distributed application design led to the development of interfaces for application identification, integration, and use based on several common standards including XML and the Web Services Description Language (WSDL). Distributed n-tiered applications became identifiable as an integration of services, many of which could be reused in other application functions.

Service-oriented architecture

The emergence of service-oriented architecture (SOA) marks an enterprise-level approach to application design. SOA utilizes a common set of guiding principles including modularity, granularity, interoperability, and reusability. Additional qualities, such as abstraction (where application function is hidden from the consuming component) and discoverability, enhance efficient use of service resources across the expanding enterprise. Application designers no longer need to know the complex data structures and processing logic required to get payroll information on a particular user; their application can simply contact the HTTP service with a `GET` call to `http://hrdata.mycorp.com/<userid>/` or directly access a Web service method: `hrdata.getPayroll(<userid>)`. SOA design includes the creation of a service registry, which can then be used to easily identify services and interoperability constraints using the service contract meta data for each registered SOA element.

Common examples for service discovery, identification, and consumption include SOAP used in Web service design and elements of Representational State Transfer (REST) software architecture methodology. The particular method and standards used in enterprises varies widely, although all include some mechanism to identify and to consume exposed services.

In additional to aiding agility in new application development by allowing reuse of existing service functions, service-oriented architectural design also aids enterprise management over legacy applications and during migration to new technology solutions. Legacy applications that don't provide transport over a secure connection can be accessed securely by creating SOA "wrappers" that hide access functionality to the legacy system behind a `GET` call over an SSL-secured hypertext transport (`https://legacyapp.someweb corp.com/clientdata/<id>/`). The SOA wrapper then handles all communications between the exposed service being accessed over the secured link and the hidden application that is never made available to the consuming client. The same functionality aids migration to new technologies by allowing SOA wrappers to provide access to new services using protocols or access methods unavailable to existing clients prior to upgrade.

Modern enterprises still employ many n-tiered distributed applications, both legacy and newly acquired. Specific enterprise markets often require specialized applications for imaging, document management, or other functions built according to specifications and preferences of third-party vendors. Monolithic applications still exist to perform special functionality for an individual user or role, while some data mining applications work on such embarrassingly large data sets that only portions of the data can be loaded at one time — returning to the days when applications and data were passed into the processing unit together and then discarded as processing progressed.

Service-oriented architectural planning can provide a bridge between all of these systems, making them available to users and consuming secondary services across the many platforms, protocols, and access requirements found in today's enterprise network.

Including Accessibility

In information technology, particularly application development, *accessibility* provides individuals with physical impairment such as restricted vision or hearing with use of and access to data and technology comparable to individuals without disabilities. To be accessible, Web content cannot depend upon only one sense or ability. For example, an image on a Web page is not accessible to people with visual impairment. In order to make that image accessible, Web developers include a text attribute in the HTML image tag that is read aloud by specialized software that allows people to hear Web pages. This text attribute is commonly referred to as an *alt tag*, like the following textual description of an image called kitten.jpg:

```
<image src="kitten.jpg" alt="A cute gray kitten playing with a ball of yarn.">
```

Other accessibility techniques include using high-contrast colors, providing text transcripts of audio files, and ensuring that keyboard commands provide comparable functionality to mouse actions.

Accessibility: What the law requires

The U. S. government has codified accessibility in the *Electronic and Information Technology Accessibility Standards.* These standards are more commonly known as the *Section 508 Rule*, because they were designed to implement Section 508 of the Rehabilitation Act of 1973.

In addition to being mandated for applications in use by Federal employees and users of information resources provided by the Federal government, accessibility may also be required for applications used by state governments and users of state information resources and institutes of high education. Even if none of those conditions apply to your organization, you should still consider making accessibility a requirement for application development, to

whatever degree you determine appropriate, particularly if those applications will be used by members of the general public.

Section 508 requires that information technology, including applications, be functional for individuals that are visually impaired, hearing impaired, speech impaired, and without fine motor control. Application-specific standards cover the use of animation, keyboard controls, display settings, electronic forms, and the use of color, among others.

You can find detailed information on Section 508, including the full text of the standards, at `www.access-board.gov/508.htm` and `www.section508.gov`.

Chapter 12

Planning for the Mobile Enterprise

· ·

In This Chapter

▶ Reviewing mobile technologies

▶ Examining mobile access in the enterprise

▶ Planning for remote mobile access

▶ Developing mobile technology policies

· ·

*J*ust as they say that everything is bigger in Texas, everything is smaller in technology. Miniaturization and high-power batteries have placed more raw-processing power into a cell phone than was used in the entire process of sending the Apollo missions to the moon and back. Plus, for most people, a cell phone is also a lifeline to the world, to Facebook friends, to music and movies when they travel, and a host of other functions wrapped in a small pocket-sized package.

This chapter focuses on the inclusion of mobile technologies in the enterprise network. The topic is a challenging one due to the rapid pace of evolution and adoption of new platforms and entirely new mobile solutions.

Introducing Mobile Computing

Many different mobile technologies exist, from Wi-Fi–enabled medical implants to automobiles with built-in, short-range Bluetooth connectivity. Even building environmental systems, security cameras, and lawn sprinklers may be connected via wireless networking solutions. Devices of all types are being configured for connectivity, so you must be constantly on the watch for the Next Big Thing that may sneak into your enterprise network disguised as a Web-enabled coffee maker or Bluetooth-enabled set of running shoes.

Figure 12-1 demonstrates this ongoing process, with the left side showing a portable computer from the 1980s, while the right side shows increasing levels of miniaturization in Apple's MacBook, iPad tablet, and iPhone devices — all of which pack thousands of times the processing power of my old machine.

Figure 12-1:
One of the first portable computers (left) and the ever-diminishing size of Apple's popular line of technologies (right).

http://commons.wikimedia.org courtesy of Jon Mountjoy

Laptops

Still the most common type of mobile device in the enterprise, laptop computers are small battery-powered computing devices capable of measurable processing power and presenting large high-resolution displays. Laptop computers have varying levels of capability, with high-end systems able to run even the most resource-intensive video games and present rich multimedia content. These systems can be very large and pack in near-desktop system performance at the cost of battery life and heat. They may cost many thousands of dollars for each system, depending on performance and hardware specifications.

Netbooks

Like a laptop, a netbook is a small battery-powered computing device. Typically, netbooks have reduced processing power and smaller displays than their laptop kin to improve battery life and reduce weight. Netbooks are generally low cost, often running only a few hundred dollars per device. By using solid-state storage devices, energy-saving processors, and low-power displays, some of these systems can operate for an entire business day on a single charge. Netbooks are lightweight, easily tossed into a bag or briefcase, and can run most user productivity suites for normal business use.

Tablets

Another trend in portable computing comes in the form of the tablet, including computing devices such as the Apple iPad as well as purpose-specific devices like the popular Kindle electronic book reader. These devices offer much of the same processing power as a netbook, but do away with the keyboard and mouse in favor of touch-screen interfaces and acceleration sensors, allowing the device itself to be used as a mobile touch control. (You may wonder why your staff members keep shaking their tablets during a meeting, but they're not angry — only refreshing their browsers.)

Cell phones

What once was a large blocky device hanging prominently in the foyer has been transformed and made smaller, portable, and loaded with so many bells and whistles it almost makes breakfast for you.

The first portable phone was the size of a small briefcase, weighed as much as a lead brick, and was notoriously unable to maintain a signal without crossing conversations with other mobile phone users. Today, cell phones are small computers capable of sending two-way e-mail, taking pictures, organizing day planners, mapping travel routes, providing remote desktop access to servers, and performing any number of other duties by simply downloading the desired application using a built-in data connection.

Bluetooth

Devices can share short-range interconnection using a variety of mechanisms, including the commonly available Bluetooth protocol. By registering device endpoints, this protocol allows the association between a computer and a variety of wireless headsets, mice, keyboards and other input devices. Bluetooth can also provide data communication between Bluetooth-enabled devices, allowing lightweight mobile WLAN sessions to be created using ad-hoc interconnection between devices.

Long-range wireless

Long-range wireless technologies such as the WiMAX (Worldwide Interoperability for Microwave Access) standard have found some use on farms and in other locations where setting up cellular data connections or more popular short-range Wi-Fi (Wireless Fidelity) transmitters isn't feasible. Figure 12-2 illustrates a mobile hotspot that we use when travelling. It connects long-range to the Internet via a cellular 3G/4G data plan and creates a short-range Wi-Fi connection for up to five devices.

Figure 12-2:
A 3G/4G
cellular data
link provid-
ing a Wi-Fi
hotspot
for WLAN
access
between
up to five
devices.

You can use the WLAN independent of cellular coverage to facilitate group data sharing, including the small on-device data chip shown in the figure. This type of technology poses a risk for highly secure locations because a hotspot with a 32GB or larger chip can be dropped near a building, allowing data to be uploaded from a Wi-Fi-enabled device within the contained area for later retrieval.

Exploring Mobile Computing in the Enterprise

Your mobile communication strategies must include local well-connected users as well as those accessing resources from locations and using devices with limitations on bandwidth or data storage. Access from a public com-puter or kiosk places your organization's data at risk due to the potential for malware on the open system or interception of data. Data stored on mobile devices also poses a risk for disclosure if lost, stolen, or seized for review by customs agents when crossing international lines.

Device interaction

Because wireless transmission systems produce signals that radiate outward from the source, they're useful for roaming devices but also present challenges for security. Broadcasts on the same frequencies can often present significant challenges to help desk personnel charged with figuring out why a user's laptop can no longer find the Wi-Fi access point across the hall. Figure 12-3 illustrates the number of devices identified during a NetStumbler capture of Wi-Fi access point identifiers within a three-block square grid of an average, middle-income residential neighborhood.

No hacking was involved; the nodes were identified by simply listening for ongoing Wi-Fi broadcasts while driving along in my truck.

During a brief drive through a local neighborhood, we were able to identify 727 unique Wi-Fi access points; 142 of these nodes lacked any security, while 381 had only Wired Equivalent Privacy (WEP) enabled — a protocol known to be subject to cryptographic compromise. Fourteen of the detected systems were machines operating in ad-hoc mode, allowing direct access to the Wi-Fi–enabled computers. Broadcast interaction was also easily seen, with channels 11 and 1 having more than 160 nodes each, channel 6 (the default) with more than 300 nodes, and other channels such as 7 and 4 with less than 5 nodes each.

Boosters and dead zones

Mobile technologies are highly susceptible to interference from the local environment. Electrical motors and fans may generate electromagnetic radiation in the same frequency range as Wi-Fi systems, while buildings constructed with steel framing members may block or reflect signals and create odd patterns of high connectivity and dead spots. If you plan to make use of wireless connectivity within the built environment, either to support mobile devices or to allow easy office reconfiguration without requiring re-cabling for connectivity, you must include a detailed site survey.

Site surveys are conducted for each type of connectivity, such as Wi-Fi and cellular data, to identify locations that might need an extra access point or a cellular signal booster (see Figure 12-4) in order to provide continuous service.

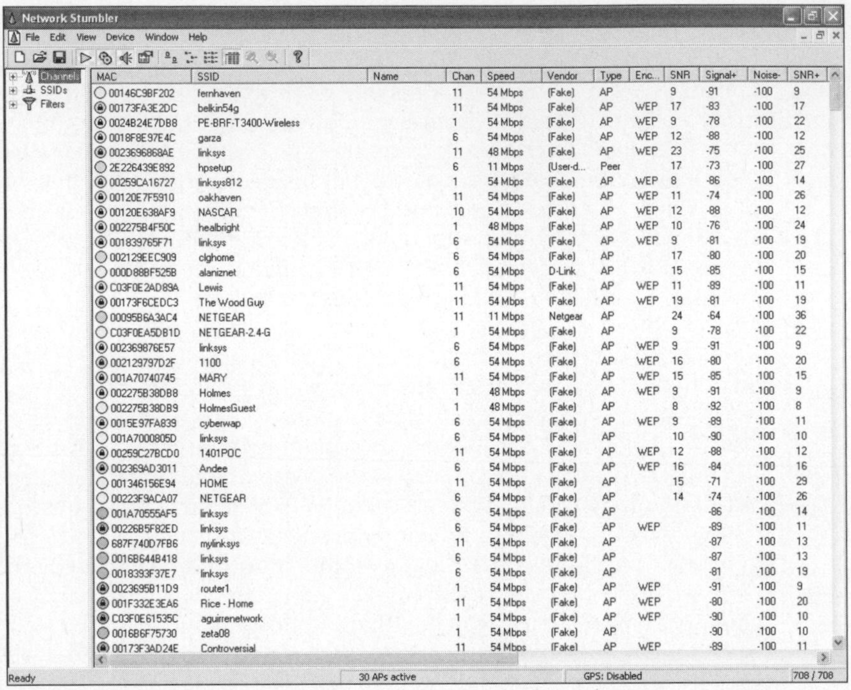

Figure 12-3:
In this image, 30 access points are within range — many of which lack even the most basic form of security against unauthorized use.

Network Stumbler

MAC	SSID	Name	Chan	Speed	Vendor	Type	Enc.	SNR	Signal+	Noise-	SNR+
00146C9BF202	fernhaven		11	54 Mbps	(Fake)	AP		9	-91	-100	9
00173FA3E2DC	belkin54g		11	54 Mbps	(Fake)	AP	WEP	17	-83	-100	17
0024B24E7DB8	PE-BRF-T3400-Wireless		1	54 Mbps	(Fake)	AP	WEP	9	-78	-100	22
0018F8E97E4C	garza		6	54 Mbps	(Fake)	AP	WEP	12	-88	-100	12
0023696868AE	linksys		11	48 Mbps	(Fake)	AP	WEP	23	-75	-100	25
2E226439E892	hpsetup		6	11 Mbps	(User-d...	Peer		17	-73	-100	27
00259CA16727	linksys812		1	54 Mbps	(Fake)	AP	WEP	8	-86	-100	14
00120E7F5910	oakhaven		11	54 Mbps	(Fake)	AP	WEP	11	-74	-100	26
00120E638AF9	NASCAR		10	54 Mbps	(Fake)	AP	WEP	12	-88	-100	12
002275B4F50C	healbright		1	48 Mbps	(Fake)	AP	WEP	10	-76	-100	24
00183976SF71	linksys		6	54 Mbps	(Fake)	AP		9	-81	-100	19
002129EEC909	clghome		6	54 Mbps	(Fake)	AP		17	-80	-100	20
000D88BF525B	alaniznet		6	54 Mbps	D-Link	AP		15	-85	-100	15
C03F0E2AD89A	Lewis		11	54 Mbps	(Fake)	AP	WEP	11	-89	-100	11
00173F6CEDC3	The Wood Guy		11	54 Mbps	(Fake)	AP	WEP	19	-81	-100	19
00095B6A3AC4	NETGEAR		11	11 Mbps	Netgear	AP		24	-64	-100	36
C03F0EA5DB1D	NETGEAR-2.4-G		1	54 Mbps	(Fake)	AP		9	-78	-100	22
002369876E57	linksys		6	54 Mbps	(Fake)	AP	WEP	9	-91	-100	9
00212979702F	1100		6	54 Mbps	(Fake)	AP	WEP	16	-80	-100	20
001A70740745	MARY		11	54 Mbps	(Fake)	AP	WEP	15	-85	-100	15
002275B38DB8	Holmes		1	48 Mbps	(Fake)	AP	WEP	9	-91	-100	9
002275B38DB9	HolmesGuest		1	48 Mbps	(Fake)	AP		8	-92	-100	8
0015E97FA839	cyberwap		6	54 Mbps	(Fake)	AP	WEP	9	-89	-100	11
001A7000805D	linksys		6	54 Mbps	(Fake)	AP		10	-90	-100	10
00259C27BCD0	1401POC		11	54 Mbps	(Fake)	AP	WEP	12	-88	-100	12
002369AD3011	Andee		6	54 Mbps	(Fake)	AP	WEP	16	-84	-100	16
001346156E94	HOME		11	54 Mbps	(Fake)	AP		15	-71	-100	29
00223F9ACA07	NETGEAR		6	54 Mbps	(Fake)	AP		14	-74	-100	26
001A70555AF5	linksys		6	54 Mbps	(Fake)	AP			-86	-100	14
00226B5F82ED	linksys		6	54 Mbps	(Fake)	AP	WEP		-89	-100	11
687F740D7FB6	mylinksys		11	54 Mbps	(Fake)	AP			-87	-100	13
0016B644B418	linksys		6	54 Mbps	(Fake)	AP			-87	-100	13
0018393F37E7	linksys		6	54 Mbps	(Fake)	AP			-81	-100	19
0023695B11D9	router1		1	54 Mbps	(Fake)	AP	WEP		-91	-100	9
001F332E3EA6	Rice - Home		11	54 Mbps	(Fake)	AP	WEP		-80	-100	20
C03F0E61535C	aguirrenetwork		1	54 Mbps	(Fake)	AP	WEP		-90	-100	10
0016B6F75730	zeta08		1	54 Mbps	(Fake)	AP			-90	-100	10
00173F3AD24E	Controversial		11	54 Mbps	(Fake)	AP	WEP		-89	-100	11

Ready | 30 APs active | GPS: Disabled | 708 / 708

Your long-term strategic plan should also call for regular site surveys to ensure that new equipment and emerging technologies using alternative means of interconnectivity continue to operate as intended.

High-density business environments, particularly in multi-level office structures, often encounter interference between devices due to poor coordination between access points. You should conduct a site survey before implementing any wireless connectivity projects, not only to identify dead zones, but also to identify existing systems that may compete for channel use. Regular reviews are necessary to ensure a bad neighbor hasn't started broadcasting on the same channel, blocking out your internal wireless access — or worse, pretending to be a valid access point in order to intercept network traffic.

Figure 12-4: This device boosts signals on the two most common cellular frequencies to improve reception in an office located between two large buildings.

Going Mobile beyond the Enterprise

When mobile users connect to organizational resources, they typically use some form of local area networking, either wired or wireless, or the global Internet. You must plan for minimum bandwidth consumption, encryption of data, and accessible technologies for both users with special needs and technology-limited devices. The popular iPhone, for example, could not process Adobe Flash-based active Web content within its browser, so organizational Web sites developed using that technology were unavailable to iPhone users.

Providing a portal or other secure Web-based intranet interface for remote clients enables them to better participate in organizational functions while on the road. Browser-based applications can perform the majority of processing functions on the server and only present the final results, and they don't require installation of custom programs on the consumer's system. This aids updates and changes to Web-based applications because the new version becomes immediately available the next time a user refreshes or visits the page.

You can also construct extranets designed for partners and suppliers as Web-accessible applications, dashboards, and portals to ensure ease in communication and availability regardless of the type of technology implemented in their organizations. Provided that care is taken in configuring browser-specific settings when programming applications, you can make resources and information securely available to external agents around the world using a wide variety of Web browsers.

Planning for mobile network access to organizational resources involves a number of facets, as described in the following sections.

Navigation

Many external navigation sites like the major search engines exist to return thousands of links for almost any topic you might happen to be curious about. We discuss some considerations for searchable sites in Part III, but it's worth noting here that mobile users are entirely dependent on external resolution of machine names through public Domain Name Service (DNS) entries and searchable entry points for organizational interaction. Corruption or lack of availability to DNS records can prevent a user from even finding the intranet site, much less being able to access its resources.

Navigation within an organization's extended network is also a monster waiting to jump out and surprise you, if care is not taken to ensure that portals and file servers are properly indexed for local search and discovery. You also must ensure that proprietary data is not accidentally exposed by overly open search engine settings.

Connectivity and bandwidth

Most mobile devices enjoy limited connectivity and bandwidth while not directly connected to the network. Although 3G/4G networks are improving transfer speeds, the mobile user typically pays more for every gigabyte of data beyond a basic service level. Applications designed for mobile devices should be constructed with the limited display size, reduced interface options (few mice are attached to cell phones), and reduced bandwidth available to clients on the go.

Many users who connect to organizational resources from home or on the road will connect over wireless networking, requiring care to ensure that proper encryption is in place to secure the data in transit.

VPN and SSL access

Encryption is also critical when transporting data between the mobile device and your organization's servers, particularly when wireless technologies are in use. Because a wireless broadcast is emitted in all directions and can be detected at significant distances, data capture and analysis is easily possible without a means to detect the snooping. Use of a secure Wi-Fi encrypted transport protocol like the Wi-Fi Protected Access (WPA/WPA2) available to most devices can aid in protecting data between the access point and the device itself.

In order to protect against interception or modification of data along the route from the mobile remote user to an organization's resources, you need to create an encrypted pipe through the public Internet. Data passing through this pipe is then concealed from capture and analysis without requiring separate encryption systems for each individual type of connection. Secure Sockets Layer (SSL) transport for Web-based access is a common example of end-to-end transport encryption, used commonly for online banking and monetary transactions. (See Chapter 17 for additional details on encryption.)

Users who need to access your organization's resources as if directly connected to the local network can connect through a virtual private network (VPN) client running on their local system. This approach allows the remote device to participate in the organization's network, creating a tunnel through the organizational firewall to allow direct access to resources and services, even when using a private address space. VPNs typically allow users access from the public Internet, but you may also use VPNs within the enterprise to isolate internal network traffic. For example, a business unit, such as research and development, may have its own VPN to provide another layer of security for highly sensitive data.

Hardware versus software VPNs

You can set up VPNs using hardware or software. Each solution has its own benefits and drawbacks, and you need to evaluate various solutions to see which is the best fit for your enterprise. When making this decision, keep the following in mind:

✔ Hardware VPNs increase complexity in the enterprise by adding more devices to the network.

✔ Software VPNs place a burden on existing devices, shifting resources to supporting tunneling and encryption.

✔ Hardware VPNs are typically more expensive than software VPNs.

✔ You may be able to reduce costs by bundling VPN with other network devices, such as switches, routers, or firewalls.

Remote desktops

Providing remote users access to their full desktop suite, settings, and files offers the experience of being in the office even while on the road. We examine remote desktop access in Chapter 13, but the process basically provides keyboard and mouse data to the remote desktop system and returns audio and video data to the client running on the user's mobile device. This strategy can provide significant benefits by allowing the remote desktop machine's processing power to perform tasks well beyond the capability of a lightweight netbook or tablet device. Because all data remains on the remote desktop host, loss of the mobile device doesn't expose operational details.

When someone is travelling internationally, personal technologies may be taken for security review and access passwords required from device owners on risk of imprisonment or fine. If the user is travelling with an inexpensive netbook configured with no software beyond an antivirus agent, a VPN client, and a remote desktop client, then the officials may examine it all they want without any chance of data loss or exposure. At worst, you can obtain another inexpensive device and configure it the same way to allow continuity of operations even if the device is seized for an extended time.

Power

Even the most efficient netbook systems eventually run their batteries down. Mobile technologies must constantly reconnect to recharge before once again roaming free from the constraint of wires and wired infrastructures. If your users travel internationally, they must also consider the impact of alternative power systems using different voltages and cyclic rates than are used when plugging in at home.

Long flights and mobile use away from a convenient wall socket can also present an issue for the modern always-connected/always-busy information worker. A spare battery or an auxiliary power source like that shown in Figure 12-5 can allow that marvel of mobile technology to avoid becoming a brick useful only as a paperweight until the next plug comes into sight.

Figure 12-5:
A power pack the size of a small deck of cards can add several hours of operation to a netbook and charge various other mobile devices while you're on the road.

Wi-Fi transmitters can consume a significant amount of power when no access point is present or when access point placement is inefficient, requiring increased power to negotiate a successful transfer of data. The Wi-Fi–enabled device will poll for available devices at maximum power in the absence of a signal. Managing device settings for power consumption and turning off wireless links when outside of service coverage helps to extend battery life for mobile devices.

Planning for SmartPhone Computing

In addition to planning for mobile application access by reducing screen size expectations, interface requirements, and bandwidth consumption, you should also include planning for dashboards that present aggregated data in a view-at-a-glance format and file system gateways to facilitate access to a user's common resources when working remotely. Avoiding large graphics as your dashboard indicators and in mobile site content is also a way to improve data plan use.

We describe some considerations for the inclusion and support of smart phones in the enterprise in the following sections.

Familiarity

Many smart phones can serve as cellular modems for a nearby computer tethered via short-range wireless connections or physical cabling. They provide users with instant access to data, e-mail, and many other elements of organizational business data. Built-in Web browsers can also allow them to access intranet portals and other resources via the Internet. Smart phones are the most common personally owned device that may be found across your enterprise, and users will expect support for their various devices when attempting to connect them to standard line-of-business services.

You must encourage the support staff to develop proficiency with newly emergent cell phone technologies or plan for lengthy sessions with irate users. Programming staff members must also familiarize themselves with the limitations and capabilities of mobile devices used within the enterprise, testing newly developed applications for compatibility and ease of use. Emulators such as the Adobe Device Central emulator shown in Figure 12-6, can aid in this process.

Planning ahead

Users who purchase their own mobile devices will often want to integrate them directly into their organizational functions, such as linking e-mail and calendaring applications or connecting to their desktop environment remotely using all manner of devices and vendor technologies. Without policies in place and mechanisms to address the emergence of the next great must-have device, your help desk will be rapidly overrun by users seeking assistance with each unique set of technologies that comes out. Such situations can be magnified when new highly anticipated devices and software are released, leading users to try out the leading edge of technology without understanding the impact they may have on the enterprise network.

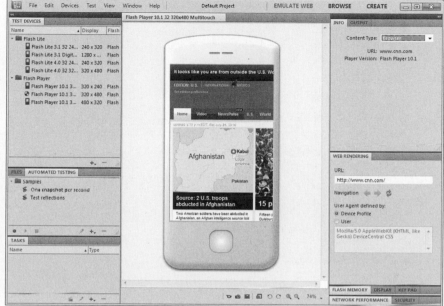

Figure 12-6:
A mobile device emulator displaying a popular news Web site using the designated device, browser, and version of Flash player.

Device locking

Because of their portability, mobile devices are easily left, lost, or stolen. The first line of defense against access is the simple process of enabling automatic device locking.

Figure 12-7 illustrates the prompt received on a smart phone before being allowed to access its contents. If the wrong answer is entered 15 times, the phone automatically wipes itself.

On-device encryption

You must develop strict policies for data storage encryption on mobile equipment, including removable storage devices like the common key fob flash drives. It is remarkable how many mechanisms can carry a tremendous volume of data, including cuff-link USB drives, data watches, and even the shared drive for MicroSD cards on a Wi-Fi hotspot.

By the nature of their use, portable devices are more subject to loss or theft than desktop systems left in the office. Encrypting data on these devices is critical to protecting against exposure due to device theft or loss.

Figure 12-7:
Logon
prompt for
smart phone
device.

Kill pills

When a device is lost or stolen, your policies for encryption may keep the data safe from inadvertent disclosure, but other data may still reside on the device. Many users leave their cell phones unlocked and configured for automatic receipt of e-mail and scheduled events, presenting a threat to operational security. If policies and technologies are in place, the e-mail system administrator can send a kill pill to the device when it next synchronizes for an update. This type of technology can either erase all e-mail on the device or render the device entirely nonoperational, depending on the configuration and options available to the specific technologies involved. Figure 12-8 illustrates this functionality in the moment before one of the author's cats accidentally converted his iPhone into an expensive brick while capturing this image. Fortunately, the device was recoverable.

Laptop LoJack

Like LoJack car-recovery system, technologies also exist that cause lost devices to call home and report their whereabouts for recovery. These systems can work, but are sometimes unreliable when facing tech-savvy criminals.

Device retrieval, beyond the lost laptop left out on the picnic table in the park, can also present challenges requiring involvement by law enforcement officials and other matters of property recovery. Unless your clients are carrying around secrets or intellectual property of significant value, these products present more problems than they fix.

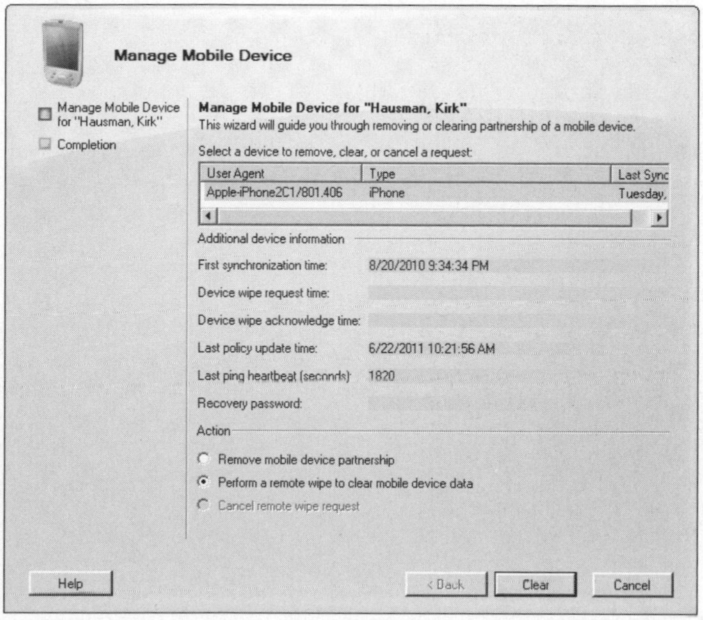

Figure 12-8:
The phone wipe interface of a common enterprise collaboration suite.

Defining Mobile Access Policy

Figure 12-3, earlier in this chapter, of the NetStumbler review of nearby mobile devices clearly shows the difficulty involved in "securing" mobile connections against detection, compromise, or misuse. Scanning an area for wireless access points, known as *wardriving,* allows identification of numerous open access points and capture of data using automated utilities to extract weak WEP encryption keys.

Common tactics, such as man-in-the-middle attacks using rogue access points configured with a known SSID or cracked WEP key, also create risk for enterprise data when accessed by mobile users in hotels, coffee shops, or home offices where the strongest signal with an expected network identifier will be selected automatically.

It's important to define policies for mobile computing, remote access, wireless use, and storage device encryption in order to provide guidance to an increasingly mobile user base. These policies must be reviewed regularly due to the high rate of change in the devices and types of mobile communication technologies that will be found in an extended enterprise environment.

Mobile computing policies

A mobile computing policy should apply to any computing device that operates from multiple locations or that connects to or hosts organizational data that is removed from the premises. The policy must include requirements for on-device encryption of stored data, requirements for securing and storing mobile devices, and requirements for updated malware defenses before connecting to the enterprise network.

Mobile device policies should include recommendations and mandates for removal of cached data, configuring device firewalls, applying updates and patches, avoiding the use of stored credentials for Web and other remote application access, and selection of only noncleartext authentication protocols. Audit rights should be clearly stated and signed by users if personal equipment is to be used for business purposes. In some states, *Open Records requests* (a legal request for information to be released under the Open Records Act) and other legally mandated discovery directives can apply to personally owned devices if also used for business purposes.

Clearly spell out liability for loss; have the user sign the agreement before transfer of organizational equipment to mobile users. Users who travel across geopolitical borders may warrant a more detailed policy, specifying remote access and data removal practices to avoid exposure of sensitive data at border checkpoints.

Remote access policies

Your remote access policy should specify the method and mechanisms for user access to enterprise resources from remote systems, whether mobile or fixed technologies outside of the organizational network. These policies define requirements for transport encryption (SSL for corporate Web sites, VPN configuration, and so on), remote authentication (EAP-RADIUS, EAL-TLS, and so on), and credentials management (such as using only nonexportable certificates for a PKI-based authentication system).

Remote access policies should detail the protocols that may be used (PPTP, L2TP, IPSec, and SSL, for example) and should reflect the environment of the remote users, to ensure compatibility with other common technologies such as NAT devices.

Wireless use policies

Wireless use policies are only required for organizations employing wireless solutions, or whose users employ those technologies in their remote access. These policies are intended to protect the enterprise against unauthorized access and interception of data. The policy should specify the technologies supported (Wi-Fi, WiMAX, and so on), allowable access modes (consider banning ad-hoc Wi-Fi to ensure that barrier defenses and network IDS function properly), and wireless encryption protocol selection, such as IPSec and WEP/WPA encryption.

The policy should include access point configuration details (consider turning off SSID broadcasts), whether MAC address restricted connection controls can be used, and audit rights. Also specify mandatory reviews conducted through site surveys and channel management mandates within the organization. Although Wi-Fi operates within unregulated frequencies, remind users to configure their personal hotspots for channels not in use within the organizational wireless plan. (Consider keeping at least one channel clear for user devices.)

Detail separation of network traffic when multiple wireless networks are present, including specifications of what data may be accessed via the unsecured guest network versus that which is available only via the authentication-required organizational network.

Part V

Obtaining Value beyond the Basic Enterprise

The 5th Wave   By Rich Tennant

GREEN IT GAME PLAN

"Well, I suppose we should plan on getting rid of those coal-burning servers."

In this part . ..

As you discover in this part, you don't have to stick with the tried-and-true to find value. You can find value in nontraditional solutions and emergent technology, such as virtualization and high performance computing solutions.

And believe it or not, you can be green in your IT practices as well.

Chapter 13

Virtualizing Enterprise Systems

In This Chapter

▶ Understanding virtualization in the enterprise

▶ Identifying server virtualization issues and best practices

▶ Recognizing user environment options

▶ Glimpsing cloud computing possibilities

*V*irtualization has become a buzzword touching many different elements of the enterprise, from virtualized servers and virtualized desktops to virtualized storage and virtual applications.

Virtualization allows an enterprise to take advantage of economies of scale and standardize platforms across a very large environment and access licensed software resources on demand, all while controlling costs. Because modern hardware is capable of running multiple operations simultaneously, servers are often underutilized and may spend most of their time idle. Instead of continuing to increase the number of physical machines, using robust hardware to host multiple virtual machines is more efficient. By using a larger percentage of the physical host machine's true capabilities, greater value is gained from the purchase of that hardware.

For example, a developer may need multiple servers to separate functions, such as database, authentication, and Web presentation, in a new application. Instead of having three systems, as would have been necessary a decade ago, a single physical server can host all three distinct systems, each with its own dedicated resources.

In this chapter, we look at the use of virtualization in server and desktop environments and application virtualization in the enterprise and in the cloud.

For much greater detail on virtualization practices and the process of configuring and deploying virtualization solutions, check out the book *Virtualization For Dummies* (Wiley) by Bernard Golden.

Getting the Scoop on Virtualization Technology

You're probably already familiar with virtualized functions within the enterprise in the form of a print spooler or server that controls jobs and access to multiple physical printers. This approach allows for replacement or rearranging of physical printers with minimal user disruption. You can configure these virtual printers for specific predetermined settings, such as duplex printing, print quality, or color use, and push them out across the enterprise.

You can extend the same flexibility to an entire user desktop so that users can easily access applications and settings from anywhere at any time. But, system virtualization involves a change in attitude toward traditional dedicated software-on-top-of-hardware installations of operating system, application, and other configuration details on a single system.

One form of system virtualization is the Preboot eXecution Environment (PXE) boot capability where computers aren't preloaded with even operating system software but instead ask a Trivial File Transport Protocol (TFTP) server over a network connection for operating system and applications at boot time (see Figure 13-1).

Preboot eXecution Environment

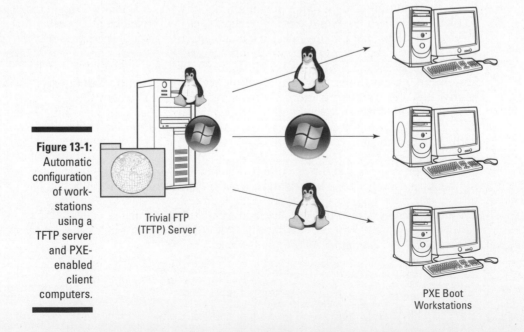

Figure 13-1: Automatic configuration of workstations using a TFTP server and PXE-enabled client computers.

Trivial FTP (TFTP) Server

PXE Boot Workstations

Another form of virtualization is the preconfigured virtual appliance or virtual machine that runs inside of a dedicated server or workstation host. These solutions include the Parallels virtual host in Macintosh platforms that is often used to make Microsoft Windows applications available as if part of the native Mac installation.

You can also virtualize individual applications so that they're automatically deployed to a client computer only when needed, such as when an associated file type is first opened. The first time a user attempts to open a .pdf file, for example, you can stream a virtualized copy of Adobe Acrobat Reader to the client's computer. You can associate different versions of a file with different versions of the same application through this process, such as when an older version of Internet Explorer and the Java virtual machine may be needed to open a legacy application Web site with a newer version available all other times.

Virtualizing Servers

One of the most effective forms of virtualization in enterprise restructuring is the consolidation of multiple servers onto a single physical host, as shown in Figure 13-2. This form of virtualization has the advantages of greater utilization of existing hardware as well as overall reduction in the number of physical devices in server rooms, saving on power and hardware purchase.

Server Virtualization

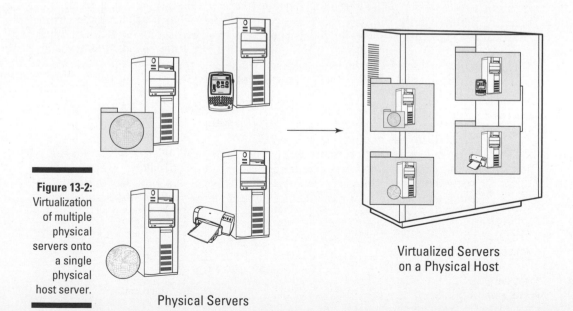

Figure 13-2:
Virtualization of multiple physical servers onto a single physical host server.

Physical Servers

Virtualized Servers
on a Physical Host

Because each virtualized machine is nothing more than a collection of files on the host server, full system backups become significantly easier. Replacing a failed system requires nothing more than restoring a copy of those files onto another host system.

You can easily move virtualized servers from one host to another, allowing for load balancing during periods of peak utilization in which the demand exceeds the resources available on a current host. Load balancing across a large virtualized server farm can be automated, enabling failover and transfer of hosting while systems are in operation.

Automatic load balancing across large virtualization farms presents challenges regarding legal motions of discovery because some investigations require forensic capture of both the current media as well as any media on which the data may have resided. In a very large virtualized farm, automatic load balancing can translate into the forensic duplication of hundreds, if not thousands, of hosts because the data may have resided on many systems as the virtual server was automatically moved among hosts.

The following topics cover issues arising from server virtualization.

Hosting virtual machines

A virtual machine (VM) may run in a host operating system configured to serve as a virtualization host, or it may run atop a minimal environment often referred to as a naked hypervisor. The *hypervisor* provides an interface between the virtualized operating system and its hosting environment, dedicating resources and creating a virtual hardware abstraction layer (HAL). Because of the HAL, server virtualization produces hardware-agnostic virtualized systems. You can move a virtualized server across host servers of different types running different operating systems or running a naked hypervisor alone, so long as the virtual machine formats are compatible and resource constraints are adjusted accordingly (see Figure 13-3).

Unfortunately, no single standard for virtual machine format exists yet, so your shop may tend to use a single virtualization vendor, such as VMware or Hyper-V, to ease compatibility between hosts. Most virtualization vendors have limited-capacity versions of their products available free or at minimal charge that can help your system's admins evaluate virtualization strategies. Virtualization vendors may also have more advanced commercial options that add features such as automatic management and reporting, load-balancing, and automatic failover.

Heterogeneous Virtualization Hosts

Figure 13-3:
A VM can be moved between virtual hosts of different types, provided the new host has a format-compatible hyper-visor and sufficient resources.

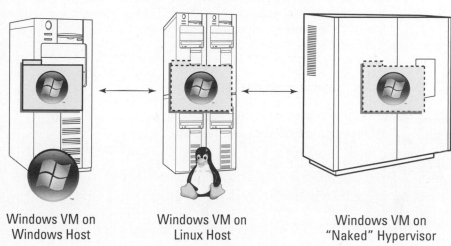

| Windows VM on Windows Host | Windows VM on Linux Host | Windows VM on "Naked" Hypervisor |

Don't leap before you look here if the evaluation environment employs a different virtualization host than the production environment, particularly if virtualized development systems are rolled directly into production use. Investigate the virtualization solutions in place both in development and production during the enterprise software survey and strive to reduce the number of virtualization hosting formats in use across the enterprise.

Separating hardware and software tech refresh planning

The ability to migrate virtualized systems from one host to the next presents a challenge for technical refresh cycles because you can retain legacy virtual machines across multiple hardware refresh cycles — immortal outdated operating systems and applications that may provide easy access for attackers due to vulnerabilities long since eliminated in more modern systems. Figure 13-4 illustrates the ability for a single virtualization host to support a wide range of virtual machine types of versions, which can create pockets of complexity in the enterprise that must be reduced in long-term planning.

Getting rid of a "perfectly good system" (as per technical staff already experienced with a cherished legacy system) becomes a challenge for you when the virtualized outdated legacy system can be moved to brand-new hardware without issue. Update cycles must stress updating software as well as hardware to ensure compatibility, security, and service across the entire software lifecycle in the face of a fully virtualized environment where you can update hosting equipment without involving outdated software encapsulated within a virtual instance.

Heterogeneous Virtual Machines

Figure 13-4: Because physical host and software refresh cycles become separated in virtualized environments, undesirable complexity can grow without planning.

Emerging best practices

Virtualization is still a relatively new practice in large data centers, but the economic and administrative advantages are so evident that a number of best practices are beginning to emerge:

✔ **Reduce bottlenecks:** A single virtualization host may support virtual machines with different use cycles, such as a Web site that receives high use during daytime hours and an inventory management server that performs warehousing updates during off-peak hours in the middle of the night. When determining resource requirements such as memory, CPU, and storage, you must include calculations for potential bottlenecks such as a shared network interface card (NIC). Existing network interfaces might be easily capable of handling the required bandwidth for one or two systems but unable to handle the load of all systems at once, particularly when off-cycle updates or maintenance may cause many systems to restart at the same time.

✔ **Identify points of failure:** Cycling individual virtual machines doesn't generally affect other VMs on the same host unless the server is overloaded or resources poorly allocated to each VM. However, loss of function of the host will cause a loss of service for all hosted virtual machines. Automated updates must be applied so that the host is not attempting to apply updates at the same time as its guest VMs, for example, adding complexity to maintenance planning in virtualized environments.

✔ **Watch the heat:** A single powerful system hosting a dozen virtualized guests generally draws less power than the original dozen physical systems, but server density in a single rack may remain constant even though each server is now providing much more processing power. This can increase cooling requirements for a data center significantly, which could be overlooked in virtualization projects combined with data center consolidation projects. Air handlers can be rapidly overwhelmed by filled cabinets running multiple multi-core systems at 50 percent of maximum capacity compared to the same space filled with single processor systems spending most of their time idling.

✔ **Virtualize first:** It's important to perform the physical-to-virtual (p2v) process first to make sure that all applications and functions are operational in their new virtual setting before adding networking, address space, and latency factors into any troubleshooting efforts. After the virtualized servers are working well, then they can be gracefully transferred to consolidated data-center hosting.

✔ **Counting boxes:** Because the number of servers no longer corresponds 1:1 to the number of physical systems in the data center, tracking inventory and licensing is more complex. Licensing is often based on the number of threads, cores, and processors that may be available to a particular VM and its applications. Updates to physical hosts or migration between hosting servers can make license calculation more difficult. In some environments, you may find that licensing at the host level for a number of VMs (or in some cases, unlimited guest virtual machines) may provide an overall reduction in licensing costs — a nice item to report to stakeholders.

Virtualizing Workstations

Another area of virtualization is the user client environment. The PXE boot process was used to illustrate one type of server-to-endpoint virtual workstation deployment solution. Although streaming all the operating system and application packages to each workstation may take too long and consume too much network bandwidth for large enterprises, you can effectively use PXE-boot systems in user training and briefing facilities where the entire system must be returned to a clean install of particular software and settings on a regular basis.

Other virtualization options exist for workstation management.

Using thin and thick clients

Another workstation virtualization option borrows from older mainframe operations, where terminals without processing or storage of their own allowed users to access resources and processing power of large computing systems. You can still find "dumb" terminals of this type in enterprises supported by mainframe or dedicated high-performance computing systems, providing administrative access to directly connected, powerful computing systems.

The user workstation equivalent of the dumb terminal connected to a mainframe involves a limited-capacity computer responsible for receiving data from a remote server and presenting that data to the user, while passing mouse and keyboard input from the user to the back-end computing environment. The front-end client system may possess significant preprocessing storage and compute power (a thick client) or may be only a simple interface passing audio/visual and data to the user and returning data and user input (a thin client).

All software resides on the remote desktop server these clients access and processing occurs entirely on the server in thin client installations or is shared between a thick client and its server. Updates to client-server environments occur at the server by updating its software packages directly. Clients' hardware systems continue in use until they fail outright, presenting challenges for users of more recent software needing larger screen sizes or removable hardware devices such as flash drives, unless tech refresh cycles are implemented for both hardware and software elements of workstation support.

Virtual desktops

Although the cost of individual workstation computing systems continues to decline, updating a workstation on each user's desktop is a significant expense and should follow strategies designed to align need against cost rather than strategies involving user desire or coolness factors. Technical refresh strategies are covered in depth in Chapter 15, but it is safe to say that users are typically most productive when using their standard desktop with personalized applications and settings configured to their preferences.

Transforming the client-server user environment into a network accessible desktop interface available to users from a variety of network-connected devices can provide similar access to applications and settings to users wherever they are. Desktop virtualization ensures that users can access the same options regardless of whether they are connecting to the virtual desktop infrastructure (VDI) servers from a desktop, laptop, netbook, thin client, or mobile device.

The client device connects to some form of *connection broker,* which is a server or group of servers responsible for controlling access to the virtualized desktop. VDI hosts run a hypervisor similar to that used in server virtualization, but it's also capable of freeing up system resources for users' desktop instances by storing idle virtual desktop instances until needed. You can customize each virtual desktop session to a particular user, providing access to applications and resources based on deployment criteria rather than as a consequence of sitting at a particular computer to access software loaded locally on that system.

Remote desktops

You can achieve VDI-like functionality through the use of remote desktop protocols, which enable users to connect to their own desktop user environments from a remote system. Processing power and storage remain on the user desktop system, facilitating mobile access without risk of data loss if the remote device is lost, stolen, or seized. Nothing remains on the remote device beyond its own operating system, VPN and anti-malware services, and a link to the remote desktop system.

Unlike the shared virtual servers of the VDI, this configuration doesn't reduce hardware costs because each user still has dedicated hardware hosting the remote virtual desktop session.

Client hosting

You can configure modern desktop and laptop devices with enough processing, memory, and storage resources to perform as virtualization hosts with their own hypervisor. This capability allows deployment of virtual appliances (virtual machines with preconfigured software and settings) or secondary operating environments suited to a user's needs. Using this type of virtualization, Macintosh users can access Windows applications natively using the Parallels hypervisor while Windows users can access a Linux suite of tools running in the Virtual PC hypervisor.

Layering of operating systems, applications, and user settings can become very complex if you don't plan accordingly, although this option can aid in testing new applications and software prior to production rollout without affecting the hosting client system's other software. User acceptance is also higher when using their own devices hosting custom business applications in client hosted VMs than when they have to install software directly onto personal systems.

Virtualizing Applications

You may want to provide a more fine-grained application deployment than client-hosted full virtual machine environments or remotely hosted VDI desktop instances. This type of deployment becomes critical when users in diverse organizational units or groups need different applications or different versions of applications in order to perform business tasks.

Application virtualization services like Microsoft Application Virtualization (also known as App-V) found in Microsoft enterprises automatically provide applications to users based on criteria such as time of day (the payroll app may be available only during business hours), location (applications and data may be restricted using GPS to systems physically within the country), and group membership (only testers using computers in the testing group get the newest version of a beta application to open a particular file type, while all others automatically use the older version in production).

Application virtualization aids in presenting updated versions of software automatically because the next time users attempt to access their software or data, their clients will request the updated software from the appropriate server. When a new version is present, users receive the update automatically, allowing forced expiration of feature sets, retirement of outdated applications, and an automatic reconfiguration of desktop options when a user changes roles within the organization.

Cloud Computing

The most highly virtualized environment currently available to an enterprise is one where every aspect of the enterprise infrastructure has been concealed from the end user, and users can simply reach out and claim resources within an apparently formless body of services termed the *cloud*. Resources such as address space, storage, database capabilities, Web site support, and a myriad of other services and functions are requested by an authorized end-user, configured, and presented back to the user entirely without involving manual effort by IT staff.

The cloud environment provides access to services and capabilities without details of resource location or configuration. Hosting servers are subject to change at any time without affecting use or availability, presenting access to the user who no longer needs to make that dreaded call to the tech help desk asking for another 10GB of storage for a quick proof-of-concept project. As with application virtualization, the requesting user can automatically ask for services and resources to be allocated based on role, group membership, or other form of resource authorization.

By accessing a simplified, nontechnical Web site, a user may call for a database-enabled Web site for sharing images of a particular size, with a storage capacity up to the requester's maximum allocation without needing to know what type of database will be used, what type of storage system is used, or where the Web server is located. Details, such as integrating the new site so that both internal users and authenticated partner organizations, are simply checkboxes in the request, rather than complex negotiated issues requiring meetings between administrative, supervisory, and technical representatives.

Cloud resources are coordinated and allocated through automated services using designated resource availability constraint policies that can be tailored to your enterprise's particular needs and culture. Cloud hosting is an attractive opportunity for many organizations and adoption of cloud computing and cloud-hosted services is proceeding quickly, including services such as the Google Docs application. Backup vendors, collaboration systems, user productivity suites, and many other forms of computing in the cloud make these functions available to users without requiring any knowledge of the back-end plumbing.

Private clouds

Public clouds are constructed from servers and services located outside of the enterprise, with pricing typically based on total storage and computer resources allocated to the organization. When more resources are needed, the cloud provider can simply add more at the back end for an incremental increase in service cost. This approach is more attractive for organizations that would prefer to reduce their own data center resources and costs in favor of outsourced cloud resources available to users from anywhere on the Internet.

Many organizations with security or regulatory constraints may find that the vague "it's in the cloud somewhere" nature of public clouds can't be easily aligned with existing service management practices. Requirements might include mandates such as use logging, mandatory encryption standards for storage and transport, or the ability to identify all users who have ever had access to data. The flexibility of automated resource allocation has led some organizations to develop internal *private clouds,* which leverage the capabilities of cloud computing across resources controlled entirely within the enterprise.

You may find that resources freed up through virtualization and data center consolidation projects can easily form the core of a private cloud. Because you can update, move, or replace resources within the cloud without affecting utility to the requesting user, older equipment retired from active service works well in a private cloud to create a proof of concept.

Best practices

A number of best practices can help guide your integration to the still developing cloud computing model:

- **Select a standard:** Cloud vendors have not yet established a common standard, so systems designed for an Amazon Elastic Computer Cloud (EC2) may not work as well (or at all) when attempting to integrate with a VMware vSphere-based cloud. As with virtualization vendors, pick a cloud computing standard for use enterprise-wide.

✔ **Migrate components together:** You can't move all applications into the cloud. Moving services from dedicated hardware to virtual cloud deployment may require changes to network protocols, resource monitoring solutions, or other deeply integrated applications that are not resident in the cloud. Identification of integrated applications is vital to avoid blocking a critical business function because one component is no longer accessible via a particular protocol.

✔ **Manage licensing from the start:** As with virtualized server environments, application licensing practices still lag cloud computing potential. Licenses that have costs per machine become problematic when a machine can either be considered as a physical host or as a single hosted virtual system. Licensing per processor or per core can be equally difficult to assess when multiple virtual systems may share a single CPU, or when a single GPU chip can contain hundreds of individual cores. Software migrated into cloud environments can be automatically shifted between hosting equipment transparently, potentially causing an organization to fall out of licensing compliance. License management can present significant risk to an enterprise if not addressed with specific controls in the cloud service contact prior to migration into a cloud setting.

✔ **Plan for mid- to long-term storage requirements:** The pay-as-you-go model used by cloud vendors requires monitoring to ensure that tiny increments to resources do not add up to unsupportable overall costs. Even small sips will eventually empty the largest vessel. When negotiating resource constraints or implementing a private cloud, plan sufficient resources to allow expansion beyond the initial inventory of requirements.

✔ **Privacy:** Because public clouds can be located anywhere and moved without notice to end-users, data stored in the cloud is at risk for loss or unexpected access. Federal investigators must ask for access to resources located in the enterprise, but may serve a warrant for access directly to your cloud service provider without notice to your organization. The opaque nature of hosted cloud services also affects data when it is moved between states or outside of the country, where privacy laws may differ and discovery motions depend on the laws where the data currently resides rather than the laws of your organization's home. Private clouds reduce this risk by keeping the back-end resources local to your operation.

✔ **Transparency:** Services hosted in the cloud do not readily integrate with many enterprise monitoring solutions, which may rely on specific transport or discovery protocols or alternative mechanisms for authentication. Logging of unauthorized access, causative analysis of loss of system uptime, and details of operation changes are maintained internally to the cloud service provider rather than being directly available to your organizational review. This can complicate internal investigations or validation of service availability when your cloud-based services are leveraged to provide services to another consumer.

Chapter 14

Facilitating High-Performance Computing

In This Chapter

▶ Reviewing supercomputing functions

▶ Identifying HPC enterprise strategies

▶ Integrating HPC with cyclic tech refresh

As computer processing power increased, text-only displays gave way to fully interactive graphical user environments. You can easily see advances in processing power when you look at the evolution of video games, from blocky 16-color blobs to modern fully immersive, 3-D interactive environments.

You can also concentrate computing power to solve complex mathematical tasks, such as weather prediction, economic forecasting, oil and gas flow modeling, visualization studies, and biochemical analysis. This chapter focuses on mechanisms for facilitating high-performance computing in the enterprise to suit a wide range of uses.

Supercomputers Rule the World

The most obvious form of high-performance computing exists in the top-of-the-line dedicated systems created as custom ultra-high-speed machines suited to a particular type of processing. You can find examples of these systems in weather modeling centers, such as the supercomputing complex at the National Oceanographic and Atmospheric Administration, in nuclear modeling systems developed for the Department of Energy, and in research facilities like the one housing the Cray X-MP supercomputer (see Figure 14-1) at the National Security Agency.

Figure 14-1:
Cray X-MP
supercom-
puter at the
National
Security
Agency.

These systems cost millions of dollars and are often designed to meet only
a single type of processing, such as the IBM Blue Gene system designed specifically for playing chess. Next-generation supercomputers will employ specialized processors that are essentially a supercomputer on each CPU, with
memory, dozens of cores, and an internal thread controller built into each
chip as in designs such as the IBM Cyclops64 architecture.

Desktop computing

Supercomputing research continues all the time at universities and research
centers around the world, with a constantly shifting upper end of what may

be defined as a *supercomputer*. Today's top supercomputer may be no more powerful than the desktop of ten years from now. The current top machine is the Cray Jaguar, which performs more than 1.75 quadrillion floating-point mathematical operations per second. Projects such as the Blue Waters super-computer being built at the National Center for Supercomputing Applications at the University of Illinois is expected to have a peak performance capability of nearly 10 quadrillion operations per second.

By comparison, today's average desktop system can reach 10 billion floating-point operations per second, up to 40 times faster still if configured with a compatible graphical processing unit (GPU). Teraflop speeds place the pro-cessing power available in a standard desktop system within the same level of performance as many of the Top-500 supercomputers less than a decade ago (many of which are still in use, if only as teaching tools).

Individual *deskside* computer systems are capable of standalone supercom-puting power by combining standard desktop systems with one or more dedicated computing boards. The Dell/Cray CX1-iWS is a good example of this technology, combining a standard Microsoft Windows workstation with multiple boards running the dedicated Windows HPC Server 2008 to provide a dedicated cluster running behind the workstation operating system.

Other systems constructed using one of the numerous the Intel X58 "Supercomputer Motherboard" configurations pack a high-end CPU onto a motherboard capable of handling four or more GPU-enabled video cards. These systems provide small-scale supercomputing power to individual desk-top systems without any complex software configuration or special power requirements. These types of systems are becoming more common in orga-nizations managing large data sets, physical models, geographic information system (GIS) applications, predictive inventory and financial analysis, as well as in medical and diagnostics settings.

Floating-point operations per second (FLOPS)

The most common measure of raw processing power is the number of floating-point mathemat-ical operations that can be accomplished per second, using a standard such as the LINPACK benchmark. One billion operations per second is a gigaflop, while today's fastest supercom-puters operate in the petaflop range or one quadrillion operations per second. Atmospheric researchers suggest that zettaflop (one billion trillion operations per second or a million times faster than today's top supercomputer) systems will allow accurate predictions of weather pat-terns up to two weeks in advance. Other per-formance measures may be also applied to high-performance computing systems, such as flops per watt efficiencies or peak performance measured against sustained throughput.

Parallel computing

Supercomputers reach petaflop levels of operation by subdividing large, complex processes into smaller procedures that can be individually calculated independently of one another to arrive at a final solution more rapidly. This process is akin to counting inventory, where a single person might take a month to count all items in a warehouse, but a team of 100 people can each take a stack of goods and quickly tally up all of the items in the warehouse in a matter of minutes. This type of processing depends on different methods for programming than traditional start-to-finish processing, to effectively divide up procedures so that one processor is not left waiting for data to be provided by another processor.

You can separate some processes, such as the rendering of pixels on a graphical display, into a number of parallel tasks without effort — each pixel is rendered individually and not as a result of calculations from its neighbors. The emergence of dedicated special-purpose graphics accelerators and GPUs made possible the remarkably realistic real-time rendering found in games and multimedia displays, packing hundreds of individual processing cores into a single chip to handle individual pixels and pixel groups in parallel.

Newer GPU chips, such as the NVIDIA general purpose computing on graphics processing units (GPGPU), can work together with the system CPU to shift floating-point operations to the high-speed parallel processing chip to improve performance of nongraphical mathematical processes such as data mining and finite element analysis.

Distributed computing

In addition to dedicated, purpose-built monolithic supercomputers, you can also achieve high-performance computing by integrating processing power from a number of separate computers to perform parallel processing tasks. By splitting up large tasks into smaller chunks and passing each piece to a separate computer over a high-speed network connection, you can divide very complex tasks into pieces and reintegrate them to rapidly provide the final solution.

Because each system has its own internal clock and possesses its own CPUs, GPUs, memory and bus architecture, individual distributed computing nodes may perform tasks more or less efficiently than other nodes. The scheduler is responsible for shifting data and processing loads to the individual nodes to provide the most efficient level of throughput overall, making this process slightly less efficient than true parallel computing within a supercomputer where all components are matched to provide optimal processing power in tightly synchronized parallel cycles.

Because distributed networks can make use of computers located anywhere in the world, very large-scale computations are possible. Early distributed computing efforts resolved 56-bit and 64-bit encryption keys and aided researchers in signal processing, looking for extra solar life by participating in the SETI program.

You can see the darker side of distributed processing power in the massive botnets created by injecting malware onto tens of thousands of computers so that their combined processing power can be turned into denial of service attacks, spam generation, and other nefarious purposes. Cyber criminals use botnets under their control to send millions of connections per second at targeted sites for extortion and sabotage and in acts of online aggression to block legitimate access to sites.

Everyday High-Performance Computing

Although your enterprise may not have the need for a top-500 supercomputer, many opportunities exist for high-performance computing using commodity off-the shelf components. Common high-performance computing uses include economic forecasting, architectural design, data mining, biochemical research, mechanical system simulations, and multimedia production (see Figure 14-2).

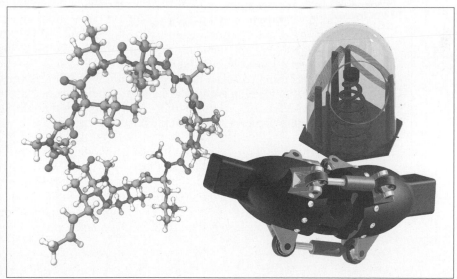

Figure 14-2: Output from common high-performance computing functions, including biochemical research and mechanical system simulations.

A number of vendors currently produce high-performance bolt-on appliances and dedicated servers that can be integrated directly into an existing network, such as the AMAX 3,500-code 4U rack mounted server. These systems approach mini-supercomputer capabilities, but may also be difficult to justify in the face of recent economic impact on technology purchasing. Another option is to purchase off-the-shelf systems in order to provide high-performance capabilities in your enterprise, often trading a slight loss of processing power over dedicated supercomputers for an economic advantage in price-per-gigaflop.

Computing clusters

A *cluster* is a group of computers that are linked together closely to perform tasks as a single unit. A *compute cluster* combines the processing power of multiple compute nodes as if the cluster were a single, large parallel processing system. Compute clusters use a supervisory head node to separate tasks and data, sending smaller packages to individual compute nodes and aggregating responses from the distributed parallel process. Many public-facing Web applications use load-balancing clusters to balance user connections across multiple servers transparently to the end user. High-availability clusters provide fault-tolerance for a server by maintaining a warm backup node that can take over operations transparently in the event of a hardware failure in the primary node to ensure continuous operations.

Many of the top 500 supercomputers are actually clustered systems, composed of equipment built around the same chips found in high-end multimedia desktop computers and gaming consoles. The U.S. Air Force is currently building a supercomputer from 2,500 Playstation3 gaming consoles to process radar imagery and simulations of human neural interaction. Figure 14-3 details the Columbia supercomputer at the NASA Ames Research Center, built from 20 SGI Altix clusters. Because individual computers vary in their internal components, even within the same production run, clusters inevitably lag slightly behind the purpose-built supercomputers but often provide similar computing power without the purpose-built price tag.

You can configure clusters in the enterprise using commodity hardware and high-speed networking, typically gigabit Ethernet, InfiniBand, or fiber channel connectivity. Jobs submitted to the head node are separated into sub-jobs and distributed to individual compute nodes for processing. Nodes typically lack storage, keyboards, or monitors, reducing power consumption and relying on network distribution of node configuration and data.

Figure 14-3: The Columbia supercomputer at the NASA Ames Research Center, made up of 20 SGI Altix clusters for a total of more than 10,000 CPU cores.

The first well-recognized commodity cluster was called *Beowulf*, and it was developed at NASA for scientific computing using personal computers. Beowulf clusters typically use some flavor of Linux together with common parallel processing libraries, such as the Message Passing Interface (MPI). They support a wide range of software optimized for clustered computing environments, such as the MPI basic local alignment search tool (mpiBLAST) used for genetic sequencing or the Point of View ray-tracing (POV-Ray) application used for photo-realistic multimedia rendering, as shown in Figure 14-4.

Figure 14-4: A POV-Ray rendering of transparent, reflective, and multi-shaped objects produced by Gilles Tran.

Courtesy of http://commons.wikimedia.org.

Numerous open-source tools exist for constructing compute clusters, such as the Rocks and Condor frameworks. Flash-key bootable options also exist such as the ClusterKnoppix Linux distribution. Commercial products include the Microsoft HPC Server and the Red Hat HPC Solution distribution.

Visualization clusters

Another common implementation for clustered computing involves the use of multiple lightweight computing nodes, whose combined processing power allows the direct representation of large images and combined data sets across multiple monitors. Small visualization systems like that shown in Figure 14-5 are commonly found in emergency resource centers, providing the capability to view large geographic areas with fine resolution not possible on individual displays.

Figure 14-5:
A small visualization cluster of three computers, each driving two monitors.

Very large visualization systems facilitate entertainment, collaboration, and the expression of extremely large data sets at very high resolution. Figure 14-6 illustrates the Stallion visualization cluster at the Texas Advanced Computing Center at the University of Texas at Austin, representing the current top-end of visualization systems.

In the Stallion installation, 24 commodity computers allow 75 monitors to act as a combined desktop with more than 307 megapixels of total display area. This enables the examination of high-resolution imagery, active video content, telepresence data sharing, and teleconferencing all at the same time.

Figure 14-6:
Stallion is the world's highest resolution tiled display at 307 million pixels. The system was deployed by the Texas Advanced Computing Center (TACC) at The University of Texas at Austin in 2008. Stallion was designed and built by members of TACC's scientific visualization and advanced computing systems groups.

Photo courtesy of Faith Singer-Villalobos of the Texas Advanced Computing Center.

Grid computing

When distributed processing systems are not well connected or distributed in multiple locations, grid computing solutions can coordinate distributed resources toward collective goals.

You can implement grid-computing solutions within an organization to suit many different uses, often using only spare capacity available when systems are idling and unused.

✓ **Storage grids:** Storage grids bring together the aggregate storage space from many systems, creating a very large virtual storage space functioning as a single location. Such solutions provide enterprise capability to handle embarrassingly large data sets that exceed storage capacity or that may exist for only a short time before being recycled. Geological surveys, weather projections, and data capture during high-speed physics experiments can produce prodigious volumes of data at a rate too high for many storage processors to spool. Storage grids configured for high capture rates can address such needs, while those configured for high-volume storage can allow data mining access across tremendously large inventory systems.

✔ **Compute grids:** Compute grids function like loosely coupled clusters by aggregating processing power across many distributed machines. Because communications may occur more slowly than in tightly connected clusters, individual nodes are generally provided data in larger chunks so that processing can occur more efficiently before results are returned and a new set of data is requested from the host.

✔ **Render grids:** Grid computing systems are commonly used in the production of imagery and digital media content. Rendering grids split up media creation tasks, such as iVideo production into smaller elements, sending frames 1 through 500 to render node 1, frames 501 through 1,000 to node 2, and so on. The supervisory machine coordinates the various nodes, compiling the final output into its completed form. This type of processing works very well with any type of process that can be segmented without one segment depending on the output of another before beginning.

✔ **Grid tools:** Although numerous commercial HPC servers have grid computing support, the most common toolkit for creating compute and storage grids on open source platforms is the Globus Toolkit. Globus includes support for resource management, information and security services, and data management in grid computing environments. Access to services and applications across the grid are made available through standard XML-based Web services.

Volunteer computing

Another form of distributed computing makes use of the spare compute cycles available when a donor's system is at idle. Owners download a volunteer computing client, which monitors the system for times when the computer is not in use and then dedicates resources such as processing power or storage to the project selected by the owner. These projects use a middleware component built around a framework like the Berkeley Open Infrastructure for Network Computing (BOINC) used in the popular SETI@home and Folding@home projects.

By volunteering their computers' idle computing capacity, participants allow their systems to be used for conducting research into genetics, astrophysics, medicine, and the search for life beyond this planet.

You can also use the BOINC framework to create local grid computing projects so that already-coded volunteer computing methods can be applied to internal high-performance computing projects in the enterprise without requiring significant development of data and code distribution systems. However, the BOINC project already lists hundreds of potential projects that can be easily configured for participation, allowing an enterprise to provide resources to high-visibility or closely associated projects already in place for community engagement and publicity purposes. Other project sites include Grid.org, distributed.net, and the World Community Grid.

Compute farms

When systems are connected in large, loosely connected groups, they're commonly referred to as *farms*. Compute farms may be comprised of end-of-life systems collected in an out-of-the-way area to provide extra processing power for proof-of-concept projects, or they may be composed of high-speed systems dedicated to a particular function, such as software compilation (compile farms) or graphic visualization (render farms).

Desktop High-Performance Computing

Whatever the purpose in your enterprise, high-performance computing does not require monstrously powerful supercomputers taking up floors of space and generating the heat output of a small bomb. The tools and resources available to you will allow the creation of clusters, grids, or other distributed processing functions using the same equipment now purchased for users to read e-mail and create presentations. The same equipment can even be shared, borrowing idle processing time and unused storage space for use across the enterprise.

A recent research project leveraged a standard cyclic replacement tech refresh cycle to provide clustered processing power in year 1, storage and compute grid functions while deployed to users' desktops in years 2 and 3, and compute farming capabilities in years 4 and 5 (see Figure 14-7) before finally retiring systems out of operation when their wattage-per-gigaflop falls below acceptable levels due to the emergence of ever-improved systems.

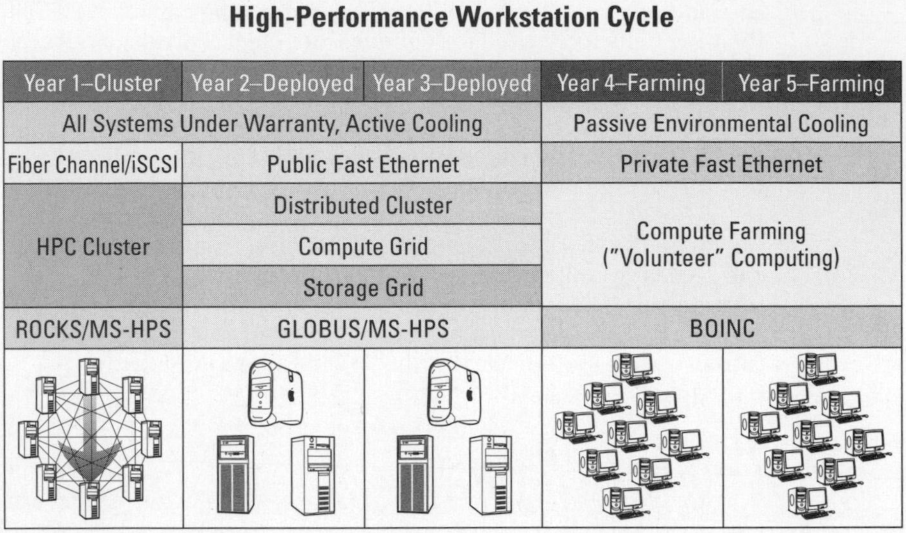

High-Performance Workstation Cycle

Figure 14-7:
High-
performance
computing
during a
five-year
research
cycle,
including
details of
toolkits and
technolo-
gies used in
each stage.

Year 1–Cluster	Year 2–Deployed	Year 3–Deployed	Year 4–Farming	Year 5–Farming
All Systems Under Warranty, Active Cooling			Passive Environmental Cooling	
Fiber Channel/iSCSI	Public Fast Ethernet		Private Fast Ethernet	
HPC Cluster	Distributed Cluster		Compute Farming ("Volunteer" Computing)	
	Compute Grid			
	Storage Grid			
ROCKS/MS-HPS	GLOBUS/MS-HPS		BOINC	

Chapter 15

Enabling Green IT

In This Chapter

▶ Reviewing hardware update strategies

▶ Upgrading components, firmware, and device drivers

▶ Planning for software updates

*L*arge data centers concentrating thousands of servers into the space of a single building consume as much electricity as a small city. Increased processing power and speed of computing devices have created an insatiable thirst for energy and the constant need for cooling necessary for continual operation. Also intensifying is the political and environmental pressure to decrease the impact of technologies on the environment, including the materials used in production, energy consumption during operation, and environmentally friendly disposal at end of life.

Green IT is a sometimes-overused term for reduced environmental impact technologies and IT practices, but it encompasses many aspects that you should consider in the face of rapidly increasing costs for power and water, together with mounting fees for excessive utility consumption. This chapter examines strategies for enacting Green IT projects for economic as well as social perception benefits for your enterprise.

Practicing Green Technology

Before examining specific technologies and their green factors, it's worth considering technology strategies that can help reduce the environmental footprint of your enterprise as a whole. Many different metrics exist for measuring the "greening" of an enterprise, from the total volume of carbon released during production and operation to the level of environmentally harmful chemicals released in production and disposal.

Another measure translates all activities into the total volume of water consumed, such as the fractional milliliter used in producing the power needed for a single search engine query — these add up rapidly when tens of millions of searches are conducted each day. Regardless of the specific metrics chosen for before-and-after comparison of your green IT projects, it can be very valuable for your enterprise to be able to demonstrate its green efforts to its clients. Reduction in power and water consumption can also translate into direct savings in operational costs for the organization.

Extended replacement cycles

One of the easiest ways to reduce the environmental impact of technologies in your enterprise is to extend the replacement cycle. More than half of a computer system's environmental effect comes from the energy consumed and chemicals produced in its manufacture, so replacing computers on a four-year cycle instead of a three-year cycle reduces equipment turnover each year and the extensive manufacturing energy requirements for replacement equipment. Chapter 16 talks about strategies for tech refresh cyclic hardware replacement. An overly extended refresh strategy can create significant problems in terms of compatibility, operational capability, and undesirable complexity. Newer systems tend to be less power-hungry with advances in power-saving options.

Telework and telecommuting

Extending your enterprise to knowledge workers in the field and in home offices can save significantly on the direct costs and amount of carbon released due to travel. Virtualized services, such as faxing and voice mail routed to an e-mail inbox, Voice over IP (VoIP) telephone services, shared workspace for online meetings, and secure remote desktop access, can provide remote workers the full experience of in-office participation without the commute to work or the air conditioning, furniture, and office space needed at a central work site.

Face-to-face communication through lightweight audio/video feeds is now readily available using simple webcams. The ability to extend a virtual workplace to agents in the field also means that your enterprise can enter new markets without anything more than a hotel room with broadband access.

Data center location

Because data centers must waste heat produced by increasingly concentrated racks of high-density servers employing multiple processors and cores, the location of data center facilities can influence cooling efficiency.

Large distributed organizations may find that shifting workloads to data centers located in northern areas during summer months can significantly reduce energy requirements for cooling because air handlers do not also have to exhaust as much heat infiltrating from the environment.

Data centers near bodies of water can allow the use of aquatic heat transfer systems to dump waste heat. Similarly, sites with adequate land access may be able to employ geothermal cooling, dumping waste heat through oil filled pipes run down into local bedrock. All such systems require careful studies to avoid affecting local wildlife while trying to help the environment.

Energy tax credits

Significant tax savings are possible for enterprises that take advantage of Federal and state incentives for reduced energy consumption, improved thermal insulation, alternative energy, and reduced hazardous materials consumption.

Many different laws and regulations provide guidance and mandates for green opportunities, including several in the USA:

- **Resource Conservation and Recovery Act (RCRA):** Addresses the proper disposal of solid waste and hazardous waste materials.
- **Toxic Substances Control Act (TSCA):** Regulates or restricts the introduction of new chemicals, based on an assessment of toxic or nontoxic characteristics.
- **American Recovery and Reinvestment Act of 2009 (ARRA 2009):** Intended to address the developing economic recession. Often referred to as the Stimulus Bill, it includes energy sector mandates and energy-related tax incentives.

Many countries around the world are implementing similar legislative and regulatory initiatives to encourage environmentally friendly operational procedures. Many of them provide tax credits for the purchase of energy efficient products, including air conditioning, computing equipment, and building materials.

ENERGY STAR

The ENERGY STAR certification program is a government-sponsored program designed to encourage the development of energy efficient products in the U.S. It has since been adopted by many other countries, along with the similar TCO Certification created in Europe. Energy efficiency translates directly into reduced energy costs, but also for reduced water consumption and greenhouse gas emission during energy production.

ENERGY STAR products must meet strict levels of energy efficiency to qualify for the designation and display the logo, the linkage phrase mark version (see Figure 15-1). ENERGY STAR products are further rated in energy efficiency using a simple precious-metal rating system (Gold, Bronze, and so on) to reflect specific levels of compliance.

Figure 15-1:
Products marked with the ENERGY STAR mark must meet ENERGY STAR specifications, including U.S. Department of Energy or Environmental Protection Agency criteria.

ENERGY STAR linkage phrase mark printed with permission from www.energystar.gov.

ENERGY STAR products for commercial buildings include specific guidelines for computers and monitors, as well as separate criteria for servers. An example of computer requirements is power supplies that are at least 80 percent efficient to meet the Bronze level of certification, while server specifications include mechanisms to measure power use, and advance power management options to conserve power when processors are idling.

According to the ENERGY STAR product guidelines, servers that meet ENERGY STAR certification requirements are roughly 30 percent more efficient than noncompliant systems. This can translate into significant savings to your enterprise, while also reducing the carbon and water-consumption footprint of the data center.

Considering Alternative Energy

Because data centers create high-density energy demands, they often place a strain on power distribution systems when located in areas formerly used for standard business or residential energy consumption. A new data center should be planned with power and cooling requirements in mind, coordinated with local utilities to ensure adequate supply and adequate infrastructure to provide for uninterrupted utilities to the enterprise or to the local area.

Alternative energy production on-site has become a popular method of addressing the concentrated energy needs of data centers, with large public projects involving photovoltaic (solar panels) and wind turbine power generation making headlines for data centers around the country. Google has even announced its interest in offshore floating data centers with their own wave-power and wind-power generation onboard.

Although current photovoltaic efficiencies are only around 20 percent maximum, the large roof surface areas of data centers and business office parks provide an excellent opportunity for solar power generation. Solar energy supports only daytime operations and in general doesn't meet the full power requirements of a data center, but it can offset peak-use energy consumption costs and often reach cost recovery in less than ten years with an average lifespan of twice that or more.

Wind turbine power generation provides additional opportunities in regions with steady winds, but presents problems for bird and bat populations as well as radar systems used for aircraft and water navigation, weather mapping, and national defense. Wind turbines are also considered a source of noise pollution making them unpopular near populated areas.

Water microturbine power generation is becoming a viable energy production alternative in locations with a steady current in a nearby water source, but this is a relatively new type of alternative energy system and its operational lifespan and long-term environmental impact remains unknown to date.

Alternative energy production installations and power storage that shifts off-peak power to business consumption during peak hours not only reduce power costs to the enterprise but can also provide tax credits and participation incentives from a number of governmental programs. These projects also boost your organization's public approval for green IT initiatives.

Reducing Consumables

One simple opportunity for IT green initiatives is to reduce the use of consumables across your enterprise. The first place to look is at the routine reports that so many enterprises produce, without purpose beyond "We've always done it this way."

Many times, paper copies of large reports are mass-distributed to preserve a copy of details as a point-in-time reference. A single copy printed and stored properly can preserve this data for audit purposes, while electronic distribution can easily fulfill the requirement for mass audience access. When dealing with sensitive information or protected intellectual property, make sure that messaging systems implement proper controls against unauthorized download and forwarding.

While the paperless office may remain forever in the future, small changes can markedly improve spending when measured enterprise-wide. Reducing the size of margins on printable output and printing in duplex (on both sides of the paper) can significantly reduce paper consumption. The use of entirely online documentation in organizational intranets and portals can further reduce printed output, while also ensuring the most recent copy of information is made available to consumers.

Technology-driven green initiatives may also include the use of rechargeable batteries in phones, pagers, and other devices with removable power cells. LED and fluorescent lighting in the place of traditional filament bulb illumination can also save a great deal of energy and cooling costs when implemented in large scale. Even consolidating consumable orders to a small number of vendors can provide green benefits by reducing costs and the environmental impact of shipping multiple smaller orders separately.

Selecting Green Hardware

In addition to buying hardware that conforms to ENERGY STAR standards, you can reduce power consumption and the environmental footprint of technologies by implementing strategies to combine functions, reduce unnecessary processing power, and select less energy-hungry alternatives. Consolidation of office equipment is a ready example of this potential, where a single multifunction device can replace printer, scanner, fax, and copier devices with one that needs only a single set of consumables and employs a single power supply for all functions.

Power over Ethernet (PoE) solutions and 12V DC power solutions can provide energy efficient alternatives to power distributed devices. For example, some PoE systems can dynamically allocate power on a per-port basis and even vary service voltage based on device need. DC power systems used in data centers can help to reduce costs by separating power supply services and passing only low-voltage into the cooled data center.

Modern graphics cards employ very powerful rendering chips called graphical processing units (GPUs), which are dedicated high-speed CPUs that consume power and produce heat similar to that of the main system processor. Unless additional power is needed for multimedia or high-performance computing purposes, you can reduce workstation power consumption dramatically by avoiding GPU-enabled graphics cards in favor of on-motherboard video. Entirely headless servers without graphics capability at all can further reduce power requirements, but require some attention to ensure adequate recovery capability if direct terminal access is needed.

Sharing a single monitor across multiple servers can help reduce the energy footprint of data center operations, using direct-cabled KVM switches or more expandable IP-based management systems. Though a few CRT style monitors are still in operation, they are being rapidly replaced by LCD displays with higher resolution and a reduced desktop footprint. LCD systems consume less power than their CRT predecessors, but more than newer LED-based displays. The backlighting element in LCD monitors remains active during operation, while LED pixels are only energized when displaying graphical information.

Other new technologies promise to reduce energy consumption on the desktop and in the data center, such as the transformation of hard drive storage from traditional spinning platters to solid-state drives (SSDs) using a variation of flash memory storage. These devices have no moving parts, so enjoy longer life cycles and reduce energy demands over drives that must spin platters to high speed before read/write operations can occur. A number of mobile devices such as Apple's popular iPhone and iPad enjoy enhanced battery life over earlier tech generations through the use of solid state drive storage.

Configuring Green Settings

Enterprise configuration of power saving options can ensure that computing power is available when needed, and minimized when unused or idle. This approach is similar to setting air conditioning systems to cool during office hours and to warmer temperatures overnight to conserve power in larger buildings. You can configure individual workstations to enter reduced-power mode when idle or to shut off entirely at the end of the workday.

Many systems can now step down their operating cycle speed when processor demand is low, including Intel chips with SpeedStep and AMD chips with PowerNow! technologies. Developed to optimize battery life in mobile devices not connected to central power, these technologies are available to many desktop systems and can reduce energy consumption during periods of operation when the processor is mostly idle by slowing down the system clock and accelerating to normal speeds when use resumes.

Additional components of workstation systems can be configured to enter into energy saving modes when unused, such as shutting off display monitors or parking hard drive storage devices after a designated delay since last access. Many enterprise-level configuration utilities allow control of power settings, including systems entering hibernation states (entirely off, but with settings stored for rapid return to function) and sleep-mode (low-power).

Workstations configured for wake-on-LAN functionality allow systems that have shut down at the end of the day to be turned on remotely using the TCP/IP network connection. This allows systems to be brought out of shut-down modes for maintenance and patching during off-peak times, without requiring systems to be left on all day.

Virtualizing Hardware

Virtualization allows a single powerful server to host multiple virtual machines. (For more on virtualization, see Chapter 13.) This process reduces hardware and consumes far less electricity than the original physical devices required for each system's operation.

Although a single virtualization host may consume more power while hosting multiple systems than when running only a single server's process load, the overhead beyond raw processing power for each system can be eliminated for the devices moved from physical to virtual hosting. Given the current ENERGY STAR target of 80 percent power supply efficiency, the energy use reduction translates into a full 100 percent per-system power savings for every five machines virtualized, just from reductions in energy waste alone.

Greater efficiencies result because CPUs will generally not operate above 60 percent of their rated capacity outside of momentary peak usage. Automatic load-balancing services such as VMWare's VMotion can shift virtual servers between physical hosts to avoid running CPUs beyond recommended levels, aiding cooling and heat dissipation strategies by ensuring hosts remain within their most efficient operational levels.

Virtualized desktops, either running headless as individual systems or as elements of a virtual desktop infrastructure (VDI), can be accessed using low-power mobile devices and thin client hardware to further reduce workstation power consumption and heat generation.

Ensuring Green Disposal

One of the earliest publically visible green efforts involved recycling, first of glass bottles and cans and later of a wide variety of plastics, paper products, and other debris that is generated by daily life. Recycling paper continues to be an easy way to reduce an enterprise's environmental impact, with services readily available for collection and secure shredding of paper prior to reprocessing. Recycling of ink jet cartridges and laser jet and copier toner cartridges can provide significant savings to your enterprise while also being environmentally friendly.

You can recycle some computer systems for parts and reuse, while you have to successfully render others into their base elements, which means extracting gold, platinum, silver, and other valuable elements used in their manufacture. Because of the materials present in computing hardware, many cities require disposal of computing hardware as hazardous waste. Batteries also are filled with reactive chemicals and may contain heavy metals and other durable environmental pollutants. Even computer cases and many internal components are made up of materials that may produce noxious gasses if disposed of incorrectly or incinerated in public waste disposal areas.

Enterprise disposal practices should include care for computer systems, monitors, and storage media. Microwaving optical media might well destroy data, but also releases significant quantities of dangerous gasses and risks the microwave oven catching fire. Other common bad practices such as drilling holes through hard drive media can expose operators to heavy metals and other chemicals present in the device.

In general, disposal of technologies should be conducted by trained personnel from a bonded third-party vendor approved for handling hazardous waste. Ad-hoc procedures create potential environmental hazards and operator risk.

Part VI
Protecting the Enterprise

The 5th Wave   By Rich Tennant

"You outsourced security to who?!"

In this part . . .

This part looks at protection strategies in more detail, including technology updates, security, and disaster recovery. We discuss hardware update strategies, common network threats and countermeasures, along with your role in Business Continuity (BC) and Disaster Recovery (DR) planning.

Chapter 16

Planning Technology Updates

In This Chapter

▶ Updating hardware

▶ Upgrading components, firmware, and device drivers

▶ Timing software updates

An enterprise employs many types of hardware and software to provide services and functionality to its clients. This array of technologies is a lot like a garden; you can't just plant it and walk away. Maintenance is critical if the systems (or tomatoes) are going to be as productive as you expect. Just like a garden, an enterprise needs continual upkeep, with outdated items removed to make way for new replacements.

This chapter examines several standard strategies for planning a technology refresh, and points out the uniquely useful aspects of each strategy.

Reviewing Hardware Update Strategies

You must update computing hardware, such as workstations and servers, regularly, implement emerging technology, and avoid age-related hardware failures if your enterprise is to remain agile. Planning, a critical first step in the hardware update process, helps minimize business disruptions. As you plan your strategy, you may find that update cycles will be affected by established criticality, function, or contractual obligations. *Tech refresh* is a commonly used term that refers to the periodic replacement of old technologies with new ones.

It can be said that there are almost as many different update strategies as there are enterprises. This statement may be an exaggeration, but determining how and when to upgrade technology is an issue of fierce debate between management and technical staff in enterprises of all sizes. Management concerns tend to be political, social, or financial, while technical staff concerns tend to revolve around security or functionality. As an enterprise architect, you need to select an approach that aligns with your organization's strategic plans, provides value, and ensures that mission-critical services remain available.

The following sections introduce several common hardware update strategies.

Keeping systems until they fail

Some organizations, particularly those that aren't well-funded or don't rely heavily on new technology, prefer to keep equipment in service until it fails. This strategy may save on computing hardware costs, but the savings may be offset as the following problems start cropping up:

- ✓ **Computing components devaluate quickly but may rise in price when manufacturing stops and demand is high.** Keeping a system around long enough may result in its replacement parts being as expensive (or more) than new parts.

- ✓ **Older hardware may not be able to run modern operating systems.** This problem can limit the applications the organization can implement.

- ✓ **Support for older hardware is no longer available.** For proprietary or specialized hardware, such as point-of-sale systems or video capture cards, vendors may go out of business, be acquired by other companies, or simply stop supporting older technology.

- ✓ **Entry-level technical staff are typically not trained in legacy technologies.** This lack of knowledge can cause problems when the enterprise needs to replace retiring workers who have legacy skill sets.

This use-it-'til-it-falls-apart strategy may create stability in the operating environment, but it's the least agile of all update approaches. Legacy computing equipment often creates roadblocks to resource integration. Enterprises using older equipment are likely to find their software choices increasingly limited as their hardware continues to age. Additionally, failures in legacy equipment are more difficult to recover from due to component availability and will generally involve longer outages than planned replacement, resulting in loss of business continuity.

Using defined replacement cycles

One of the most preferred strategies is to have a defined replacement cycle that is linked to strategic funding cycles, computing hardware warranties, or software life cycle. Benefits of cyclic replacement include

✔ **User acceptance:** Replacements are assigned based on age of the machine or the point in time in the cycle, and not because of organizational politics or personal reasons.

✔ **Budgeting ease:** Because the cycle of replacement is predictable and regular, year-to-year cost fluctuations are minimized.

✔ **Standardization:** Cyclic replacement minimizes technology variations within the enterprise and, in turn, reduces complexity and simplifies test, update, and end-user support.

These cycles can involve full replacement of hardware every few years or a partial replacement every year.

Full replacement

In a *full replacement cycle* (shown in Figure 16-1), all systems are replaced in the same fiscal year. The cycle's length is typically linked to warranty. If the full replacement cycle exceeds Moore's and Kryder's Laws (see Chapter 10), life-cycle costs increase toward the end of each replacement cycle because all equipment in the enterprise will be out of date, near end of life, and prone to unexpected failure. Shortened cycles avoid the problem of dealing with older equipment, but while shortened cycles increase agility, they also increase costs.

Figure 16-1: A simple example of a full replacement cycle illustrating server, desktop, and laptop devices.

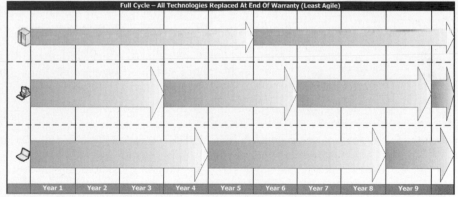

Full Cycle – All Technologies Replaced At End Of Warranty (Least Agile)

| Year 1 | Year 2 | Year 3 | Year 4 | Year 5 | Year 6 | Year 7 | Year 8 | Year 9 |

If your replacement cycle extends beyond three or four years, the enterprise's systems become increasingly outdated. Eventually, your hardware resources won't be up to the task of running modern software, which is designed to work with latest-generation, higher-capacity hardware. Cycles extending beyond warranty periods and vendor service plans become more expensive to maintain because parts are less available after four years.

The main benefit to this strategy is its lack of operational complexity, which results in decreased support and administrative overhead, as we discuss in Chapter 4.

Drawbacks to this strategy are primarily budgetary and staff-related. Although the enterprise becomes less complex, the budgeting process becomes more intricate. Most years, there will be no budget for replacement technology. The year the cycle ends, however, the budget must account for systems replacement throughout the enterprise. If other critical issues arise during that year, other business units may try to scavenge system replacement funds to address their needs. If that happens, you may have to justify your funding requirements to senior management.

Additionally, if expansion, merger, or acquisition requires the purchase of additional systems off-cycle, those newer systems will need to be replaced on the next cycle, which may be wasteful, or on the cycle after that, which means that those systems will be older, more likely to fail, and probably out of warranty.

Staffing requirements are high during replacement years, and your organization may need to hire temporary or contract workers to supplement permanent technical staff. This places an additional burden on both Human Resources and IT, in the form of in-processing and training. If you don't hire additional personnel, your organization risks having other projects delayed. When funding allows, ensure that your strategy includes these additional personnel costs when planning the overall budget.

Only use this strategy in very small enterprises or in highly specialized environments, due to the impact of disrupting the entire workforce during the enterprise-wide replacement rollout and the extreme variation in budgetary requirements between years with replacements and those without.

Partial/staged replacement

In a *partial or staged replacement* strategy (shown in Figure 16-2), a percentage of systems are replaced each year. This strategy has several benefits over the full replacement strategy, including less variable budgets and staffing requirements. Having a predictable yearly technology replacement budget makes strategic planning easier, and hardware-related staffing requirements remain consistent throughout the cycle. This strategy is more complex than a full replacement one (see preceding section) because it involves purchasing a portion of the hardware each year for several successive years. However, complexity is minimized within each purchase cycle because all machines in a particular year are the same. A partial/staged cyclic replacement plan is generally considered optimal.

Figure 16-2:
A simple example of a partial replacement cycle illustrating server, desktop, and laptop devices.

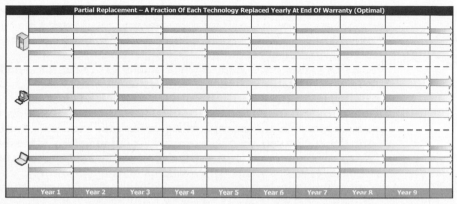

In Figure 16-2, a portion of each system type will reach maximum life each year and be replaced, with another fraction only one year old in service. Budgeting is simplified due to predictability and can be handled as a stabilized cost-of-business rather than a varying budgetary line item. Limited variation (one vendor's product in each category per year) allows testing updates for a minimum number of configurations.

You can use this strategy for both workstations and servers, although servers typically enjoy a longer lifespan before being replaced.

The percentage of workstations you will replace each year is linked to the length of time each system remains in production, which in turn is typically linked to warranty. For example, if systems have a four-year warranty, 25 percent of systems should be replaced every year in order to ensure that all systems in the enterprise are under warranty. If systems have a three-year warranty, 33 percent of systems should be replaced every year.

Employing a partial or staged replacement cycle also aligns with Moore's Law, which states that processing power will double every 18 months. Because of the impact of Moore's Law, software development practices, and standard warranty options, the most common cycle for user workstations involves purchasing midrange systems on a three-year cycle. Many standard warranties follow three-year replacement cycles because the design lifecycle of hardware and standards for software resource minimums follow the same cycle. Extending warranties to a fourth year or longer results in diminishing returns on investment because software, accessories, and storage requirements continue to expand in the intervening time and older equipment is prone to failure.

To save money, some organizations replace 25 percent of workstations every year, but purchase systems with three-year warranties. This approach results in some systems being out of warranty for a time. Even so, replacing components on an as-needed basis for the out-of-warranty systems may be significantly less expensive long-term than the cost of the extra year of warranty. Whether your organization would benefit from such a plan depends on your hardware's failure rate, your technical staff's proficiency with hardware, and the environment in which the systems are used.

A five-year cycle for server replacement is common within enterprises because server-class hardware is more robust and vendors may offer longer warranties on servers than on workstations. Additionally, a five-year cycle corresponds to common manufacturing strategies such as the evolution of new blade chassis formats. Many vendors maintain the same blade form factor of their server-class products for five years before updating to the next generation of blade chassis and server blade configuration.

Riding the cutting edge

Technology is said to be *cutting edge* when it is new, advanced, and state-of-the-art. Enterprises with adequate financial resources, as well as incentives, may replace systems frequently (even more than once per year) so that users always have the benefit of the newest and best technology. Whether this strategy has any benefit depends upon the nature of the enterprise and its motivations for replacing systems so frequently. For example, being able to advertise the use of cutting-edge technology may figure into the company's marketing plan.

Additionally, organizations that want to use workstations for high-performance or grid computing initiatives may find a constant influx of new systems helpful (see Chapter 14). This strategy is also highly agile, as the newer an organization's base technology is, the easier it is to implement emerging technologies. Design and architectural firms are common examples of organizations that can benefit from cutting-edge replacement strategies.

The cutting-edge replacement strategy (shown in Figure 16-3) definitely has drawbacks, however, particularly with regard to user disruption. Even if data is stored on a centralized server and the IT staff loads applications prior to switching out a user's workstation, frequent disruptions may be detrimental to productivity, particularly for users with highly customized systems.

In the simplest form, shown in Figure 16-3, all devices are replaced when a new version becomes available. Budgeting is complex due to the unpredictable period between new product releases. Systems are replaced together, so all devices of the same type can be updated together.

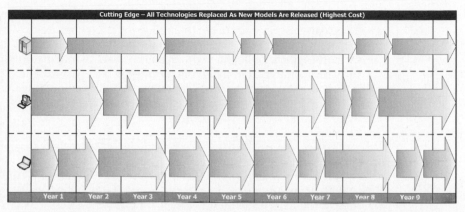

Figure 16-3:
An example
of a cut-
ting edge
replace-
ment cycle
illustrating
server,
desktop,
and laptop
devices.

If you are considering this strategy, remember that the more often systems are replaced, the more time technical staff must spend ensuring that data is securely removed (see Chapter 10) and that drivers are available for existing software. Additionally, beware of making the transition from cutting edge to *bleeding edge*, which occurs when the technology is so new that it is considered experimental, unreliable, or incompatible with existing technology. The newer the technology, the greater the risk.

Employing trickle-down replacement

In the *trickle-down replacement strategy,* you identify key personnel or functions and replace the systems associated with them first. You then use the displaced systems to replace other systems, and this process continues until you remove the oldest systems from service.

A common practice for organizations using this strategy is to upgrade executive and management systems first (tier 1), transfer old tier-1 systems to full-time employees (tier 2), and transfer old tier-2 systems to part-time employees (tier 3). Another common practice involves replacing mission-critical systems first and then shifting all systems in a cascade of replacement based on system age.

This strategy maximizes utilization against cost by placing the newest, most powerful systems where they are needed, then rolling each strata of systems down one level so that all staff members experience a small upgrade each year. This approach can be effective approach in some enterprises, such as those whose primary functions are engineering or multimedia, or others that require greater processing power.

The biggest drawback to this strategy is user disruption because all systems are shifted after every purchase. Depending on the percentage of computers replaced each time, the trickle-down plan may also result in complexity from having many system builds in service, some of which may be outside their warranty period. Additionally, if this strategy is based on political hierarchy instead of need, you gain additional complexity without adding value.

Relying on surplus technology

Some organizations, such as charities or not-for-profits, rely on donated equipment. In an enterprise, some underfunded units may be not be able to afford new equipment and can replace their systems only with ones that are retired from other units. This strategy is likely to suffer the drawbacks described in "Keeping systems until they fail" section, earlier in this chapter, without any of the benefits. This type of environment offers little stability, as systems are often kept in service beyond not only warranty but expected life span. Additionally, a high level of technology maintenance and support is required due to the high level of complexity from having a wide variety of equipment and also because these organizations tend to have a higher incidence of component-level replacement in order to conserve resources.

While you can place this strategy into limited use for development — such as testing proof of concepts — in general, this strategy should be used enterprise-wide only if no other strategy is feasible.

Using technology as a reward

Some organizations use technology as a reward, replacing systems based on an employee's job performance, position, or status. It's also not unheard of for new workstations to be offered in order to gain political support. Enterprises that engage in these behaviors have difficulty taking advantage of economies of scale, both in purchasing and support, and minor differences between systems purchased in an ad-hoc manner create further complexity (see Chapter 4). Additionally, the morale of employees who rarely receive upgrades may decline. This reward strategy is normally seen only in immature enterprises, where a single individual is responsible for purchasing and deploying technology without being subject to IT governance requirements (see Chapter 2).

As it has no real benefit, you should avoid this strategy.

Replacing technology in an ad-hoc manner

Replacing technology in a random or ad-hoc (because of a new project or unplanned sudden development) manner is not truly a strategy at all, but instead only a reaction to events such as equipment failure, new hires, or a sudden influx of unexpected funds. In response to such events, management buys systems in small numbers or even individually. This approach is often taken in immature enterprises in which technology purchases are not coordinated, such as small businesses or home office environments. It is also common in educational or research settings, where units are funded independently and money not spent during a fiscal year is lost.

It can be argued that an enterprise that works this way is not an enterprise at all, but an extended workgroup with multiple operational silos of equipment. These environments, shown in Figure 16-4, can be highly complex and face significant difficulties when trying to implement any type of centralization or integration strategy. Reactionary or on-the-fly procurement is not cost-effective because technology purchases aren't aligned with the organization's overall purchasing strategy and can't gain economies of scale possible through coordinated purchasing.

Figure 16-4:
An example of an ad-hoc replacement cycle illustrating server, desktop, and laptop devices.

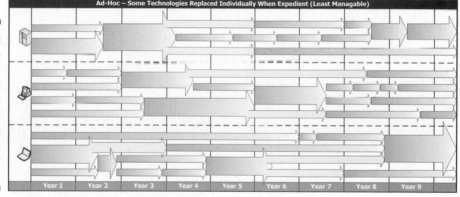

In Figure 16-4, devices are acquired or replaced based on individual project or departmental-level events and may be retained well past warranty periods and expected equipment life cycles. Budgeting is complex due to the unpredictable nature of both quantity and cost of individual devices acquired to meet each new requirement. Significant variety of system age, vendors, and product types makes this solution the most difficult to patch and update systemwide and may create pools of systems unable to implement new software packages due to device driver variation or system resource limitations.

Because there may be little control over procurement, a reactionary strategy may result in the purchase of equipment that technical staff cannot support adequately. Lack of proper support can easily result in loss of productivity when problems can't be solved in a timely manner. It also raises the risk of a security-related incident, such as a release of confidential information, because support staff is not familiar with the proper security controls for that particular system.

For all these reasons, you could argue that this is the worst type of update solution and is not supportable in a well-integrated enterprise. It creates significant complexity due to the large variety of individual devices types and vendor products that may be in place at any time and places barriers to gaining efficiencies through economies of scale and centralized update solutions.

Planning for Sub-System Updates

While you're selecting strategies for updating entire systems, remember to plan for upgrades and updates to components, firmware, and device drivers.

Upgrading components

Although upgrading components is no longer as common as it once was, some enterprises find it necessary to upgrade system memory, video cards, processors, or other components. This need may arise from failure of components that are out of warranty, the desire to improve system performance, or hardware specifications required by a new application.

It may not seem that adding more memory or upgrading a processor is a significant change, but prior to allowing component-level upgrades, you should be aware of several issues:

✔ Some software products use system hardware information as part of their copy protection and registration process. For this reason, a component upgrade may require you to re-register your software or contact the vendor's technical support staff.

✔ Configuration settings may have to be adjusted both on the system itself and in applications running on that system.

✔ New device drivers may need to be installed, and those drivers may conflict with other applications or operating system components. In some cases, drivers may not yet be available for cutting-edge devices, requiring a period of time before they can be deployed.

In addition, to thoroughly test software upgrades and deployments on all hardware present in the enterprise, the organization needs to maintain a component-level inventory of systems instead of simple make and model information. This task alone may negate any cost savings gained by replacing a component, as opposed to replacing the whole system.

This issue mainly applies to workstations. Servers typically have longer production lifespans than workstations, so vendor-approved and tested parts are available for longer periods of time.

Updating firmware

Firmware refers to the internal software (also called the *instruction set*) that a device uses for operation. Firmware can reside in read-only memory or programmable read-only memory, neither of which is generally user-accessible. The most common example of firmware is a computer's basic input/output system (BIOS), which contains the instruction set that runs when the computer is turned on. You can also find firmware in switches, routers, wireless access points, and other network infrastructure devices, as well as at the component level in servers, such as storage controller and video cards. Hardware vendors typically do not release firmware updates very often, and the updates usually fix bugs or add new functionality.

A failed firmware update can render a device unusable or "bricked." Because of this risk, any update plan should allow for thorough research and testing of new firmware before it's installed in expensive or mission-critical hardware. Further, technical staff should ensure that the update is truly necessary by carefully reviewing any information related to it. Some firmware updates may apply only to certain batches of components or should be installed only if users are experiencing certain problems.

Many small to mid-size organizations do not have the resources to test updates on spare systems. If this situation applies to your organization, procedures should mandate applying firmware updates only when necessary and updating non-mission-critical systems first, if applicable. Due to the extensive amount of work involved, you may find that it is feasible to apply firmware updates on a regular cycle, such as quarterly or yearly, instead of as they come out.

Updating device drivers

Software that facilitates the operation of hardware devices is referred to as a *device driver*. This software allows other software programs that operate at a higher level, such as operating systems or office productivity software, to interact with devices. Drivers are updated on a fairly regular basis by hardware vendors, and these updates, like firmware updates, fix bugs and add new features. Unless systems are experiencing acute problems, you should handle driver updates along with other software updates.

Planning Software Updates

Just as it is preferable to have minimal complexity in hardware, you should strive for minimal complexity in software. As discussed in Chapter 4, reducing operating system and application variation decreases support skill requirements and improves the user experience.

You must update software regularly to ensure the confidentiality, integrity, and availability of information resources, as well as to meet business needs. A vendor may release new major versions of software that add functionality every two to three years. They may release updates and patches, however, far more often in order to fix bugs or remediate vulnerabilities.

Software update strategies must balance security with productivity. The IT staff must ensure that software is updated regularly and in a timely manner, while also ensuring that there is minimal impact to users during peak usage times. The strategy you choose is likely to depend on the applications and operating systems in use in your enterprise. Regardless, all update strategies should include procedures for testing, deployment, and maintenance.

Understanding the need for testing

It is critical to test new software — whether it is an update, patch, upgrade, or new installation — prior to deployment in your enterprise. Deploying untested software is risky, and may result in disruption of operations. Testing is performed in a test network, which is a smaller-scale replica of the enterprise that is comprised of the same software and configuration settings being used in the production environment. This allows technical staff to develop update procedures specific to the software being installed and troubleshoot problems ahead of time, without risking disruption of the production environment.

Because software vendors can't test their products in every possible environment, it isn't unusual for installations or upgrades to fail — in some cases, catastrophically. Obviously, it's better to discover such failures in a contained test environment.

Small to medium-sized organizations may not have the resources to have an extensive test network, particularly due to the cost of hardware, but some of this cost can be offset by using virtualization technologies to create a test environment with a small number of physical systems. We discuss this and other uses of virtualization in Chapter 13.

Exploring deployment strategies

In small organizations or immature enterprises, IT staff may spend a great deal of time installing or upgrading software one system at a time, often displacing the user while the work is being performed. This displacement reduces employee productivity. Ad hoc deployment is not a functional strategy for a mature enterprise or ones supporting a large number of machines or frequent updates. You should use one-at-a-time upgrades only in very small enterprises or when required by software licensing constraints, such as those that require physical keys (dongles).

Consider more appropriate strategies for deploying software that encompass procedures for initial system deployment, software version upgrades, and system recovery in the event that a system needs to be reloaded.

The following sections examine widely used deployment strategies and an emergent strategy.

Using a standard base

Deployment options that depend on a standard base can increase efficiency in medium-sized to large enterprises. In this strategy, a standard software load consisting of the operating system, security software, and standard required utilities or applications is used for all systems. Additional software can then be loaded based on needs such as function, workgroup, or location. Management solutions such as Microsoft System Center Configuration Manager or Novell ZENworks can assist with this, where applicable, as can customized batch files or similar solutions.

This type of deployment requires detailed planning, but allows you to use the same mechanism for initial deployment as well as later updates. Because software installation can be group-based, it is highly flexible. Users can be given a wide variety of software (subject to licensing), which they can choose to install or not, or pre-selected configurations can be loaded automatically the first time a user logs in or prior to first login.

Image-based deployment

Chapter 4 introduced the concept of image-based deployment in the context of standardization. In this form of deployment, a system is loaded and configured, an image or "snapshot" is saved, and then that image is copied to other systems.

Images may contain fully configured operating systems and all necessary software applications, or may consist of standard loads that are modified as needed after deployment. Both of these methods are more efficient than installing software on systems individually. Regardless of which method is used, variations in hardware and software may require multiple images to be created.

It is not enough to create images to prepare for initial deployment of systems into the production environment. To be useful for system restoration, the images must be maintained and updated with new versions of software, patches, and security updates.

I recommend that you consider establishing a *nursery* — a protected network in which systems can be brought online, loaded, and configured in relative safety. Loading systems in a nursery allows IT staff to ensure that anti-malware software is up-to-date and all patches are applied before they are exposed to threats typically found on a publicly accessible network.

You can deploy images over a network connection, provided that it has sufficient bandwidth and the threat of malware infection is low, such as in a nursery or in a well-defended enterprise. If full system network deployment isn't feasible, you can load systems offline using removable media such as thumb drives, external hard drives, or optical media such as DVDs.

Considering virtualized solutions

Application and desktop virtualization solutions (see Chapter 13) allow the automatic provisioning of system, service, and application suites based on specific assignment. Because no hardware pre-configuration is required, automatic distribution of virtualized applications can be the fastest setup option for highly mobile business units or during disaster recovery efforts. Once the servers and DNS namespace have been restored to direct access to a new data center, any commodity hardware systems supporting the proper remote protocols can be connected and updated functionality accessed automatically on the virtualization host.

Updates applied to the desktop virtualization host or updated packages replacing older packages in an application virtualization service will be automatically available to users upon the next access without requiring update to the end-user device, although this can present a risk for data compromise if not properly secured and maintained.

Planning for software maintenance

In a production environment, software must be maintained beyond the initial load. New vulnerabilities are discovered almost daily, and threats and exploits evolve continuously, requiring both periodic and emergency updates to installed software. Additionally, business needs are often best served by upgrading to current software versions in a timely manner.

Major commercial software vendors typically release new versions of their software every three years, with the exception of security and mobile software, which has a much faster release cycle.

While you need to plan for major software upgrades every three years or so, upgrade strategies are highly vendor-dependent. Some vendors provide upgrade packages that simply add features while allowing configuration settings to be carried over, while others require that the old version be uninstalled prior to installing the new one.

Upgrades to applications may also involve structural upgrades to their associated databases consumed by client/server applications or middleware components within n-tier enterprise application environments. In this situation, it is important not only to first conduct the upgrade in a test environment, but also to ensure that adequate backups are performed prior to deploying the upgrade in the production environment in case a rollback is necessary.

Software vendors regularly release updates to their applications in order to fix bugs, mitigate vulnerabilities, and add new features. These updates may be referred to as security updates, patches, or hotfixes, depending on the vendor and the type of update. Vendors may also release *service packs*, which contain multiple patches rolled into a single, easily deployable update package. Service packs may also be more than just the sum of their parts and often include new functionality. For this reason, service packs require more testing than basic updates or patches prior to deployment, to ensure that operations are not disrupted.

Chapter 17

Planning Security Strategies

In This Chapter

▶ Recognizing potential threats
▶ Preparing countermeasures

The always-on, network-connected enterprise provides a ready target for attack. The concept of security through obscurity is worthless in an age of automated tools capable of profiling public-facing networks and attacking any identified vulnerabilities. This chapter examines some of the most commonly encountered network threats — malware, application vulnerabilities, and directed network attacks — and identifies strategies useful in defending against them.

Throughout this chapter, *attackers* are people, groups, or other entities that attempt to circumvent security controls. Although an attacker is typically a malicious outside person, such as an industrial spy, it can also be an internal individual, such as an employee trying to bypass security to make his job easier.

Identifying Threats to the Enterprise

Threats to the enterprise can come from internal or external sources and can target particular operating systems, applications, organizations, or even users. The following sections look at common enterprise threats.

Malware

Malware is malicious or unwanted software that is placed on computers without the owner's informed consent. A computer with malware installed on it is said to be *infected*. Malware infections can result in destruction or alteration of data, confidential information (including login credentials) being exposed, network disruptions, and reduced employee productivity.

Beyond keeping systems patched, the best defense against malware is anti-malware software, which we discuss later in this chapter.

The following sections take a look at several common types of malware you may encounter.

Viruses and worms

Viruses and worms spread differently but have similar results. *Viruses* move from system to system by copying and executing infected files, whereas *worms* seek out other systems to infect on their own. A virus typically carries a payload, which is code that is executed once the virus successfully infects a system.

Virus creation kits are freely available on the Internet and they require very little programming knowledge to use. Anyone can now create and distribute a virus.

Trojans

Like the mythical Trojan horse, this type of malware appears to be something beneficial but is actually damaging. Users are tricked into running the Trojan because this malware appears to be legitimate or at least interesting. They may infect computers via malicious Web sites with executable content, e-mail attachments, or software downloads. Attackers may also take advantage of vulnerabilities in applications that make them vulnerable to Trojan installation. Trojans, particularly those used to steal passwords or personal information, are often utilized by criminals and criminal organizations simply because it's relatively easy to hit thousands, if not millions, of victims in a short amount of time using the Internet.

Spyware

Spyware is monitors a user's activity, such as Web surfing habits. Spyware that collects form data is particularly dangerous, since it may pass along login credentials to unauthorized persons. In addition to collecting information, spyware may interfere with the functionality of the operating system or Web browser by adding icons to the desktop, opening browser windows without warning, modifying the user's home page, adding browser helpers, changing system settings, or disabling legitimate software.

Spyware is often installed unintentionally by users who think they are installing free games, Web helper tools, screen savers, desktop wallpaper, or other types of "fun" software that has no place in a secure enterprise.

Botnets

A botnet is a collection of malware-infected computers that are controlled by an individual referred to as the owner or herder. Individual computers in the botnet are also called zombies or drones, and the owner controls them remotely via communication medium such as Internet Relay Chat (IRC). The owner may have a dedicated IRC server, called the command and control server, or may take advantage of existing servers. IRC is the preferred medium because it's simple to use and largely unregulated.

Botnets have many malicious purposes, but the most common appear to be conducting distributed denial-of-service (DDoS) attacks, which render computing resources unavailable by flooding them with communication requests, and sending unsolicited commercial e-mail, usually referred to as *spam*.

It is critical to keep bots out of your enterprise, not only because you do not want your organization's systems used for illegal activity but also because there can be a heavy financial impact. Although actual computing hardware is not damaged, it may take a significant amount of time to bring the infected computers back to a secure state. In addition, botnet infection leads to a loss of productivity from network slowdowns that can occur during the initial infection and afterward as the systems are manipulated by the attacker.

Application vulnerabilities

Malware can take advantages of vulnerabilities in applications caused by software flaws (see preceding section). Attackers can also exploit these vulnerabilities manually. Some common flaws include

- **Unsanitized input:** Software that fails to validate user input may be vulnerable to injection attacks, in which malicious code is input and processed by the server.

- **Overly verbose error messages:** Any error message seen by the user should contain only information that user needs to know. It should not contain debugging information, such as codes, information about the file structure, or platform information. This information is helpful to attackers.

- **Defaulting or failing to an insecure state:** Applications whose settings aren't secure by default may allow unauthorized access to data or functionality in the event of faulty logic or programming errors.

- **Unlimited resource allocation:** Most applications allocate resources in some fashion and failure to implement limits can lead to denial of service. An attacker could establish multiple sessions and use all available client connections, or an employee could accidentally use all available disk space by uploading a very large file.

The preceding list is only a tiny sample of possible software flaws. For a more complete listing, refer to sites such as

- SANS Top 25 Most Dangerous Software Errors (www.sans.org/top25-software-errors)

- Open Web Application Security Project Top Ten (www.owasp.org/index.php/Category:OWASP_Top_Ten_Project)

- Common Weakness Enumeration (www.cwe.mitre.org)

Directed network attacks

Attackers may attempt to attack the enterprise network directly using techniques such as

- ✔ Intercepting unencrypted network traffic
- ✔ Scanning the network for open ports in order to identify services
- ✔ Forging, or *spoofing*, IP addresses, in order to appear to come from a trusted host
- ✔ Launching DDoS/DoS attacks

Selecting Appropriate Countermeasures

Threats and countermeasures have a complicated relationship. Sometimes a single countermeasure can protect against a variety of threats. Alternatively, you may need to implement multiple countermeasures in response to one threat. For example, directed network attacks, such as those mentioned in the previous section, are countered by applying multiple countermeasures such as encryption and firewalls, at a minimum.

When planning a security strategy, you may want to consider bundled solutions, as they may be more cost-effective. Buying a single network device that serves several purposes (such as router, virtual private network, and firewall) may be less costly than purchasing individual devices, particularly when you take maintenance contracts and training costs into account.

The countermeasures discussed in this section are basic protections suitable for most enterprises.

Malware protection

Many anti-malware vendors such as McAfee (www.mcafee.com), Symantec (www.symantec.com), Trend Micro (www.trendmicro.com), Microsoft (www.microsoft.com/forefront/), and AVG (www.avg.com) offer solutions that protect against multiple types of malware, including viruses and worms, Trojans, spyware, and phishing e-mails.

Although you may be tempted or pressured to select low-cost or free standalone antivirus solutions, saving money doesn't outweigh the benefit of using a managed enterprise-level anti-malware solution. Managed solutions allow you to control update frequency, scanning frequency, and configuration from a central console. You can easily determine which computers are behind on malware definition files, and your security staff can receive alerts when malware is detected within the enterprise.

If a system becomes infected, it is usually safer to reload the system rather than attempt to clean it, particularly if it is a workstation. Virus removal tools are not always successful and remnants may remain.

Secure application development

You can address vulnerabilities in vendor software by regularly applying patches and updates. Evaluate applications developed in-house for vulnerabilities using platform-appropriate manual and automated testing techniques such as penetration testing, vulnerability scanning, manual input validation, or code analysis.

Data loss prevention

Data loss prevention (DLP) solutions are used to protect data in use, data at rest, and data in motion. DLP systems can be network-based or host-based. Network-based solutions are installed at the enterprise's gateway and monitor all network traffic, searching for any unauthorized transmission of protected data out of the network, such as by e-mail or over the Web. Host-based solutions install agents on workstations and servers that identify attempts to copy protected data to unauthorized devices such as USB drives.

DLP solutions are very useful in organizations that manage valuable proprietary data, trade secrets, financial data, health records, or other types of confidential and mission critical data. In some enterprises, prevention of a single data breach more than pays for the cost of the DLP system. There are a number of DLP solutions available and features may vary, but all solutions require you to identify the data to be protected. This can be a time-consuming process requiring a great deal of planning and testing before implementation to ensure that appropriate data is blocked and false positives do not negatively affect business.

DLP solutions are most effective in a mature enterprise, so you may wish to hold off on implementing wide-scale DLP until resources are centrally managed (see Chapter 4) and appropriate data storage policies have been implemented (see Chapter 10).

Encryption

Encryption should be used on confidential or sensitive data such as password files, medical or financial information, or proprietary business information. Employing encryption helps prevent the release of data if computing equipment is stolen or if unauthorized persons gain access to files. In a nutshell, encryption uses an algorithm and a key to transform data from something readable to something unreadable without the key. A user can encrypt a file, a folder, or even the entire disk, although full-disk encryption may slow the computer down noticeably if there are multiple applications open at once. Some operating systems have their own built-in encryption, and many third-party solutions are available.

There are two basic types of encryption:

- **Symmetric:** In *symmetric* encryption, also known as *secret-key encryption*, a single key is used to encrypt and decrypt data. This type of encryption is popular with home users and in smaller enterprises and there are some very strong symmetric encryption algorithms available, such as Advanced Encryption Standard (AES). This algorithm is used widely in programming and built-in encryption for portable devices such as USB drives. Other algorithms include Data Encryption Standard (DES), 3-DES, RC4, and Blowfish.

- **Asymmetric:** *Asymmetric* encryption is also referred to as *public-key encryption*. In this type of encryption, key pairs are used instead of a single shared key. These key pairs consist of public and private keys. The public key is available for general use, while the private key is kept secure and not revealed. Data encrypted with a public key can only be decrypted with its companion private key and vice-versa. For example, if Alice wants to send an encrypted message to Bob, she obtains Bob's public key, encrypts the message with it, and sends it to Bob, who decrypts it with his private key. This is illustrated in Figure 17-1. Bob's public key can be openly published without risking compromise of the encryption, because the public key can only be used to encrypt data. A separate private key is required for Bob to decrypt the encrypted message and retrieve the information Alice sent him.

To prevent *man-in-the-middle attacks*, in which an attacker intercepts traffic between Alice and Bob by substituting their public keys for his own, a trusted third party is used as a certificate authority (CA). The CA verifies the identity of Alice and Bob by creating digital certificates for them that verify their identity. In this manner, Alice and Bob can prove their identity to each other and any attempts by an attacker to inject nonvalidated keys will fail.

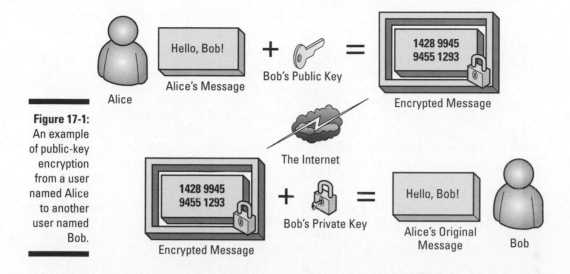

Figure 17-1:
An example of public-key encryption from a user named Alice to another user named Bob.

Using encryption in the enterprise

In addition to the approaches already mentioned, you may wish to consider the following encryption strategies:

✓ **Secure Sockets Layer (SSL):** SSL is used to encrypt data communications, particularly over the public Internet. You can use SSL to provide security for Web traffic, using the HTTPS protocol, as well as for e-mail and file transfer. SSL is a widely used example of hybrid encryption. It uses asymmetric encryption to establish a session between the client and the server, and then uses symmetric encryption to encrypt the data being transferred.

✓ **Digital signatures:** Digital signatures use asymmetric encryption to verify the identity of the sender of a message and the message itself may or may not be encrypted. Digital signatures can be used on electronic documents in the same way physical signatures are used on paper documents. In addition, digital signatures can also verify that a message has not been altered in transmission. Because the encryption process for the digital signature incorporates the message, the digital signature is invalidated if the message changes.

✓ **Public-key infrastructure:** If you plan to use encryption throughout the enterprise, you will want to consider implementing a *public-key infrastructure (PKI)*. PKI facilitates the use of digital certificates and a PKI system issues, verifies, publishes, and manages certificates and their associated keys. Implementing PKI adds both cost and complexity to the enterprise and requires extensive planning and research to obtain the best value and ensure that solutions in use within the enterprise are compatible with the PKI solution selected.

Your organization can act as its own CA for internal communications, including internal Web sites, because you can easily push out root certificates to systems in your enterprise. You should use trusted third-party certificate authorities — such as VeriSign (www.verisign.com), Thawte (www.thawte.com), and GoDaddy (www.godaddy.com) — for public-facing servers, however, because they are already trusted by client software and operating systems.

Although Bob and Alice are commonly used as an example to explain how public key encryption works, it is more of a teaching tool than a real-world example. Because asymmetric encryption is slow, it is often used to transmit symmetric keys so that faster symmetric algorithms can be used to encrypt the actual data.

For more detailed information on encryption, we recommend *Cryptography For Dummies,* by Chey Cobb (Wiley Publishing).

Firewalls

At its most basic, a firewall is a boundary. It can be likened to a medieval city gate guard or a modern border patrol station in that it controls who or what passes through it in either direction. Firewalls can be used to protect an entire network from the public Internet or protect network segments from each other as well as the Internet. They can be hardware-based or software-based. Hardware firewalls are network appliances that may also include other functionality, such as routing, switching, or virtual private networking. These firewalls can protect the entire enterprise or network segments. You can install software firewalls on workstations or servers and integrate them with the operating system.

Figure 17-2 shows a basic firewall protecting an organization's network. This firewall resides on the boundary between the private protected network and the public Internet, and some services may be exposed.

Figure 17-3 illustrates a dual-firewall configuration creating a demilitarized zone (DMZ) in which a public-facing Web server is segmented from the rest of the protected private network. In the event that the Web server is compromised, an attacker cannot use it to gain access to the rest of the network.

You should consider layering multiple firewalls to provide additional security for sensitive data. Using multiple firewalls is a delaying mechanism because the exploit that worked on the one firewall isn't likely to work on another, provided the firewalls use different platforms. This allows intrusion detection software, if used, more time to detect the unauthorized activity and alert security personnel.

Some common types of firewalls are explained in the following sections.

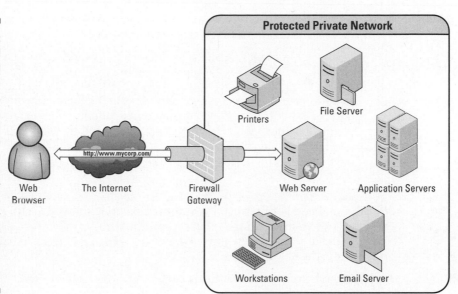

Figure 17-2: A firewall configured as a gateway, allowing external users to access the corporate Web server but blocking all other access to the protected private network.

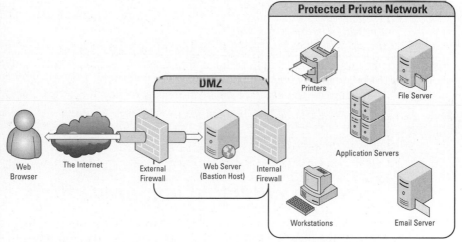

Figure 17-3: A dual-firewall configuration in which two firewalls separate the partially exposed DMZ network from the internal network.

Packet-filtering firewalls

Packets can be filtered in two ways:

> ✔ **Stateless:** In *stateless* packet filtering, the firewall simply analyzes the packet based on the current rule set and either denies or allows the packet access to the network. Because it operates in such a simple way, there is little overhead and packets are analyzed at high rates of speed.

Unfortunately, it does not maintain session state, which means that it does not associate inbound and outbound traffic.

This type of packet filtering is useful for controlling network access. For example, the firewall could block incoming traffic on port 80, thereby making sure that any development Web servers in their default configuration were not accessible from outside the local network. It could block all ICMP traffic, preventing anyone from outside the network from pinging machines inside the network, or it could block all traffic from a particular IP address or network. It can also be used to keep network users from contacting particular networks or types of servers, such as FTP servers using port 21.

✔ **Stateful:** In *stateful* packet filtering, the session state of network communication is maintained. The firewall analyzes inbound and outbound traffic to make sure that packets entering the network were originally requested from inside the network, as well as making sure that they follow the defined rules.

This type of packet filtering is useful to protect against Trojans or other types of malicious attacks that may be successful in getting around the stateless packet filter and be caught only because a computer inside the network did not request the packets.

Content-filtering firewalls

Firewalls are also capable of performing content filtering. Typically, content filtering is performed in order to block access to undesirable or unauthorized Web sites and is managed by linking the firewall to an external rules server that contains the list of blocked addresses or keywords or by downloading these lists and rules to the firewall. A company may choose to block access to pornographic Web sites, sites that offer illegal music or video downloads, gambling sites, or others deemed inappropriate for work.

Intrusion detection and prevention

An intrusion detection system (IDS) identifies attempts to circumvent security controls. IDS is a passive technology that does not attempt to block intrusion. It merely identifies and reports it. With regard to information technology, there are two main types of IDS: network-based and host-based. Network IDS monitors network traffic and examines packets for suspicious activity, while Host IDS limits its monitoring and alerting to a specific device, such as a workstation or server. An intrusion prevention system (IPS) reacts to detected attempts at intrusion and seeks to prevent them, typically by terminating the source connection.

Examples of IDS and IPS solutions include

- GFI Events Manager (www.gfi.com/eventsmanager)
- HP TippingPoint (www.tippingpoint.com)
- McAfee Host Intrusion Prevention (www.mcafee.com)
- Open Source Hot-based Intrusion Detection System (www.ossec.net)
- Snort (www.snort.org)
- Tripwire (www.tripwire.com)

In addition to identifying intrusions from external sources, IDS can be used to detect intrusions from internal sources. In this way, you can use IDS as an internal auditing tool to identify employees who are violating security policies by attaching unauthorized devices to the network or running prohibited software. IDS can also be used to identify malware-infected systems.

Network address translation

Network address translation (NAT) is a process by which computers and other devices on a network are assigned private IP addresses that are not visible outside the network. They will not resolve over public networks and will be dropped by routers. Internal IP addresses are usually special unregistered addresses specifically set aside for private networks. These address ranges are

- 10.0.0.0–10.255.255.255
- 172.16.0.0–172.31.255.255
- 192.168.0.0–192.168.255.255

The router that provides NAT service presents public (or outside) IP addresses to the external network and translates them to the proper internal IP addresses during communication. It does so by changing the IP address in the packet header so the transmission appears to be coming from the external address, not the internal address. This process is illustrated in Figure 17-4, in which a group of privately addressed workstations share a single public routable address. The NAT device manages outgoing sessions, returning response packets to the proper workstation.

NAT does not protect internal systems from internal users who are also on the same private network. If this type of protection is desired, separate private networks must be configured.

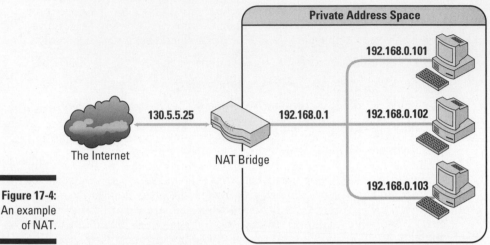

Private Address Space

192.168.0.101

192.168.0.102

130.5.5.25   192.168.0.1

The Internet   NAT Bridge

192.168.0.103

Figure 17-4:
An example
of NAT.

Static and dynamic NAT

There are two types of NAT:

- ✔ **Static:** In *static* NAT, internal IP addresses can be mapped to external IP addresses. This is performed on a one-to-one basis, so if 10 internal computers need to communicate with an external network, 10 external IP addresses must be available.

  Static NAT is useful if internal resources, such as Web or e-mail servers, need to be accessed by external users.

- ✔ **Dynamic:** In *dynamic* NAT, internal IP addresses are mapped to a pool of external IP addresses. The mapping is also one-to-one, but the mappings are not reserved. Any internal computer can use any available address in the pool.

  Dynamic NAT is useful in that it provides additional security (by obscurity) because an internal system may not always present the same external IP address.

The main advantage of NAT in general is that it hides the IP addresses of internal devices, such as servers, computers, printers, and switches, from outside attackers. Even if an outside attacker were to discover the private address of an internal device, that address would not be routed properly across a public network. Also, dynamic NAT can reduce costs by limiting the number of public IP addresses that must be leased from an Internet service provider (ISP).

In static NAT, every internal node that needs to access resources outside the internal network, such as the Internet, must have a corresponding external address. In dynamic NAT, fewer external addresses are needed, reducing the cost as mentioned previously; however, if there are only 10 external addresses, only 10 internal nodes can access external resources at any given time.

Benefits and drawbacks of NAT

As already mentioned, the primary benefits of NAT are extending the available range of IP addresses and hiding internal IP addresses from the outside world. Before considering implementing NAT in the enterprise, you should be aware of the drawbacks, some of which include the following:

- ✔ NAT may interfere with applications that require end-to-end connectivity, such as File Transfer Protocol (FTP) and similar applications.
- ✔ When used with high bandwidth solutions such as videoconferencing, the NAT device may create a bottleneck, causing performance to suffer.
- ✔ NAT increases complexity in the network (see Chapter 4 for complications of complexity).

You may find after examination, as many organizations do, that the benefits of NAT outweigh the drawbacks, at least in certain scenarios. Even if you do not wish to employ NAT across the enterprise, you may choose to employ it for certain specific purposes such as setting up test networks or temporary training areas or creating a secure "nursery" in which to load systems.

Port address translation

Port address translation (PAT) is a type of dynamic NAT that allows the network to present a single IP address beyond the enterprise by assigning a different port number to each internal node that accesses external resources. It does this by taking advantage of multiplexing, a TCP/IP feature that allows for concurrent connections using multiple ports. The router running the NAT service maps internal IP addresses to port numbers in its address table and each internal node keeps the same port number for the duration of the connection with the external system.

PAT can be used to extend the number of available IP addresses on an as-needed basis. For example, if an organization with only 5 available IP addresses needs to set up 20 computers all needing network access for a week-long training session, it could put those 20 computers on a switch behind a NAT device. Also, PAT devices are particularly useful when loading new systems. New machines can be loaded behind them fairly safely and not brought out into the main network until they are fully secured.

PAT does have its disadvantages, however. Because only one IP address is visible externally, two public Web servers both operating on port 80 could not be placed behind the PAT device because the PAT device could only route port 80 to one server. In this type of scenario, static NAT would be more appropriate.

Network monitoring

Network monitoring is important to measuring overall network health, which is relevant to both network operations and security. Poor performance can indicate a technical problem, such as failing or misconfigured hardware, or a security problem, such as a denial of service attack.

Examples of network monitoring solutions include

- Big Brother (www.bb4.com)
- Cisco Network Management (www.cisco.com)
- Nagios (www.nagios.org)
- Spiceworks (www.spiceworks.com)
- What's Up Gold (www.whatsupgold.com)

Please note that this is a very small sample list of network monitoring solutions and that there are many commercial and open source solutions available.

Chapter 18

Planning Business Continuity and Disaster Recovery

In This Chapter

▶ Knowing the difference between continuity and disaster planning

▶ Creating a business continuity strategy

▶ Planning for recovery from disaster

▶ Choosing a backup business location

▶ Keeping the lines of communication open during a crisis

A key subject throughout this book is how to align information technology with business objectives. Many of the solutions that you will implement will have a significant effect on business processes and may even create new ones. Changes in business processes and their accompanying technological solutions can antiquate your organization's established business continuity and/or disaster recovery plans, requiring regular testing and revision.

This chapter explores your role in business continuity and disaster recovery planning, which should include not only information technology personnel, but also key representatives from all other business elements in the organization. You need to remember that the resulting plan is not a goal, achieved and then never reviewed. It will be a living document and a constant challenge as you move forward with enterprise architectural projects and technology modernization practices.

Defining Business Continuity and Disaster Recovery

Planning for recovery operations includes two different aspects: disaster recovery and business continuity (also called continuity of operations). *Disaster recovery* (DR) involves the recovery of lost capabilities, often through outright replacement in the event of disasters, such as fire or flooding.

Business continuity provisions address strategies necessary to keep the organization in operation during times of difficulty — whether physical, as during a hurricane, or purely electronic, as with an extended denial of service attack. Both recovery efforts require a prior risk assessment that identifies elements of the network enterprise and their relative value to operations so that the most critical systems are recovered in the most effective order (such as authentication, followed by collaboration systems or community notification Web sites followed by authentication services).

Planning for recovery is useless without communicating policies throughout the organization and testing recovery plans on a regular basis to ensure that staff members are skilled at their assigned tasks and that backup practices produce effective recovery alternatives.

Some disasters, such as Hurricane Katrina, are so widespread that they overcome even the best planning, necessitating changes to recovery planning that must be communicated across the workforce through a mechanism outside of the afflicted zone. Without careful planning, implementation, maintenance, and communication of alternative means to connect with coworkers, a relatively simple recovery process can fall into chaos at the smallest deviation from the original plan.

Keeping Your Business in Business: Continuity Planning

Because business continuity planning affects technology as well as business processes, you, as an IT architect, are likely to participate in the creation and maintenance of your organization's plan. The degree of your participation depends on your organization's internal workings, but it is critical that you have a seat at the table. You should have a very clear understanding of how the changes you have made will affect business processes, and your knowledge is essential to conducting two critical elements of continuity planning: the business impact analysis (BIA) and the risk assessment, which are covered in the following sections.

Participating in a business impact analysis

BIA is conducted to identify critical business processes and determine the impact of any disruption to them. It is important to remember that BIA is performed on business processes, not on applications or servers. While there is certainly an effect if the e-mail server, database server, or customer relations management application is down, that impact exists only because it interferes with a business process.

Because BIA is driven by business processes, executive and management support is critical. More than likely, you will not be conducting a BIA yourself, but you will participate in the process as a technical resource. You will be asked to identify any IT resources that support critical business processes. These assets can be internal to the organization, such as resources residing in the data center, or external, such as data feeds from partners or other outside entities.

When performing a BIA, it's helpful to think in terms of fixed periods of time and determine the consequences of a resource loss in time periods such as one hour, one day, two days, five days, one week, and two weeks. It is important to ensure that all resources are analyzed using the same periods of time so that their impact may be compared. This will help to decide the recovery priority. Unless it's dictated by technical requirements, such as ensuring that directory services are restored prior to any solutions that require login, priority will be determined by business needs.

You may also be asked to assist in determining the recovery point objective (RPO) and recovery time objective (RTO) of specific information resources.

Recovery point objective

The *recovery point objective* is the point in time to which data should be restored following an incident. It is, quite simply, a determination of how much data your organization can afford to lose. This number is going to be based on the criticality of the business process that the data supports and should align closely with your backup schedule. If the RPO is one business day, then daily backups are required. On the other hand, if the RPO is four hours, then backups must be conducted more frequently.

For particularly critical business processes, such as financial trades or high-volume online retail sales, the RPO is likely to be the point of failure. In this scenario, data must be restored to the point at which the failure occurred.

You can achieve this RPO with backups alone. It requires a highly resilient and redundant architecture. Chapter 18 discusses backup strategies.

You need to know if your organization has any point-of-failure RPOs when planning the realignment because that information will play a major factor in data center consolidation efforts (see Chapter 4) and data storage policy development (see Chapter 10).

Recovery time objective

The recovery time objective is the length of time in which a business process can be down before unacceptable consequences occur. Consequences vary, based on the organization and the business process, but can include contract violations, noncompliance issues, fines, penalties, loss of sales, loss of competitive advantages, loss of trust, and negative publicity. In certain industries, consequences may also include harm (including loss of life) to personnel or the general public.

RTO is an objective, not a mandate, and it may not always be possible to meet the desired RTO. It is not always essential that a process be restored to full functionality within the RTO. It may be appropriate in planning to meet RTO by invoking manual workarounds for other operational elements or providing a reduced level of service, as long as an appropriate level of business functionality has been restored.

Participating in risk assessment

Business continuity planning also includes identification of risk. Risk assessments are performed on critical information technology to determine the probability of loss or disruption and as part of recovery strategy development.

If your organization has dedicated or contracted risk management personnel, you are likely to be a participant in the risk assessment process. If not, you may be responsible for completing the risk assessment. Regardless, it is important that you understand at least the basic concepts, which I discuss in Chapter 6.

Preparing a Recovery Plan

As an enterprise architect, you will take a key role in disaster recovery planning (DRP) and business continuity planning (BCP), as many logistical and control functions within an organization are technical in nature. DRP and BCP, in a nutshell, involve the preparation that is necessary to recover or continue information technology resources supporting the critical business processes identified in the BIA.

The complete process is beyond the scope of this book, so if you don't have experience with disaster recovery planning, I recommend *IT Disaster Recovery Planning For Dummies,* by Peter Gregory, CISA, CISSP, and Philip Jan Rothstein (Wiley Publishing).

Developing scenarios

Changes to technology will also involve changes to the scenarios in your DR and BCP plans. Scenarios are used to ensure that recovery strategies cover all disasters that are likely to occur. Scenarios should include short-, medium-, and long-term outages and range from restoration of an individual service or server to a regional disaster requiring evacuation of the facility. Sample scenarios include

- Loss of an individual server
- Failure of power or environmental controls

✔ Loss of the data center

✔ Loss of key IT personnel

✔ Loss of access to the information systems facility

✔ Significant weather event (such as a hurricane or flood) resulting in evacuation

✔ Terrorist attack

✔ Outbreak of a pandemic (see the nearby sidebar "Planning for a pandemic")

Incorporating virtualization strategies

Virtualization strategies (see Chapter 13) play a key role in business continuity and disaster recovery planning. Because virtualized systems are nothing more than a set of files interpreted by the host, they can be easily moved with operating system, settings, and applications intact. The *hypervisor* (an element of the virtualization host software that allocates resources to each virtual machine) provides a generic environment for the virtualized systems, meaning that it is not necessary to obtain identical equipment for the disaster recovery site.

Planning for a pandemic

Unlike natural catastrophes in which personnel are evacuated, disasters such disease and chemical or biological contamination may prevent your personnel from leaving their homes or traveling. Planning for large-scale pandemics will involve extending resources from the business location to users at home. Recent concerns over avian flu (H5N1) and swine flu (H1N1) have caused many organizations to implement pandemic plans.

The mobile strategies presented in Chapter 12 may need to be leveraged to a far larger portion of the user base than for normal day-to-day operations. Planning for greater bandwidth consumption at the server end, as well as intermittent or limited connectivity on the user side, will affect the efficiency of telecommuting employees. It is important to stress-test the infrastructure and to train users in proper practices for operating in this environment.

Although unpleasant to consider, pandemic planning must also take into account continuity of operations in the event that a significant portion of the workforce is incapacitated or deceased. Administrative credentials as well as operational knowledge must be preserved in a way that can be transferred in an environment where travel may be restricted and the facility physically unavailable. Cross-training and password escrow services may aid this process. It may also be helpful to identify non-IT employees with technical skills in the event that those skills become necessary. Potential IT personnel may be found in the internal audit department or business units that may contain employees with degrees in Management Information Systems.

You can use older systems or those with lesser capacity with the original virtualized systems distributed according to capacity, hosting resources, and business requirements. Systems that you've removed from service during consolidation efforts (see Chapter 4) and retained can continue to provide value by serving as alternative-site recovery platforms — a more cost-effective solution than trying to maintain identical new equipment in both operational and recovery sites. It is also significantly less expensive than attempting to obtain replacement hardware of a particular type on short notice.

Figure 18-1 illustrates this capability, including the use of external hosting providers, provided that the same hypervisor is used and limited customization of the virtualization host has been performed.

Virtualization in BC/DR Operations

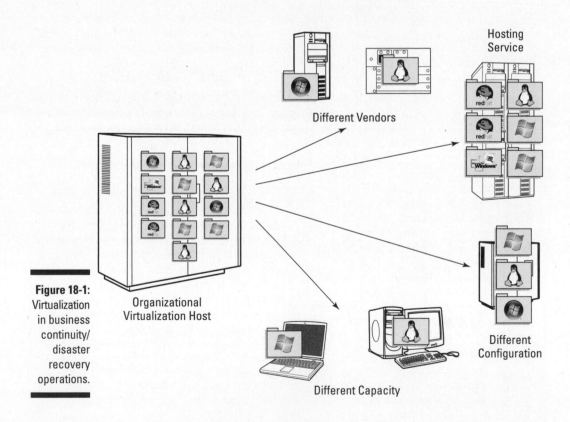

Figure 18-1: Virtualization in business continuity/ disaster recovery operations.

In a pinch, an organization's virtualized systems could be restarted for limited use on very underpowered hardware purchased over the counter when even the planned backup site is unavailable. Response time will degrade, but business can continue in the face of failure in the primary and backup sites provided that the backup and hosting application media are available and sufficient equipment can be acquired. Name service changes may also be necessary to redirect browsers to new IP addressing in the alternative location, which can delay access for users whose local ISPs have cached the old contact details.

Testing the plan

Testing is an important part of disaster recovery planning to ensure that a working plan will be used in the event of a disaster. Changes to the enterprise may also affect the plan's testing procedures, particularly those changes involving application integration and consolidation.

Following are a few standard testing methodologies:

- **Walkthrough, checklist, and simulation:** Walkthrough, checklist, and simulation testing do not affect normal business operations because production information systems are not involved. These methodologies entail reviewing and discussing the plan, making sure all steps are present, and simulating various types of disasters. In simulation testing, vendors and other external personnel may be contacted and alternative sites tested.

- **Full interruption:** Full interruption testing involves moving operations into disaster recovery mode, using production data and personnel. This type of testing has the potential to significantly disrupt business, is time consuming, and may be costly. Prior to integration, full interruption testing may have been used for specific services such as e-mail or Web, or for specific business units. Post integration, this type of testing may not be possible or practical, or may carry too much risk to your organization's operations.

Updating the plan

All disaster recovery plans should have provisions for maintenance, which includes a review and update schedule. Because enterprise architecture realignment can produce significant changes, it will be necessary to update the disaster recovery plan with these changes when they occur, even if it is outside the normal schedule. Some of the things that should trigger an update include

✔ Changes in hardware platforms, such as from standardization initiatives (see Chapters 3 and 4)

✔ Retirement of legacy applications or hardware

✔ Implementation of technologies using virtualization (see Chapter 13)

✔ Implementation of new collaboration solutions, such as groupware and portals (see Chapter 8)

Every time you implement a significant change to the enterprise, there is always the possibility that the project will not go as planned, and you will need to invoke the disaster recovery plan to roll back the changes by instituting recovery procedures. As such, it is in your best interest to ensure that the disaster recovery plan is up-to-date.

Using Alternative Sites

As the realignment progresses, you may find it beneficial to investigate the use of alternative sites. Whether your organization needs an alternative site depends on business need, the nature of the enterprise, and available funds. If your organization has regional offices, for example, it may be prudent for operations to move to an office in a location not directly affected by the disaster. Options for alternative sites are discussed in the following sections.

Selecting the right type of site

In addition to identifying secure locations outside of areas vulnerable to other disasters (or even similar ones), the enterprise architect should ensure any alternative site has a low rate of service interruption for power, water, and network service. There are three main types of alternative sites: cold, hot, and warm. The type of site that you select depends on RPO, RTO, and available funds. Generally speaking, the faster operations must be restored, the more expensive restoration will be.

✔ **Cold site:** A *cold site* is little more than an available location with basic infrastructure such as power and phone, which may or may not have network connectivity. It has no computers, servers, telecommunications lines and equipment, or even furniture.

A cold site is the cheapest form of alternative site; however, it takes the most effort to be brought to a functional state. This type of site should be used for longer RTOs, such as days or weeks. Even with advanced preparations, it will take some time to acquire or configure the necessary computing hardware and restore your data from backups.

✔ **Hot site:** A *hot site* is a fully functional alternative site that can be ready to take over operations immediately or shortly thereafter. In addition to power and phone, this site has all necessary computing hardware and software, as well as data and telecommunications networks and equipment. Everything is fully configured, and data should be either current or recent. How often data is replicated to the hot site should be based on a combination of RPO and RTO.

A hot site is the most expensive form of alternative site, but the cost may be justified for critical or high-risk business processes. This type of site should be used when business must be resumed quickly.

✔ **Warm site:** A *warm site* falls somewhere between a cold site and a hot site. In addition to power and phone, this type of site generally has the necessary computing hardware, as well as data and telecommunications networks and equipment, to restore operations fairly quickly, but this equipment may or may not be configured. In addition, data will have to be restored from backups.

The cost of this type of site falls between that of cold and hot sites, as does recovery time, which can range from hours to days.

Managing the alternative site

You have the option of managing your own alternative site or outsourcing that function. Although managing the site yourself offers you more control, it burdens your organization with additional cost and time.

If your organization does not possess alternative facilities under its control that meet the qualifications for a disaster recovery site, it's usually easier to contract this function with an established disaster recovery vendor. Vendors can generally offer hot, warm, or cold site recovery options at a reduced cost because cost for the facility and infrastructure is spread out among many customers.

When outsourcing, consider elements such as bandwidth and power, service level agreements, availability of facility personnel, and whether equipment is shared or dedicated.

Regardless of whether you manage your own recovery site or outsource it, the location of the site is critical. The site should be remote enough that it would not be affected by the same disaster as the primary site. If your organization's primary site is at risk of disruption due to certain weather events, such as hurricanes, it may be necessary for your recovery site to be in a completely different geographic region.

You should also consider the logistics of moving personnel to the disaster recovery facility. Transportation, housing, and basic amenities will be necessary for key business and technical personnel. You cannot simply assume there will be adequate hotel space during a large-scale disaster.

Communicating During a Disaster

After Hurricane Katrina, one of the first problems that businesses encountered was difficulty communicating with dispersed personnel. Once outside the area lacking access to the Internet, many individuals attempted to contact supervisors or coworkers, but because their companies' servers were still in the affected area, communication was difficult. E-mail was not relayed in a timely manner, if at all, and personnel were unable to determine current contact information.

Even businesses with detailed continuity and recovery plans found that key personnel had been redirected to different locations by evacuation authorities, while others found themselves in shelters and other facilities with limited access to Internet and even cell service in some cases. Coordinating personnel in possession of backup media with personnel responsible for performing restoration posed many challenges.

The preceding scenario is a good illustration of how even good plans can go awry when emergency communication isn't planned. This planning may include advance arrangements for

- A Web site hosted by a third-party vendor that facilitates threaded discussions and file exchange. This site isn't the recovery site, but rather a simple communications point of contact. You should develop it using the simplest methods possible. This site must be

  - Accessible by personally owned cell phones, smartphones, laptops, and other devices.

  - Secured with technologies, such as SSL, that do not require the installation of special software.

Businesses located in areas subject to disasters, such as those along coastlines, along geopolitical borders, or in areas of geological instability, should contract with a third-party vendor well outside their own area.

✔ Travel arrangements for key personnel to alternate sites or satellite offices, if available.

✔ Two-way radios that can be issued to key personnel in the event that cellphone communication isn't possible. Extra batteries are a must.

Avoid using any development technologies that are dependent on specific browsers or plugins and optimize graphics and files for low-bandwidth connections. Plain text is a perfectly acceptable means of communication. The site is not meant to be pretty; it is meant to serve as a starting point for recovery.

Users should be trained in access procedures for the site as part of their regular security awareness training. This site should be activated during disaster recovery testing and during a disaster, but should remain inactive and secure until needed.

Part VII
The Part of Tens

The 5th Wave   By Rich Tennant

"I didn't know they made skins for mainframes."

In this part . . .

Every *For Dummies* book ends with The Part of Tens, which provides useful information in easy-to-digest lists of ten. In this book, we include a list of ten challenges you are likely to face when trying to architect an existing enterprise and ten low-hanging fruit opportunities that may provide both a quick return on investment and obvious improvements to the enterprise.

Chapter 19

Ten Challenges for Redesigning an Existing Enterprise

In This Chapter

▶ Getting executive support

▶ Dealing with change

▶ Overcoming other common issues

---

*I*n this book, we identify numerous areas for enterprise realignment, which can provide many benefits from economic efficiency to enhanced data sharing. These changes don't come without cost, even if it is only that isolated IT shops may have to learn to work with others. If you're charged with realignment of an existing enterprise, here are ten challenges that you may face.

Dealing with Lack of Executive Support

One of the most soul-crushing situations is to finally be assigned the responsibility for re-architecting the enterprise, only to discover that you don't have the authority to make this redesign happen. This situation can easily happen in enterprises that lack cohesive IT governance, where projects are sponsored, approved, and implemented without support for enterprise-wide completion.

Anytime the CIO doesn't have a seat at the table of the executive organizational governing body, it's all too easy to develop strategies for efficiency, cost savings, and improved service only to encounter opposition from local, controlling IT managers with their own revenue streams who simply refuse to participate without a mandate.

Enterprise architecture must be a component of organizational strategic planning and supported by executive-level mandates, or it will fail. Negotiated solutions and opt-in at will strategies create greater complexity, reinforce existing silos, and complicate attempts to achieve economies of scale.

One way to gain executive support is to tie new initiatives to cost savings and perceived value. Communication of strategies, policies, and opportunities with executive staff play a key role in achieving success, as discussed in Chapters 2 and 17.

Handling Opposition to Change

Many technologists, as well as end users, resist change with the stubbornness of a mule. No amount of new features, bells and whistles, or improved efficiencies will persuade them that adopting change is a good thing. Technologists tend to defend solutions within their comfort zone and past technology decisions with all the passion of a mother bear defending her cubs. End users may scream when even the slightest change is made to their desktop background or the Web site's color scheme.

Communication, education, and demonstrations can help these individuals adapt to new technologies and the opportunities they present. After reading about the new technologies in the monthly newsletter, for example, these users may find some of the "new" worn off by the time the technology appears on their desktop.

Remember, as mentioned in Chapter 4, communication is critical.

Deciding on a Platform: Open Source versus Closed Source/Commercial Off-the-Shelf

If the organization is running both open source and closed source/commercial off-the-shelf software, trying to implement any kind of platform standardization is going to be a major challenge. While opposition to change is to be expected, people seem to be particularly passionate about open source versus commercial, and the proponents of each always seem to be able to spout off a myriad of reasons why their choice is better.

Realistically, you need to evaluate the use of both open and closed source software within your enterprise and determine which is best based on functionality and value and which best supports critical business processes. A product that is familiar and easy to use by the client base is generally going to be better than a really nifty equivalent that requires learning before use.

Platform standards must align with strategic business goals.

Chapter 3 looks at benefits and drawbacks of both open source and closed source software and may assist you with determining which is most appropriate for your enterprise.

Eliminating Resource Silos

Perhaps the most difficult issue in the enterprise revolves around the concept of personal ownership or proprietary control over technologies. While users easily accept a new telephone or a new water cooler, they become rabidly protective of their computers, printers, scanners, or other technical devices when confronted with policies that may change, remove, or alter their use.

Technical staff members may exhibit a near-religious fervor when asked to examine a solution that doesn't fit with their "One True Way." Loss of administrative autonomy may also be strenuously resisted, complicating consolidation efforts. To the typical system administrator, loss of administrative privilege translates to demotion.

As with many other tasks, communication is the key. Administrators must feel that their perspectives, skills, and knowledge have been taken into account when developing larger strategies. Users must be assured that changes won't prevent them from performing their tasks. Implementers must be given clear guidelines and policies to work from.

Chapter 4 provides guidance on standardization and consolidation practices that should result in elimination of resource silos.

Integrating Legacy Systems

Few architects are presented with a blank canvas, able to create the enterprise entirely from scratch. Legacy, outdated, unsupported, and sometimes unknown technologies within the enterprise are major challenges to integration. Proprietary protocols, embedded operating systems unable to be updated, and end-of-life software may all be found in an existing enterprise.

One way to address the continued use of legacy systems and protocols involves employing Service Oriented Architecture practices, as discussed in Chapter 11.

On a related note, loss of source code behind compiled applications in production can become troublesome when faced not only with integration, but with the need to change or update functionality. Changes or updates become particularly difficult when the original authors are no longer available to serve as a reference for what the application should be doing.

When Change Doesn't Happen Fast Enough

In contrast to users who stubbornly oppose all change, you may also encounter a small group of highly vocal users who constantly want to employ the latest, greatest, and most interesting technologies. These tech-savvy users will often ask for new and wonderful devices before your technical staff has even heard of them.

Nothing is ever good enough for these users, who seek the bleeding edge of technology — the newest, fastest, and most powerful computing resources — even if their only use is reading e-mail and browsing the Web. They demand regular upgrades, the most recent hardware, and continued replacement as matter of course.

You can address this incessant demand for the best and newest of everything by standardization enterprise-wide and communication of the advantages and cost-efficiencies gained as a result. As discussed in Chapter 16, implementing a regular hardware replacement cycle may also address this problem. When nobody has the bigger and better machine, then these users' need to be at the leading edge can be tempered.

Maintaining Compliance throughout the Process

The modern enterprise is surrounded by a vast and complex set of regulatory and legal mandates, as discussed in Chapter 6. Because the act of change involves movement from a known state to a new state, transitional practices may create conflicts with these mandates. During a server consolidation project, data may be housed on temporary shared servers even when regulatory guidelines mandate a separation. When transitioning from one operating system standard to another, logging requirements may become difficult to sustain for users working in both environments.

Thorough documentation of all mandates, together with a risk assessment of the realignment project, will help you identify problem areas and potential conflicts and may present solutions. Solutions should be identified for each problem before project implementation and management should always be made aware of any action that might result in noncompliance.

Dealing with Separate Revenue Streams

In any enterprise larger than a mom-and-pop single facility location, individual revenue streams will be used to procure updates and new technologies. When consolidating enterprise resources, you must remember to identify the source of funds for licensing, equipment, and service support in order to ensure that any constraints on each revenue stream are included in the planning process.

Strategies to obtain economies of scale (see Chapter 4) often involve aggregating purchasing previously conducted at the individual business unit level, requiring contributions toward the mass purchase. Clear communication with purchasing agents and accounting staff will aid in the process of funding the new consolidated purchase.

Supporting Personally Owned Equipment

Where once computers existed as large monolithic devices kept in cold rooms and supported by a staff of highly trained technicians, computing devices are now readily available in many forms. The proliferation of technologies that may integrate with the enterprise will present you with a significant challenge to long-term planning. New technologies may sell millions of devices in the first month of availability and cause users to expect immediate integration of their new devices with their business functions.

Keep an eye out for new technologies and obtain examples of popular devices so that your support staff can develop a familiarity as quickly as possible, before user support calls start rolling in. Rapid evolution and turnover in technology is particularly evident with mobile devices, as covered in Chapter 12.

Alternatively, it may be necessary to develop policies and mechanisms for communicating with users when some devices simply cannot be (or should not be) integrated into the enterprise. Many enterprises are opting to provide a fixed stipend for mobile devices used in part for organizational purposes so that they can avoid the capital expense for devices and accessories or the widely variable monthly costs of data and use plans. This strategy avoids the need for users to carry multiple devices in order to separate business use and personal use functions and allows users to update their personal technology as per their personal mobile service contracts without having to wait on an organizational tech refresh.

Know Your Limits

The complexity of a modern enterprise network may well exceed your knowledge and skills. While it's critical that you continually expand your skill set, there may come a time when additional expertise is absolutely necessary in order to conduct a new project. Too many technologists feel that bringing in additional expertise translates into admitting defeat. It is important to know your own limitations, but also to keep in mind that expertise is simply a resource, and bringing in external help does not constitute a loss of power. Although the IT Enterprise Architect's functions align closely with those of a business leader, the architect must be deeply experienced in a wide range of technologies in order to understand their application within the enterprise, together with their interdependence and impact on other solutions in use or planned for use. This skill requires constant update to enable the inclusion of emergent solutions and evolved versions of older technologies. A pure business leader or project management leader

- ✔ Can't effectively address technical concerns that will be raised in opposition to changes.
- ✔ Can't plan effectively for second- and higher-order opportunities and interoperability challenges.
- ✔ Can't lead or drive the evolution of the enterprise unless they also possess updated technical skills and an understanding of current systems and services in the enterprise.

Business leaders without personal technical skills can't communicate effectively and authoritatively with implementation staff, data resource planners, and application development architects responsible for implementing new enterprise architecture projects.

Technical, leadership, and communication skills are mandatory for effective enterprise realignment (see Chapters 1 and 2). The best plans can still fail if any of these is entirely lacking.

Chapter 20

Ten "Low-Hanging Fruit" Opportunities

. . . .

In This Chapter

▶ Reducing and consolidating extra resources

▶ Taking advantage of technology with updates, upgrades, and more

▶ Thinking green to save money

. . . .

*E*nterprise architectural projects encounter many obstacles, from lack of support to long implementation cycles. Beginning an enterprise-wide architectural project portfolio is a time-consuming and difficult process, which must find a way to prove its worth as early as possible.

In this chapter, we identify a few of the enterprise strategies that can provide a rapid return on investment. These ten "low-hanging fruit" opportunities may present themselves during an enterprise architecture project.

Eliminate Resource Silos

Perhaps not the "lowest-hanging fruit" possible, eliminating resource silos and breaking down barriers between elements of your extended enterprise will provide the greatest payout by making many other projects possible. Although technical administrators may fight tooth and nail to retain control over "their" silos, each segment of the network is a barrier to efficiency and service advancement.

Silos prevent effective resource sharing, isolate both services and technical support, and create costly undesirable redundancies. By starting this project early, you'll be able to better implement any later changes and policies enterprise-wide.

Standardize the Workstation Environment

Take a look at the workstations in your enterprise. If a clear majority of them have the same operating system, you may find it fairly easy to standardize your workstation environment. Likewise, if a majority of users are already using one particular office productivity suite, such as Microsoft Office or Star Office, then standardization on that suite may also be a fairly simple decision. The same logic applies to other applications, such as utilities, browser plug-ins, and document viewers.

The more you can standardize your workstation environment, the more you can

- Improve the efficiency of help desk personnel by allowing them to focus skills on fewer products.

- Improve your security posture, because it is easier to secure a large number of similarly configured workstations than large numbers of dissimilar workstations.

- Reduce costs by taking advantage of economy of scale with regard to software licensing.

Don't try for 100 percent compliance right off the bat; 80 percent (or as close as you can get) is a good target to aim for at the start. You're likely to encounter some legitimate exceptions, and enterprise planning must allow for them wherever possible.

Create a Centralized Data Center

If your organization doesn't already have a centralized data center, you may want to tackle this project fairly early in the realignment process. If you have no data center, there will be a number of information technology silos in the organization under the control of various business units; even if your organization is not ready to consolidate functionality, moving all the server hardware into a centralized facility is a good first step. This project can be considered low-hanging fruit if you already have a suitable location that just needs modifications or if your enterprise is fairly small and can make do with a server room instead of a data center.

You can find guidance for facility planning in Chapter 4.

Consolidate Resources Already Within the Data Center

If your organization is fortunate to already have a centralized data center (see preceding section), you may be able to achieve quick success by simply consolidating resources already within the data center. The most likely complaint — not wanting to relinquish control over the physical machine — is unlikely to rear its ugly head, and you should have little opposition to consolidating redundant servers already in the central data center.

A reduction in the number of physical servers leads to decreased complexity, reduced operating costs, and possibly lower licensing costs. Consider cutting the number of redundant similar servers. For example, if you have multiple servers running the same database solution, such as Microsoft SQL Server or MySQL, it may be a fairly straightforward task to reduce the number of database servers. You should also consider implementing virtualization, which we discuss in greater detail further down in the list and in detail in Chapter 13.

Even if new hardware needs to be purchased, you're still likely to get a fairly quick return on investment. Remember that any machines removed from service can be used in a test environment or to implement desired redundancy, as discussed in Chapter 4.

Implement Automated Update/Patch Management Solutions

If they're not already in place, implementing automated software update and patch management solutions will improve the security of your enterprise and free up technical staff for more useful projects.

Most operating systems have some type of automated patch management system. Following are some examples for common operating systems:

✔ You can manage Microsoft updates for both servers and workstations using Windows Server Update Services (WSUS) or the more robust System Center Configuration Manager (SCCM), which you can also use to update third-party products as well as Microsoft-specific technologies. Employing this solution involves setting up a server to run the WSUS service, turning on automated updates on the computers and pointing them at your WSUS server. Instead of having to patch all machines individually, technical staff can review updates as they are received from Microsoft and determine which updates should be pushed out to which computers. You may want to have different update schedules for servers and workstations in order to avoid applying an untested patch on a server, which could result in disruption of service.

- ✔ Novell servers using SUSE Linux can be updated automatically through the YaST Online Update (YOU) or the openSUSE Updater applet. Both solutions allow you to apply updates to your Novell server by directly connecting to the vendor site through the application and installing relevant patches and updates instead of having to manually browse for patches and updates and then determine which are appropriate.

- ✔ Computers running Red Hat Enterprise Linux can be updated automatically through the Red Hat Network (RHN), which is a fee-based service.

- ✔ Computers running other versions of Linux also have the ability to perform automatic updates through various native and add-on tools.

- ✔ Mac OSX computers can be set to update automatically through the Software Update pane in System Preferences.

 It's just as important to have a patch management solution for applications as it is for operating systems. Some applications support automated update functionality, while many require technical staff to download updates and push them out across the network via login script or other mechanisms.

Implement Enterprise-Level Anti-Malware Solutions

If your enterprise is without malware protection such as antivirus or anti-spyware software, implementing an enterprise-level anti-malware solution is not only low-hanging fruit, but is also a priority. Even enterprises with anti-malware software that are set to update automatically can benefit from an enterprise-level solution.

Managed solutions allow you to control update frequency, scanning frequency, and configuration from a central console. You can easily determine which computers are behind on malware definition files and your security staff can receive alerts when malware is detected within the enterprise. Additionally, a managed enterprise-level solution typically disallows end users from changing settings or putting off virus updates.

Use Risk Assessment Results to Find Easily Fixed Vulnerabilities

A formal risk assessment will identify security vulnerabilities in your enterprise. These vulnerabilities can be natural or environmental, electronic, or human, and you may find that quite a few of them can be mitigated by simple, low-cost countermeasures such as the following:

- ✔ Installing anti-malware software
- ✔ Implementing a patch management solution
- ✔ Installing network monitoring software

Chapter 17 discusses these and other countermeasures in detail. You may also find that you can mitigate risk by applying more secure configurations to servers and applications, such as requiring strong passwords (see Chapter 7).

You can find more detail on the risk management process in Chapter 6.

Schedule Workstation Replacement

If your organization doesn't already have a defined replacement cycle, consider implementing one. Provided that it aligns with your organization's strategic plan, the optimal replacement strategy is a partial or staged replacement cycle, in which a percentage of systems are replaced each year. Having a predictable, yearly technology replacement budget makes strategic planning easier and hardware-related staffing requirements remain consistent throughout the cycle.

As discussed in Chapter 16, the percentage of workstations you'll replace each year is linked to the length of time each system remains in production, which in turn is typically linked to warranty. For example, if systems have a four-year warranty, 25 percent of systems should be replaced every year in order to ensure that all systems in the enterprise are under warranty. If systems have a three-year warranty, 33 percent of systems should be replaced every year.

Depending on your current purchasing strategy, you may have a higher cost during the first year, but even so, the long-term benefits will outweigh the short-term costs. Some organizations may find that equipment leasing options can be a cost-effective option, if technology refresh is included in the contracted price. However, most leased equipment strategies don't allow an enterprise the flexibility of delaying tech refresh for a year if economic constraints simply don't allow for technology update funding. Leased equipment will simply be recovered if payment is not forthcoming.

Implement Virtualization

Virtualization can be implemented wide scale or in a limited fashion. You can use virtualization to reduce hardware and power consumption in the data center, and this approach may be the best use of virtualization technology if you're early in the enterprise architecture project.

If you're considering implementing any type of virtualization, it is important to review the various virtualization solutions available in order to select the appropriate one for your enterprise. Virtualization projects are often combined with data center centralization projects, but care should be taken to virtualize first and make sure that everything is working before following up with the centralization of the now-virtualized servers to avoid having too many things changing at the same time.

Virtualization concepts, benefits, and considerations are discussed in Chapter 13, and you can read about virtualization in greater detail in *Virtualization For Dummies* (Wiley) by Bernard Golden.

Reduce Cost from Consumables by Implementing Green IT Practices

You can reap a significant amount of savings, often with minimal user disruption, by reducing consumables, such as paper, ink, and energy. Following are a few easy, cost-saving opportunities:

- **Change your font.** Although it may sound silly, selecting a "green" font can decrease costs by reducing the amount of ink used. Making the change from an ink-heavy to ink-light font can save up to 25 to 30 percent less ink. The use of smaller font sizes or nonblock, nonbold, and sans-serif line fonts can affect cost savings when measured enterprise-wide.

- **Make duplex printing the default.** You can reduce paper costs up to 50 percent on print jobs with multiple pages by implementing duplex printing as the default. You can still allow people to print single-sided, but they'll have to make an effort to do so.

- **Change quality settings.** Draft-mode printing selection can reduce consumption of toner and ink when presentation-quality reproduction is not necessary. When printing slides or handouts, using blank or lightly toned backgrounds can significantly reduce consumption over large dark-colored backgrounds.

✔ **Print only when necessary.** While making the transition to a paperless office isn't quick or easy, you can take steps in that direction by encouraging users to print only when necessary. You may want to specifically target employees that insist on printing every e-mail; there's always at least one in every office. Using only grey-scale or black-on-white printing is also much more cost-effective than printing in color unless necessary.

✔ **Take advantage of power-saving features.** Allow equipment to go into power save mode when not in use, particularly outside normal working hours. You can configure many systems centrally to reduce power consumption by turning off monitors, parking hard drives, and reducing the processor cycle when idle.

✔ **Buy ENERGY STAR products where possible.** During the next replacement cycle, make ENERGY STAR compliance one of the purchasing requirements, since they can be up to 30 percent more energy-efficient than noncompliant equipment.

✔ **Use alternative cooling in the data center.** Data centers consume a disproportionate amount of energy because they must simultaneously power dense computing hardware and remove heat in order to maintain hardware function. Cold-aisle/hot-aisle air cooled strategies may not be enough to manage the heat generated by high-density, highly virtualized data centers. You may need to use other options, such as a larger space, open-air environmental cooling.

Water cooling solutions also provide a more efficient transfer of waste heat than forced air circulation by directly transferring heat through a liquid medium to remote cooling systems. Water cooling is much quieter, reducing noise in the data center, and allows you to separate cooling operations from data center primary space, which is typically very valuable. Secondary cooling loops extending into nearby waterways or using geothermal cooling can further reduce energy consumption where available based on data center location.

✔ **Use alternative energy production.** Because many data centers are located in remote or isolated areas, recent efforts in solar and wind-powered local generation have managed to offset data center energy costs and impact on the distribution grid. As alternative energy systems become more efficient and available, this strategy may provide opportunities for the evolving data center as well as potential energy tax credits for the organization as a whole.

You can find more strategies for finding value in Green IT in Chapter 15.

Glossary

· ·

80/20 rule: A management principle evolved from observations of Italian economist Vilfredo Pareto. It states that 80 percent of consequences are derived from 20 percent of causes.

access controls: Rights or permissions that users have to access information resources.

access token: An electronic device that provides information to the requesting user or directly to the authentication service. Examples of access tokens include smart cards and radio frequency identification (RFID) cards.

accessibility: In information technology, accessibility refers to the ability of individuals with disabling conditions, such as impairment of vision or hearing, to have comparable use of and access to data and technology as do individuals without disabling conditions.

agile programming: A rapid application development (RAD) strategy that involves very short timetables applied to incremental programmatic output, with overall goals often measured in weeks with daily meetings to measure progress. Typically, the code tests are developed first, followed by the code to suit those tests. Each small code segment is added to the whole until all pieces have been completed.

anti-malware software: Software designed to protect information systems against malware.

application programming interface (API): A set of instructions provided by software vendors, particularly operating system vendors, and used by software programmers to develop applications for use in a particular environment.

application stack: The operating system, applications, services, user applications, and other solutions that together form the operating environment for a computer. Also referred to as a technology stack.

asymmetric encryption: Also known as public-key encryption. Key pairs are used instead of a single shared key. These key pairs consist of a public and private key. The public key is available for general use, while the private key is kept secure and not revealed. Data encrypted with a public key can only be decrypted with its companion private key and vice-versa.

asynchronous communication: In asynchronous communications, people can communicate over a period of time because real-time interaction is not required. Like older physical means of information exchange, modern electronic systems allow parties to transmit or post information in threaded and community discussion forums whenever opportunity allows. Asynchronous communication mechanisms aid in the development of online communities, moving beyond simple back-and-forth conversation by allowing participants to conduct research and use forethought before posting their comments.

ATA over Ethernet (AoE): A lightweight Storage Area Network (SAN) protocol that operates using an Ethernet connection, but does not utilize the full TCP/IP protocol suite. AoE devices can be connected directly to servers or plugged into network switches.

authentication: The process of determining whether identification credentials, such as username and password, and a requested resource are valid.

authorization: The process of determining whether a user is allowed to access a requested resource, and with what permissions.

availability: One of three core principles of information security that states that data must be available for authorized use when needed.

biometrics: Methods of uniquely recognizing humans for the purpose of identification. Some examples of biometric traits that are used for authentication to information technology resources include fingerprints, palm prints, and hand geometry.

bleeding edge technology: Technology that is so new as to be considered experimental, unreliable, or incompatible with existing technology.

blog: A form of online publishing that can be used to post news stories, personal journal entries, or commentary on a variety of topics. This term evolved from the phrase "web log." Posts are typically displayed in reverse chronological order, with older items rolling off or being archived. Some blogs also allow readers to comment. Blogs can contain authentication and access controls to limit both reading and commenting ability. Public blogging is popular with individuals and organizations of all types, and some organizations have moved to blog format for their public-facing Web sites.

Bluetooth: A wireless communication standard used to transmit data over short distances. It is typically used by cell phones, video game consoles, telephone headsets, and personal digital assistants (PDAs).

bot: Also called a zombie or drone, a bot is a single computer in a botnet. *See also* botnet.

botnet: A collection of malware-infected computers that are controlled by an individual referred to as the owner or herder. Individual computers in the botnet are also called zombies or drones, and the owner controls them remotely via communication medium such as Internet Relay Chat (IRC).

brute-force attack: A type of electronic attack against a computer or application with a password-based identification system in which all possible combinations of numbers, characters, and symbols are tested sequentially in an attempt to guess the password.

Business Continuity Planning (BCP): The preparation and planning that is necessary to ensure that critical business processes and functions remain available.

business impact analysis (BIA): A type of analysis performed during Business Continuity Planning. It identifies critical business processes and determines the impact of any disruption to the process.

Certificate Authority (CA): In encryption, a trusted third party that verifies the identity of users, computing resources, or other entities on the network.

clearing: A process of data removal that makes data inaccessible to software tools, but not to laboratory recovery processes.

client-server architecture: A type of application architecture in which the user interface is separate from processing or data storage.

closed source: Proprietary software in which the source code is not provided by the vendor. Commercial software is often closed source.

cloud computing: A form of highly virtualized computing where users may request and be provisioned access to remote computing resources automatically, based on their role and assigned quota limits rather than through manual action on the part of the IT support staff. Cloud resources can typically be expanded using a pay-as-you-go model, making cloud services highly effective when transitioning from proof of concept to production levels of capacity.

cluster: A group of computers that are linked together closely to perform tasks as a single unit.

COBIT (Control Objectives for Information and related Technology): A highly detailed governance model developed by the Information Systems Audit and Control Association (ISACA) and managed by the IT Governance Institute (ITGI). It defines control objectives (high-level requirements) for 34 processes to assist with managing and controlling information in order to support business objectives. It also provides guidance on using metrics to determine a maturity model for an organization's IT processes.

cold site: In Disaster Recovery Planning (DRP), a cold site is an alternative site that is little more than an available location with basic infrastructure such as power and phone, but may or may not have active network connectivity. There are no computers, servers, telecommunications lines, and equipment, or even furniture.

collective intelligence: Collective intelligence arises when groups of individuals, through collaboration and cooperation, create a body of knowledge that is greater than the sum of each individual's knowledge. It is seen frequently in nature, most often in social insects or herd animals, but it also exists in human society in forms such as political parties, juries, and crowds.

commercial off-the-shelf (COTS): Commercial software that can be installed without significant configuration to achieve operational function.

compliance: Conformance to rules, standards, mandates, or the terms of a contact.

compute cluster: Clusters that use a supervisory "head" node to separate tasks and data, sending smaller packages to individual compute nodes and aggregating responses from the distributed parallel process.

compute grid: Grids that function like loosely coupled clusters by aggregating processing power across many distributed machines. Because communications may occur more slowly than in tightly connected clusters, individual nodes are generally provided data in larger chunks so that processing can occur more efficiently before results are returned and a new set of data is requested from the host.

confidentiality: One of three core principles of information security that states that data must be protected from being accessed by unauthorized entities.

content filtering: A type of firewall technology in which content is analyzed and allowed or disallowed into the network based on rules. Typically, content filtering blocks access to undesirable or unauthorized Web sites and is managed by linking the firewall to an external rules server that contains the list of blocked addresses or keywords or by downloading these lists and rules to the firewall.

contingency plan: Actions to take in the event of a specific occurrence, such as a data loss or breach.

Control Objectives for Information and related Technology: *See* COBIT.

countermeasure: Action taken in order to prevent vulnerabilities from being exploited. Examples of countermeasures include anti-malware software, applying security patches and updates, firewalls, and encryption.

Cutting-edge technology: Technology is said to be cutting edge when it is new, advanced, and state-of-the-art. It differs from bleeding edge only in terms of stability, where cutting-edge tech represents stable tested products and solutions.

cyclic replacement: A process in which a percentage of resources are replaced yearly.

daemon: A service that runs on a UNIX or Linux-based system. *See also* service.

data breach: The inadvertent release of sensitive or protected data.

data center: A facility that houses enterprise computing resources, such as servers, storage systems, and telecommunications systems.

data de-duplication: The process of identifying files that are identical, creating a master file, and turning other copies into links to the master.

data loss prevention (DLP): Solutions that protect data in use, data at rest, and data in motion and can be network-based or host-based.

data mining: A process that identifies patterns in data. In business, it is often used in marketing to analyze patterns in retail sales data or other types of analysis involving large, complex, or disparate data sets.

data warehouse: A repository that includes not only data, but also a data dictionary (metadata) and tools to extract and analyze data.

degaussing: A process of data removal that uses a strong magnetic field to erase data on magnetic media such as video tapes, hard drives, floppy disks, and magnetic tape.

Demilitarized Zone (DMZ): A subnet created in a buffer area between the trusted internal network and untrusted external network. Public-facing servers, such as Web servers, are placed in this zone.

device driver: Software that facilitates the operation of hardware. This software allows other software programs that operate at a higher level, such as operating systems or office productivity software, to interact with devices.

dictionary attack: A type of electronic attack against a computer or application with a password-based identification system in which common words and manipulated versions of common words, such as replacing letters with numbers, are tested in an attempt to guess the password.

digital certificate: In encryption, a verification of identity created by a Certificate Authority (CA). You can also use certifications to establish identity in authentication systems or nonrepudiation in communication suites.

digital signature: Digital signatures utilize asymmetric encryption to verify the identity of the sender of a message and the message itself may or may not be encrypted. Digital signatures can be used on electronic documents in the same way physical signatures are used on paper documents. They can also verify that a message has not been altered in transmission. Because the encryption process for the digital signature incorporates the message, any changes to the message will invalidate that digital signature.

direct attached storage (DAS): Storage devices and arrays (groups of storage devices) attached directly to a computer, either internally or externally.

directory: A database of valid identities, services, and registered resources that is used in identity management and authentication. Common directory implementations include Microsoft's Active Directory, Novell's eDirectory, IBM's Tivoli, and the open source OpenLDAP.

Disaster Recovery Planning (DRP): The preparation and planning that is necessary to recover or continue information technology resources supporting the critical business processes identified in the business impact analysis.

discovery: A pre-trial process in which an organization can be required to supply information or documentation.

distributed computing: A method of high-performance computing in which processing power from a number of separate computers is integrated to perform parallel processing tasks and rapidly provide the final solution.

distributed denial of service (DDoS): An electronic attack that renders computing resources unavailable by flooding them with communications requests. The targets are often commercial Web sites and attackers have been known to demand money from site owners to restore service.

economy of scale: The concept that it is cheaper to buy in bulk.

embedded system: A computer system found in equipment such as security systems, telecommunication systems, network infrastructure components, or highly specialized systems such as medical or manufacturing equipment.

encryption: A process of transforming data using an algorithm and a key from something readable to something unreadable without the key.

ENERGY STAR: A government-sponsored certification program designed to encourage energy efficient product development in the USA.

enterprise: All technologies and tech policies that affect consumption and service availability for clients, partners, and consumers of services provided during an organization's operations.

enterprise architect: The role assigned responsibility and authority to conduct realignment of enterprise resources to meet emerging business requirements and operational efficiencies.

enterprise architecture: The process of identifying opportunities for enhancing performance, extending service offerings or improving efficiencies by configuring, coordinating, and/or restructuring enterprise resources.

enterprise architecture framework: An enterprise architecture modeling system that describes how to identify and organize the structure of an enterprise.

Ethernet: A local area network (LAN) communication technology. Modern Ethernet networks use special twisted pair cables or fiber to connect devices to the network.

exploit: Something that takes advantage of vulnerability. In information technology, they are often software-based, such as viruses.

Extensible Authentication Protocol (EAP): An authentication protocol developed for point-to-point connections between remote systems, widely used by modern wireless solutions. The Wi-Fi Protected Access (WPA) standard implements this protocol to facilitate cross-manufacturer secured interconnectivity.

Extensible Markup Language (XML): A standardized way of describing data. It is especially useful in service-oriented architecture (SOA).

extranet: An extranet is an intranet that is also accessible to business partners, such as vendors or clients.

extreme programming: A rapid application development (RAD) strategy that involves time boxed deadlines, iterative code releases, and common practices such as pair programming. Extreme programming attempts to simplify code to the very basics, preferring operational minimally feature code over more complex application design that takes longer to provide a useful product.

factor: In authentication, each different type of category of identification is known as a factor. Common schemes, such as logon/password combinations, represent a single factor because both come from the "something users know" category. Two-factor systems involve two types of authentication, like a logon/password combination and a token such as a smart card, and are much more secure. Authentication schemes using more than two factors are referred to as multi-factor.

failover: The capability to transfer functionality from one computer to another in the event of a failure or disruption.

farm: When systems are connected in large, loosely connected groups, they are commonly referred to as farms.

fault tolerance: A fault tolerant system has the capability to respond to an unexpected failure and continue operations.

Fibre Channel: A fast communication technology that is used for connecting servers to storage area networks (SANs) and for connectivity within SANs.

file repository: A logical location (as opposed to a physical location) for saving files.

file versioning: The process of having multiple versions of the same document available in active file storage areas.

firewall: A hardware-based or software-based technology that protects networks from unauthorized access based on a set of rules configured by firewall administrators. Firewalls determine whether to block content based on examination of packets or content.

firmware: The internal software, also called the instruction set, which a device uses for operation. Firmware can reside in read-only memory or programmable read-only memory, neither of which is generally user-accessible. The example most often used when discussing firmware is computer's system BIOS, which contains the instruction set that runs when the computer is turned on. Firmware can also be found in switches, routers, wireless access points, and other network infrastructure devices, as well as at the component level within servers, such as storage controller cards or video cards.

floating-point operations per second (FLOPS): The most common measure of raw processing power in the number of floating-point mathematical operations that can be accomplished per second, using a standard such as the LINPACK Benchmark.

forum: A communication method that utilizes threaded discussions.

free open-source software (FOSS): Software in which the source code is available for review and modification, free of charge.

full replacement: A hardware replacement strategy in which all resources are replaced in the same fiscal year.

Gartner Research: A well-known information technology research and consulting organization.

global positioning system (GPS): A satellite-based navigation system maintained by the U.S. Air Force. Service is provided to both civilian and military users, allowing them to determine their exact location.

graphical processing unit (GPU): An embedded graphics processor.

Green IT: Describes reduced-environmental impact and sustainable technologies and IT practices.

grid computing: Resources from multiple computers are combined to work on a single task, such as processing or storage.

groupware: Loosely defined as a class of software that allows groups of people (workgroups or teams) to work together regardless of location by using integrated tools that facilitate communication, conferencing, and collaborative management.

hardware abstraction layer (HAL): In software programming, the layer that defines the interface between physical hardware and software.

high-availability cluster: Provides fault tolerance for a server by maintaining a warm backup node that can take over operations transparently in the event of a hardware failure in the primary node.

high-performance computing: Supercomputers and clusters used for functions such as scientific research, data warehousing, and data mining.

hot site: In Disaster Recovery Planning (DRP), a fully functional alternative site that can be ready to take over operations immediately or shortly thereafter. It has power, phone, and all necessary computing hardware and software, as well as data and telecommunications networks and equipment. Everything is fully configured and data should be either current or recent.

hotspot: A hotspot provides wireless Internet access on a free or for-pay basis. They are typically found in coffee shops, hotels, libraries, airports, book stores, and other public places.

Hypertext Transfer Protocol (HTTP): A protocol used for Web-based communications.

hypervisor: In virtualization, the hypervisor monitors virtual machines on the host system, allowing them to share hardware resources. Hypervisors can be native, running on the host system's hardware, or hosted, running as software within a host's own operating system.

identification: The process of determining the identity of a user. Credentials are presented that identify the requesting user or service to the enterprise authentication service. Examples of these credentials include a username and password or an access token (such as a smart card) and a personal identification number.

identity and access management (IAM): A combination of identity management and access controls. It is used to facilitate resource availability and prevent undesirable exposure.

identity management: The software, processes, and procedures used to handle user identification and authentication.

IEEE 802.11: A set of standards for wireless local area networks (WLANs).

InfiniBand: A type of bidirectional high-speed communications link used in high-performance computing. InfiniBand uses a switched-fabric network topology allowing every device to be connected to any other device over a switched circuit, rather than across a hierarchical system of shared circuits as with Ethernet connectivity.

information technology (IT) governance: Management of technology-related decisions, involving coordination and communication between business roles.

Information Technology Infrastructure Library: *See* ITIL.

instant messaging (IM): A synchronous communication mechanism that allows two or more people to communicate in real-time. IM sessions are primarily text-based, but some messaging solutions allow users to transfer files, insert graphics, display a photograph or avatar (graphical representation of a user), or display webcam video.

integrity: One of three core principles of information security that states that data must be protected from modification or deletion without authorization.

internal IP address: Special unregistered addresses specifically set aside for private networks. These address ranges are 10.0.0.0–10.255.255.255, 172.16.0.0–172.31.255.255, and 192.168.0.0–192.168.255.255.

International Organization for Standardization: *See* ISO.

Internet: A decentralized collection of networks that spans the globe and communicates using TCP/IP.

Internet Messaging Access Protocol (IMAP): A client/server protocol that allows clients to access and manipulate e-mail stored on a mail server without downloading it to the local device. It also allows multiple users to access a single mailbox at once and stores message state information (such as read, unread, forwarded, or replied) on the server.

Internet Protocol (IP) address: A sequence of numbers assigned to a device on a network. The most common type of IP address is IPv4, which uses a 32-bit address typically displayed in dotted-decimal notation (xxx.xxx.xxx.xxx). An example of an IP address is 192.168.0.1.

Internet Protocol Security (IPSec): A suite of standards for transactions based on Transmission Control Protocol/Internet Protocol (TCP/IP), capable of encrypting and authenticating all data packets transmitted between endpoints. This standard includes protocols for transaction integrity, authentication, and confidentiality.

intranet: An organization's internal network, accessible only to the organization's staff, members, and other authorized personnel. Also used to refer to a company's internal Web site.

intrusion detection system (IDS): A passive technology that identifies attempts to circumvent security controls without attempting to block intrusion.

iSCSI (Internet Small Computer System Interface): A SAN protocol that can be used to link SANs in different geographic areas or to provide SAN access over local area networks, wide area networks, or the Internet.

ISO (International Organization for Standardization): An international standards body that also publishes technical reports and specifications.

ITIL (Information Technology Infrastructure Library): A framework of best practices covering IT services and operations management developed by the Office of Government Commerce (United Kingdom) and the IT Service Management Forum. This model requires strong management support and commitment and may require three to five years to implement fully.

Kerberos: A time-synchronized protocol that authenticates endpoints against a trusted third source. Because this protocol underlies the authentication mechanism within Microsoft and many Linux networks, it is widely used in modern enterprise environments.

Kryder's Law: An extension of Moore's Law that states that storage density doubles every two years. It was postulated by Mark Kryder, a former Seagate Corp. Senior Vice President and current Carnegie Mellon University professor.

Layer 2 Tunneling Protocol (L2TP): A network tunneling protocol used in the operation of virtual private networks (VPNs).

Lightweight Directory Access Protocol (LDAP): A very popular lightweight authentication protocol derived from the X.500 standards. This is perhaps the most widely used protocol in environments with up to a half-million identities per database.

line-of-business (LOB) applications: Applications that are crucial to the operation of the business, such as inventory control.

LINPACK Benchmark: A standard measure of a computer's floating-point computing power by measuring the speed at which a computer solves specific linear equations. It is used to rank high-performance computers.

load balancing: Allows high-demand solutions to spread the workload over multiple servers to avoid disruptions in service.

load-balancing cluster: Balances user connections across multiple servers transparently to the end user.

local area network (LAN): A network consisting of computers and network-enabled devices in fairly close proximity to each other.

malware: Malicious or unwanted software that is placed on computers without the owner's informed consent. A computer with malware installed on it is said to be infected. Malware infections can result in destruction or alteration of data, confidential information (including login credentials) being exposed, network disruptions, and reduced employee productivity.

man-in-the-middle attack: An electronic attack in which the attacker intercepts traffic between two parties by substituting their public keys for his own.

Metcalfe's Law: Metcalfe's Law states that a communication network's value increases exponentially with its size . . . specifically, value=n2, where n is the number of users. According to Metcalfe's Law, the value of the network may quadruple even though the number of users only doubles.

microblogging: A combination of blogging and texting. Instead of log posts, microbloggers can post short text-based messages to their site from desktop applications, Web browsers, or mobile phones. Popular microblogging services like Twitter and Facebook are used primarily by individuals, but companies are beginning to use these services for advertising and promotions.

Moore's Law: Transistor density on integrated circuits doubles every two years.

multiplexing: A TCP/IP feature that allows for concurrent connections using multiple ports.

multitiered architecture: A type of application architecture beyond client-server, in which application clients communicate with middleware applications instead of directly with the server.

network address translation (NAT): A process by which computers and other devices on a network are assigned private IP addresses that are not visible outside the network.

network attached storage (NAS): A server that provides only file storage services. It runs on a scaled-down operating system, in order to provide a file system, and utilizes direct attached storage.

n-tier application architecture: A type of multitiered application architecture in which additional tiers are created by separating business logic from data access services.

offshoring: A form of outsourcing in which a business function is transferred to a foreign entity.

open source: Software in which the source code is available for review and modification. Not all open source software is free of charge.

open standards: Various definitions of open standards exist; however, it is generally defined as being approved in some fashion, published, and available to the general public. An example of an open standard is Hypertext Markup Language (HTML).

operational planning: Short-term planning that occurs at the business or workgroup level and is concerned with day-to-day operations. Operational plans are developed from tactical plans.

outsourcing: Transferring a business function to another entity.

overwriting: A process of data removal that writes over data on a storage device with random data, or a combination of 0s and 1s.

packet: A block of data that consists of control information, such as the sender and receiver, and user data.

parallel processing: The process of dividing a large or complex task into smaller components that can be processed individually by multiple systems simultaneously and then combined for the final result.

Pareto Principle: *See* 80/20 rule.

partial replacement: A hardware replacement strategy in which a percentage of resources are replaced each year.

patch: A software update released by the vendor that corrects flaws or bugs.

Personal Area Network (PAN): Used for communication among personal technological devices such as personal computers, cell phones, printers, and personal digital assistants (PDAs). Connectivity is achieved through USB or FireWire connections or wirelessly using Bluetooth or infrared.

personal digital assistant (PDA): A mobile device that was originally designed to be an electronic organizer, including capabilities such as calendaring, contact lists, and to-do lists. It has been expanded to include media players, Internet connectivity, Global Positioning System (GPS) functionality, and cellular phone service.

platform: In information technology, a hardware or software framework. Examples of platforms include operating system, hardware, programming environments, database management systems, and desktop or server configurations.

platform architecture: The establishment of suitable standards for the body of technologies used by the enterprise.

podcasting: A relatively new communication mechanism named after Apple's iPod. Podcasts are rich media files (audio and/or video) that are episodic in nature and are published through feeds, which is what differentiates them from simple streaming media files. Podcasting is used heavily by major corporations, news services, the entertainment industry, educational institutions, and even individuals to provide rich content to a mobile audience.

Point-to-Point Tunneling Protocol (PTPP): A network tunneling protocol used in the operation of virtual private networks (VPNs).

port address translation (PAT): A type of dynamic network address translation (NAT) that allows the network to present a single IP address beyond the enterprise by assigning a different port number to each internal node that accesses external resources.

portal: In enterprise architecture, a virtual entrance into an organization's information resources. It aggregates content from multiple sources, bringing it all into one place for easy access and creating a single point of contact. Many portals use a Web-based interface, which allows the portal to be platform independent and accessible from a variety of devices, from desktop computers to mobile devices.

portlet: Software components that can be plugged into portal pages in order to display dynamic content.

Post Office Protocol (POP): An older e-mail protocol used for communication between e-mail clients and servers, in which the client is connected to the server only long enough to download messages.

probability: The likelihood that a threat will materialize into an actual event.

project management: Involves breaking projects into planned stages, each with its own specific activities and requirements, identifying roles, and budgeting costs. General project management elements include initiation, planning, implementation, monitoring, and completion.

prototype: In a system development life cycle (SDLC) model, developers create a basic version of the application based on requirements analysis. This prototype is tested by developers and users, and then reworked based on user feedback. The cycle continues until the prototype is acceptable and can be used to create a final product.

public-key encryption: *See* asymmetric encryption.

public-key infrastructure (PKI): Revolves around the use of digital certificates. A PKI system issues, verifies, publishes, and manages these certificates and their associated keys.

purging: A process that removes data and makes it inaccessible to both software tools and laboratory recovery processes.

qualitative analysis: An analysis of risk using non-numeric values such as Low, Medium, or High.

quantitative analysis: An analysis of risk using numerical values for probability and impact.

rapid application development (RAD): A software programming methodology that emphasizes prototyping over planning.

Really Simple Syndication (RSS): Also known as a news feed or Web feed, RSS is an XML-based publication of electronic headlines and articles. Typically, only a snippet of the article is included in the publication to streamline the feed and make it easy for individuals to review large quantities of information in a short time and pick out items of interest. Many news and informational Web sites publish RSS feeds, sometimes many, on various topics of interest. For example, a news site may have feeds for local news, health, technology, and world news. Retail and vendor sites also make use of RSS feeds as a way of informing customers and partners of new products or promotions.

recovery point objective (RPO): The point in time to which data should be restored following an incident. This number is going to be based on the criticality of the business process that the data supports and should align closely with the backup schedule.

recovery time objective (RTO): The length of time in which a business process can be down before unacceptable consequences occur. Consequences vary, based on the organization and the business process, but can include contract violations, noncompliance issues, fines, penalties, loss of sales, loss of competitive advantages, loss of trust, and negative publicity.

redundancy: In information technology, duplication of resources such as hardware, software, services, files, or functionality. Redundancy can be desirable, such as through failover solutions, or undesirable, such as multiple copies of the same file.

redundant array of independent disks (RAID): A data storage system in which multiple hard drives are used to provide fault tolerance in the event of a hard drive failure.

remote desktop: A remote session established to a physical or virtual machine, which passes keyboard and mouse input from the remote client to the target remote computer and returns audio and video output to the client.

resource silo: An individual island of resources that cannot be shared and prevents an enterprise from taking advantage of economies of scale in operational support. It is the outcome of having separate systems for authentication and resource access control. Unless present to enforce a specific regulatory or legal mandate for operational separation, silos should be eliminated to improve enterprise-wide operational control and transparency of operation.

risk: The measure of loss due to the likelihood of a threat or vulnerability and its impact.

risk acceptance: Risk acceptance is a risk management strategy in which risk is identified, examined, and accepted, provided that the impact is fully understood and recognized.

risk assessment: The process by which threats are analyzed in order to determine probability and impact.

risk avoidance: Risk avoidance is a risk management strategy in which risk may be avoided by selecting an alternative option that does not include the same level of risk or by not engaging in the risky behavior.

risk homeostasis: A condition that occurs when changes made to reduce risk result in people acting in a more risky manner. An example of this would be users writing down passwords due to requirements for complexity and frequent changes.

risk management: A process by which risk is assessed and addressed. Strategies for addressing risk include acceptance, avoidance, mitigation, and transference.

risk mitigation: A risk management strategy in which risk may be reduced to an acceptable level by implementing additional protections or by altering the parameters producing the risk.

risk transference: A risk management strategy in which risk is transferred to another responsible party, such as through outsourcing or insurance protections.

Scrum programming: A rapid application development (RAD) strategy that begins by identifying requirements that are added to the product backlog. These are broken into sprint goals with very short timetables, which are facilitated by the ScrumMaster. A sprint might last 30 days, with meetings every 24 hours to identify progress or barriers that must then be addressed by the master. The end goal of a sprint is to produce a working increment of the final application, which is not necessarily operational by itself like the increments in Extreme programming.

Secret-key encryption: *See* symmetric encryption.

Secure Sockets Layer (SSL): A type of encryption used to protect Web sites. It uses asymmetric encryption to establish a session between the client and the server, and then uses symmetric encryption to encrypt the data being transferred.

security: The processes, procedures, and countermeasures used to protect the confidentiality, integrity, and availability of an information system. This includes protections against data loss or corruption, disruption, and unauthorized access.

service: An application that runs in the background and performs functions that are designed to work without direct user interaction. These applications range from basic, such as file and print, to complex, such as e-mail and database.

service-oriented architecture (SOA): Focuses on communication between services, such as dissimilar applications. Simple Object Access Protocol (SOAP), Extensible Markup Language (XML), and Web services are examples of SOA technologies.

service set identifier (SSID): A name given to an 802.11 wireless local area network (WLAN) for the purpose of identification. The SSID can be broadcast so that wireless clients can find it when searching for networks.

Short Message Service (SMS): A communication method that allows people to send short text messages between mobile phones in order to carry on a conversation asynchronously. It is also referred to as text messaging or texting.

Simple Mail Transfer Protocol (SMTP): The standard protocol used to deliver electronic mail (e-mail).

Simple Object Access Protocol (SOAP): An XML-based open standard that allows for communication between dissimilar applications or hosts using Web-based protocols such as Hypertext Transfer Protocol (HTTP).

social engineering: Psychological attack techniques that involve manipulation, deceit, impersonation, and other psychological tactics. Social engineering is commonly used to get login credentials.

Software Development Life Cycle (SDLC): *See* Systems Development Life Cycle (SDLC).

spam: A colloquial term that refers to unsolicited commercial e-mail (UCE).

spiral model: A Systems Development Life Cycle (SDLC) model that's a combination of the waterfall and prototyping models.

spyware: A type of malware that monitors a user's activity, such as Web surfing habits. Spyware that collects form data is particularly dangerous since it may pass along login credentials to unauthorized persons. In addition, spyware may also interfere with the functionality of the operating system or Web browser by adding icons to the desktop, opening browser windows without warning, modifying the user's home page, adding browser helpers, changing system settings, or disabling legitimate software.

staged replacement: *See* partial replacement.

standards: The rules and guidelines that the organization uses when making decisions regarding information technology and related acquisitions, procedures, configuration specifications, and policy.

stateful packet filtering: Firewall technology in which both inbound and outbound packets are analyzed in order to make sure that packets entering the network were originally requested from inside the network, and that they follow the defined rules.

stateless packet filtering: Firewall technology in which packets are analyzed and then either allowed or denied to access the network. Session state is not maintained, so it does not associate inbound and outbound traffic.

storage area network (SAN): Storage without a file system, using specialized protocols and dedicated network connectivity to allow high-speed communications between storage devices and servers. The storage devices that make up a SAN are seen by servers as locally attached devices.

storage grid: Storage grids bring together the aggregate storage space from many systems, creating a very large virtual storage space that can be addressed as a single location.

storage survey: Identification of the size, type, configuration, location, and age of all elements of storage in the enterprise network. It also includes identification of the type of data is being stored on each storage device and the relevant legal, regulatory, and security requirements.

strategic planning: Long-term planning, at least 3 to 5 years out, that encompasses the entire organization and occurs at the executive level.

streaming media: Buffers audio and video files as it downloads them, allowing them to be played while they are downloaded. Both live and on-demand content may be accessed through streaming media, such as on news or entertainment Web sites.

subnet: A subnet is a part of a computer network. Subnetting is used in order to divide the network into smaller units in order to use IP addresses more efficiently or to separate different physical or logical components of the network.

supercomputer: A system conforming to the current highest level of processing power. Because this target constantly moves forward, the term is somewhat fluid.

symmetric encryption: A single key is used to both encrypt and decrypt the data. It is also known as secret key encryption.

synchronous communication: Both parties are connected and have the capability to communicate at the same time. This type of real-time online communication can replace or supplement face-to-face meetings or telephone calls, and is particularly useful when the individuals involved are in different geographic locations.

Systems Development Life Cycle (SDLC): A formal process or methodology for application development ensuring that software projects are planned, managed, and controlled and that quality and security are incorporated into each phase of development.

tactical planning: Medium-term planning, 1 to 2 years, that occurs at the middle management level. Tactical plans are developed from strategic plans.

TCP/IP (Transmission Control Protocol/Internet Protocol): The standard for Internet and local area network communications.

tech refresh: The periodic replacement of old technology with new.

technology monoculture: A homogenous technology solution, such as a network of computers running the same operating system or application suites from a single vendor.

technology stack: *See* application stack.

telecommuting: Working outside the traditional office while accessing organizational resources, such as working from home or while traveling. Also called teleworking.

teleworking: *See* telecommuting.

tethering: Using a mobile device to provide Internet access for another mobile device. A common example of tethering is to use a cellular phone to provide Internet access for a laptop computer.

text messaging: *See* Short Message Service (SMS).

thick client: In client-server architecture, this type of client has more processing power and storage resources than a thin client and can act independently of the server.

thin client: In client-server architecture, this type of client has minimal processing power and only provides the user interface. All processing, including the operating system, is provided by a server.

threat: A negative event that can lead to a loss. Threats can be natural or environmental, electronic, or human.

tiered data storage: Moving data among various storage solutions based on time since last access, file type, file size, or other constraints. Tiered storage solutions allow older legacy storage technologies to be retained and continue to provide value to the enterprise by forming the base level of archival storage, provided sufficient measures have been taken to ensure fault tolerance.

timebox: A term used in agile programming to refer to rigid time constraints.

trickle-down replacement: A hardware replacement strategy in which key personnel or functions are identified and systems associated with them are replaced first. The displaced systems are then used to replace other systems, and this process continues until the oldest systems are removed from service.

Trojan: A Trojan is a type of malware that first appears to be something beneficial but is actually damaging. Users are tricked into running the Trojan because it appears to be legitimate or at least interesting. They may infect computers via malicious Web sites with executable content, e-mail attachments, or software downloads. Attackers may also take advantages of certain vulnerabilities in applications.

tunneling: A technology that creates a secure channel of communication between hosts across public or unrelated networks.

videoconferencing: Enables groups or individuals in different locations to participate in two-way audio/video communication in real-time. Individuals may participate from their local computers (including their home computers, if telecommuting) with the proper equipment (audio and video input sources) or from specially configured rooms.

virtual machine: The complete set of files that define the operating system, service files, data and configuration settings for a computer that has been virtualized. The virtual machine can be moved between hosting physical servers by simply copying these files to the new destination.

virtual private network (VPN): Extends the firewall to remote users and is helpful when your organization has mobile users, satellite offices, or partner entities that need access to internal resources from outside the network. A VPN is a private network running over another network, which uses tunneling protocols such as Layer 2 Tunneling Protocol (L2TP) or Point-to-Point Tunneling Protocol (PPTP) to encrypt and isolate the VPN traffic from the rest of the network.

virtualization: The process of capturing a computer system's operating system, service files and operational characteristics and translating all elements into a set of files that can be hosted on a virtualization host, operating as if the virtualized system were still installed on its own hardware. A single physical computer will typically host multiple virtual servers, ensuring that power and other computing resources are used more efficiently.

virtualized application: An application constructed from components running on several computers, coordinated into a new functionality or mode of operation. Web-based virtualized applications can be consumed by end users without requiring installation of programs on the users' systems, performing all processing tasks on the server hardware and then presenting the results to the users' browser.

virtualized desktop: A user's workstation environment that has been virtualized as a series of files containing operating system, application files, and user data running on a physical host. Access to a virtualized desktop is accomplished from a remote device running a remote desktop client or via "thin client" hardware without requiring significant client processing power or storage.

virtualization host: The physical system on which virtual machines operate.

virus: A type of malware that moves from system to system by copying and executing infected files.

Voice over Internet Protocol (VoIP): A communication technology that uses TCP/IP connectivity over data networks to provide similar functionality to traditional telephone service.

vulnerability: A weakness in a system that, if exploited, can lead to loss or harm. In information technology, vulnerabilities are often associated with bugs in software or with misconfigured systems.

warm site: In disaster recovery planning (DRP), a warm site falls somewhere between a cold site and a hot site. In addition to power and phone, this type of site generally has the necessary computing hardware, as well as data and telecommunications networks and equipment, to restore operations fairly quickly, but this equipment may or may not be configured. In addition, data will have to be restored from backup.

waterfall model: In this System Development Life Cycle (SDLC) model, all development phases are sequential, without overlap or iteration. There are distinct deliverables with fixed deadlines, which simplifies scheduling and task management.

Web conferencing: A type of electronic conferencing in which browser-based technologies allow people to communicate. Some Web conferencing features include: voice communication, chat, registration, polls, presentations, and archiving.

Web service: A Web-based application service that allows different applications to communicate with each other using technologies such as Simple Object Access Protocol (SOAP), Extensible Markup Language (XML), and Web Services Description Language (WSDL).

Web Services Description Language (WSDL): A standardized XML-based method of describing what Web services are offered by an enterprise.

webinar: A type of Web conference that has defined presenters and audience members. The presenter controls the display and audio, and audience members may have limited communication in the form of chat or audio. They are widely used by vendors for product demonstrations and industry-specific organizations for training or continuing professional education.

wide area network (WAN): A network that is geographically dispersed, such as between branch offices of an organization.

Wi-Fi: A trademark of the Wi-Fi Alliance, a nonprofit association that certifies wireless equipment.

Wi-Fi Protected Access (WPA): A newer set of wireless security standards with personal and enterprise modes. Personal mode utilizes a shared key in the form of a passphrase, and enterprise mode uses certificates. Encryption is required.

wiki: A Web site that coordinates information provided by various contributors and provides a single location for each subject.

Wired Equivalent Privacy (WEP): An older form of wireless security that is no longer considered secure.

wireless access point: Allows devices to connect to a wireless network, acting as a communication hub. Often, the wireless access point will connect to a wired network.

wireless local area network (WLAN): A local area network that links devices using wireless communication technologies. Typically, devices connect to an access point that then connects the network to a larger network, such as an enterprise's private network or a public network such as the Internet.

worm: A type of malware that moves from system to system of its own volition, actively seeking out other systems to infect.

zero-day threat: A security vulnerability that is exploited before a security patch is released.

Index

• *Numbers* •

12V DC power, 224
80/20 rule
  applying, 48–49
  defined, 289
  Scrum programming, 170
  SSO projects, 105

• *A* •

abstraction, 172
acceptable-use policy, 72
acceptance strategy, 89
access, root, 13
access control, 96, 123–124, 289
access rights, assigning, 108
access token, 98–99, 289
accessibility
  in closed source software, 36
  defined, 289
  in FOSS, 35
  hardware for, 45
  including in application development,
    173–174
  Rehabilitation Act of 1973 (Section
    508), 83
ad-hoc replacement, 239–240
administrative access, 13, 72
Administrative management
  permissions, 107
Adobe Device Central emulator, 186, 187
Advanced Encryption Standard (AES), 252
aggregation, content, 124
agile programming, 169, 289
alt tag, 173
alternative data center locations, 60

alternative energy, 222–223, 287
alternative sites, 268–270
American Recovery and Reinvestment
  Act of 2009 (ARRA), 221
announce-only lists, 131
anti-malware software
  choosing solution, 250–251
  and cost saving, 284
  defined, 289
  fixing security vulnerabilities, 285
  in security policy, 73
antivirus updates, 62
AoE (ATA over Ethernet), 155
API (application programming interface),
  172, 289
application
  effects of choosing, 14
  incompatibility due to
    standardization, 54
  virtualization of, 197, 203–204
  vulnerabilities in, 249
application architect, 21–22
application architecture
  multitiered architecture, 171–172
  overview, 171
  SOA, 172–173
application development
  accessibility, including, 173–174
  addressing vulnerabilities in, 251
  application architecture, designing,
    171–173
  overview, 163
  RAD strategies, 168–171
  SDLC, 164–168
  as source of complexity, 45–46
application programming interface (API),
  172, 289

application rights, 107
application stack, 44, 289
aquatic heat transfer systems, 221
Arbitrated Loop topology, 154
architect, 20–22
ARRA (American Recovery and
    Reinvestment Act of 2009), 221
asymmetric encryption, 252–253, 289
asynchronous communication,
    127–128, 290
ATA over Ethernet (AoE), 155, 290
attack. *See specific attack by name*
attacker, 247
auditing, IAM, 112
authentication
  boundaries, 109
  central, 103–104
  cross-realm, 105–106
  defined, 290
  directory, 103
  federated, 104
  IAM, 96
  overview, 102
  within portals, 123–124
  portals, 123–124
  review of before IAM implementation,
      110–111
  SSO, 104–105
  standards for, 102–103
authorization, 106–107, 111, 290
authorized software, 73
automated system, 63
automation
  of backup systems, 63
  of data center, 61–63
  update/patch management, 283–284
availability, 159, 290
avoidance strategy, 89

• *B* •

backup
  automatic solutions, 63
  data storage protection, 158–159
  including media in storage surveys, 144
  physical protection of media, 159
  RPO, 263
  testing, 63
  of virtual machines, 198
backward-compatibility of open
    standards, 38
bandwidth, 183
basic input/output system (BIOS), 241
batteries, 184–185, 224
BCP (Business Continuity Planning),
    264, 291
behavioral identification, 101–102
Beowulf, 213
Berkeley Open Infrastructure for
    Network Computing (BOINC),
    216–217
BES (Blackberry Enterprise Server), 57
BIA (business impact analysis),
    261–264, 291
biometrics, 99–101, 290
BIOS (basic input/output system), 241
Blackberry Enterprise Server (BES), 57
bleeding edge technology, 237, 278, 290
blog, 133, 290
Blue Waters supercomputer, 209
Bluetooth, 177, 290
BOINC (Berkeley Open Infrastructure for
    Network Computing), 216–217
booster, 179–181
bot, 85, 290
bot herder, 129

botnet
  defined, 291
  electronic threats, 85
  IRC, 129
  overview, 248–249
  processing power used for, 211
bottlenecks, virtualization, 200
breach, data, 66–67, 293
bricked device, 241
broadcast communication
  overview, 138
  podcasting, 139
  RSS, 139–140
  streaming media, 140
browser-based application, 182
brute-force attack, 97, 291
bulk discounts on licenses, 30
business architect, 22
business continuity
  business impact analysis, 262–264
  overview, 261–262
  risk assessment, 264
Business Continuity Planning (BCP),
    264, 291
business impact analysis (BIA),
    261–264, 291
business intelligence tools, 126
business staff, 16

• C •

CA (Certificate Authority), 252, 254, 291
caching, 58, 60
CAS (Central Authentication Service),
    103–104
case sensitivity, 54
cellular phone, 132, 177
cellular signal booster, 179, 180

central authentication, 103–104, 110–111
Central Authentication Service (CAS),
    103–104
centralized data center, 61, 282, 283
Certificate Authority (CA), 252, 254, 291
character set, 35
chat, 128–129
checklist testing, 267
chief architect, 20–21, 27–28
Chief Information Officer (CIO), 20, 275
Children's Online Privacy Protection Act
    (COPPA), 82–83
CIO (Chief Information Officer), 20, 275
circuitry-embedded keys, 98
Cisco Network Management, 260
classification, data, 18, 72
clearing, 159, 291
client hosting, 203
client protocols, 130
client-server architecture, 291
closed source software
  benefits of, 36–37
  defined, 291
  drawbacks, 37–38
  versus open source, 276–277
  overview, 33, 36
cloud computing, 77, 204–206, 291
cluster
  computing, 212–214
  defined, 291
  load-balancing, 300
  visualization, 214–215
CMMI (Capability Maturity Model
    Integration), Carnegie Mellon's, 15
CMS (Content Management System), 124
COBIT (Control Objectives for
    Information and related
    Technology), 24–25, 291

cold site, 268–269, 292
collaboration solutions
  groupware, 120–122
  networks of trust, establishing, 113–116
  overview, 113
  portals, 123–126
  social media, 116–120
  technology, 76
collective intelligence, 118–119, 292
Columbia supercomputer, 212, 213
commercial off-the-shelf (COTS)
      software, 33, 276–277, 292
commercial open-source software, 33, 34
communication
  about automation of systems, 63
  about opposition to consolidation
      projects, 56
  asynchronous, 127–128, 290
  during disasters, 270–271
  effective, 19
  eliminating resource silos, 277
  ensuring with IT governance, 24
  importance of in receiving support, 276
  networks of trust, developing, 115
  in RAD strategies, 168
  synchronous, 127–128, 307
communication technology
  broadcast communications, 138–140
  classes of communication, 127–128
  collaboration in portals, 124
  community sites, 132–135
  conferencing, 135–138
  groupware, 120–122
  messaging, 128–132
  overview, 127
community sites, 132–135
compatibility, 54, 111
complexity
  application development, 45–46
  application stack, 44
  connectivity, 46

hardware, 44–45
  identity management, 45
  legislative and regulatory mandates, 46
  overview, 44
  of password, 97, 99
  as security measure, 68
  in security systems, 72
complexity reduction
  complications of complexity, 46–47
  consolidation, planning for, 47–52
  data center automation, 61–64
  data center consolidation, 56–61
  with IAM, 109
  overview, 43
  sources of complexity, 44–46
  standardization concerns, 53–56
compliance, 109–110, 278–279, 292
components, updating, 240–241
compute cluster, 292
compute farms, 217
compute grid, 216, 292
computer system recycling, 227
computing cluster, 212–214
concentric-ring security, 69
conferencing technology
  overview, 135
  videoconferencing, 135–136
  virtual reality, 136
  VoIP, 137
  Web conferencing, 137–138
confidentiality, 159, 292
confidentiality, integrity, and availability
      (CIA), 159
connection broker, 202
connectivity, 46, 183
consolidation
  80/20 rule, 48–49
  economies of scale, 49
  funding for, 55
  help desk functionality, 51
  overview, 47–48

skill concentration, 51–52
technology end of life, planning for, 49–50
consumables, reducing, 223–224, 286–287
content aggregation, 124
content filtering, 292
content management, 124
Content Management System (CMS), 124
content-filtering firewall, 256
contingency plan, 91, 292
continuity of operations. *See* business continuity
Control Objectives for Information and related Technology (COBIT), 24–25, 292
convergence, 110
cooling requirements, data center, 61, 201, 220–221, 287
COPPA (Children's Online Privacy Protection Act), 82–83
cost
  full replacement cycle, 233
  increases in with complexity, 46–47
  of open-source software, 36
  of standardization, 31, 33
  sunk, as factor in purchase decisions, 47
cost benefit analysis, 92
cost-saving opportunities
  anti-malware solutions, 284
  automated update/patch management solutions, 283–284
  centralized data center, 282
  data center consolidation, 283
  green IT practices, 286–287
  with groupware, 121, 122
  with IAM, 109
  overview, 281
  resource silo elimination, 281
  risk assessment, 285
  virtualization, 286

workstation replacement, 285
workstation standardization, 282
COTS (commercial off-the-shelf) software, 33, 276–277, 292
countermeasure
  for common threats, 90–91
  data loss prevention, 251
  defined, 292
  encryption, 252–254
  firewalls, 254–256
  intrusion detection and prevention, 256–257
  malware protection, 250–251
  NAT, 257–259
  network monitoring, 260
  overview, 250
  secure application development, 251
Cray Jaguar supercomputer, 209
Cray X-MP supercomputer, 207
credentials, IAM, 96
cross-platform SSO services, 105
cross-realm authentication, 105–106
customization of commercial software, 37
cutting-edge replacement, 236–237
cutting-edge technology, 293
cyclic replacement, 50, 293

• D •

daemon, 107, 293
DAS (direct attached storage), 153, 294
data
  breaches, 66–67, 293
  categories, 145–149
  disposal of, 73
  protection of, 66–67
  requirements, identification of, 18
  RPO, 263
data architect, 22–23
data breach notification laws, 66–67, 76

data center
  alternative locations, 60
  automation, 61–63
  centralized, 61
  cooling requirements,
    61, 201, 220–221, 287
  defined, 293
  location and environmental impact,
    220–221
  planning for centralized, 61
  using alternative energy for, 222–223
data center consolidation
  additional benefits, 59
  implementing desirable redundancy, 60
  improved document recovery, 58
  improved resource use, 57–58
  improved security, 58–59
  overview, 56–57, 283
  planning the centralized facility, 61
  reducing complexity through
    virtualization, 59
data classification, 18, 72
data de-duplication, 156–157, 293
data loss prevention (DLP), 251, 293
data mining, 293
data processing, outsourcing of, 78
data removal, 159–161
data storage
  with cloud computing, 206
  data categories, identifying, 145–149
  overview, 143
  protecting data, 157–161
  redundancy in, 60
  storage policy, creating, 149–152
  storage requirements, determining,
    143–145
  storage system design, 152–157
data warehouse, 293
database, 146–147
database rights, 106

DDoS (distributed denial of service),
    249, 294
dead zone, 179–181
de-duplication, 156–157, 293
defense in depth, 69
degaussing, 160, 293
deleted items, removing, 150
Demilitarized Zone (DMZ), 254, 255, 293
deployment, 62–63, 243–244
design phase, SDLC model, 164
desirable redundancy, 60
deskside computer system, 209
desktop computing, 208–209, 217–218
desktop
  remote, 184, 203, 304
  sharing, 138
  virtual, 202–203
destruction methods, 160
destruction policy, 160–161
device driver, 240, 241–242, 293
device interaction, 179
device locking, 187
dictionary attack, 97, 293
digital certificate, 293
digital signature, 253, 294
direct attached storage (DAS), 153, 294
directed network attack, 250
directly applied access tokens, 98
directory, 103, 294
directory services, 45
disaster recovery
  alternative data center locations for, 60
  alternative sites, 268–270
  in closed source software, 36
  communicating during disaster,
    270–271
  cost of, 47
  data storage protection, 158–159
  overview, 262–263
  recovery plan, preparing, 264–268

Disaster Recovery Planning (DRP), 264, 294

discoverability, 172

discovery, 83, 294

discussion board, 133–134

discussion list, 131

disk mirroring, 158

disposal practices, 226–227

distributed computing, 210–211, 216–217, 294

distributed denial of service (DDoS), 249, 294

distributing storage policy, 151–152

DLP (data loss prevention), 251, 293

DMZ (Demilitarized Zone), 254, 255, 293

DNS (Domain Name Service), 182

document management, 124–125

document recovery, 58

Domain Name Service (DNS), 182

draft-mode printing, 286

driver, device, 240, 241–242, 293

DRP (Disaster Recovery Planning), 264, 294

duplex printing, 286

• **E** •

EAP (Extensible Authentication Protocol), 103, 295

EC2 (Amazon Elastic Computer Cloud), 205

economy of scale
as benefit of standardization, 30, 49
with consolidation, 59
defined, 294
Security as a service model, 78
strategies to obtain, 278

efficiency, 30

Electronic and Information Technology Accessibility Standards, 174

electronic threats. *See* threat

e-mail
issues related to selection of platform, 13–14
kill pills, 188
overview, 129
phishing, 85
planning use in enterprise, 129–130
protocol, choosing, 130–131
spam, 249, 306
storage requirements, 147–148

embedded system, 18, 294

emulators, 186, 187

encryption
asymmetric, 289
of backup media, 159
defined, 294
in mobile device data, 183
on-device, 187–188
public-key, 303
secret-key, 252, 305
in security policy, 73
in security systems, 67, 68
symmetric, 252, 307
types of, 252–254

ENERGY STAR, 221–222, 287, 294

energy tax credits, 221

enterprise, defined, 9–10, 294

enterprise architect, defined, 295

enterprise architecture certification, 25

enterprise architecture, defined, 295

enterprise architecture framework
defined, 295
FEAF, 26
Gartner Enterprise Architecture Framework, 26–27
overview, 25
TOGAF, 26
Zachman Framework, 26

enterprise planning
  defining enterprises, 9–10
  defining success, 14
  finding best solutions, 10
  issues in enterprises, 11–13
  overview, 9
  preventing failure, 15–16
  providing leadership, 10–11
  technological connections, 13–14
  using maturity models, 15
enterprise-level storage strategies,
    153–155
environmental threat, 85
error message, 70, 249
Ethernet, 295
executives
  commitment to security policy, 74
  lack of support from, 16, 275–276
  understanding of security program, 68
expiration, password, 97–98, 99
exploit, 295
extended replacement cycle, 220
Extensible Authentication Protocol
    (EAP), 103, 295
Extensible Markup Language (XML), 295
extension of trust, 114
extranet, 182, 295
extreme programming, 170, 295

facial recognition, 101
factor, 295
failover, 60, 295
farm, 217, 296
fault tolerance, 158, 296
FCIP (Fibre Channel over IP), 154
FEAF (Federal Enterprise Architecture
    Framework), 26

feature creep, 165, 168
Federal Educational Rights Protection
    Act (FERPA), 82
Federal Enterprise Architecture
    Framework (FEAF), 26
Federal Information Processing
    Standards, 71
federated authentication, 104
feedback, prototype model, 166
FERPA (Federal Educational Rights
    Protection Act), 82
Fibre Channel, 154, 296
Fibre Channel over IP (FCIP), 154
file repository, 145–146, 296
file rights, 106
file versioning, 58, 146, 296
fingerprint test, 100
fire suppression system, 61
firewall, 68, 73, 254–256, 296
firmware, 241, 296
floating-point operations per second
    (FLOPS), 209, 296
font, 286
forum, 133–134, 296
FOSS (free open-source software),
    33–36, 296
framework, enterprise architecture,
    25–27, 295
framework-specific certification, 25
free open-source software (FOSS),
    33–36, 296
full interruption testing, 267
full replacement, 233–234, 296
functionality, effect of standardization
    on, 53–54
funding, consolidation project, 55

• G •

gait identification, 101
Gartner Enterprise Architecture
     Framework, 26–27
Gartner Research, 118, 296
general purpose computing on graphics
     processing units (GPGPU), 210
geothermal cooling, 221
gigaflop, 209
GLBA (Gramm-Leach-Bliley Act), 82–83
global positioning system (GPS), 296
GPGPU (general purpose computing on
     graphics processing units), 210
GPS (global positioning system), 296
GPU (graphical processing unit), 297
Gramm-Leach-Bliley Act (GLBA), 82–83
graphical processing unit (GPU), 224, 297
green IT
   alternative energy, 222–223
   data center location, 220–221
   defined, 297
   disposal practices, 226–227
   ENERGY STAR certification program,
      221–222
   energy tax credits, 221
   extended replacement cycles, 220
   hardware, selecting green, 224–225
   overview, 219–220
   reducing consumables, 223–224
   reducing cost from consumables with,
      286–287
   settings, configuring green, 225–226
   telecommuting, 220
   telework, 220
   virtualizing hardware, 226
grid computing, 215–216, 297
grid tools, 216
groupware, 120–122, 297

• H •

HAL (hardware abstraction layer),
     198, 297
hand geometry identification, 100
hardware
   discounts on licenses, 30
   disposal practices, 226–227
   ENERGY STAR certification,
      221–222, 287
   extended replacement cycles, 220
   failover capability of servers, 60
   firewalls, 254
   lease or warranty replacements, 161
   personally owned equipment, 279–280
   platforms, 12–13
   power saving options, 225–226
   green, selecting, 224–225
   as source of complexity, 44–45
   tech refresh planning, 199–200
   theft of, 66
   updating in virtual environments, 200
   VPNs, 184
hardware abstraction layer (HAL),
     198, 297
hardware update strategy
   ad-hoc replacement, 239–240
   cutting-edge replacement, 236–237
   defined replacement cycles, 232–236
   keeping systems until failure, 232
   overview, 231–232
   surplus technology, relying on, 238
   technology as rewards, 238
   trickle-down replacement, 237–238
hazardous waste, 227
Health Information Technology for
     Economic and Clinical Health
     (HITECH) Act, 67, 76

Health Insurance Portability and
Accountability Act (HIPAA),
46, 82–83
help desk functionality, 51
hidden obsolescence, 50
high-availability cluster, 297
high-performance computing
compute farms, 217
computing clusters, 212–214
defined, 297
desktop, 217–218
grid computing, 215–216
overview, 207
supercomputers, 207–211
visualization clusters, 214–215
volunteer computing, 216–217
HIPAA (Health Insurance Portability and
Accountability Act), 46, 82–83
HITECH (Health Information Technology
for Economic and Clinical Health)
Act, 67, 76
homeostasis, risk, 91
host server, 197
host-based IDS, 256
hosting
client, 203
of groupware, 122
virtual machines (VM), 198–199
hot site, 269, 297
hotfixes, 245
hotspot, 177–178, 191, 297
human threat, 86
Hypertext Transfer Protocol (HTTP),
130–131, 297
hypervisor, 198, 199, 203, 265, 297

• *I* •

IAM (Identity and Access Management).
See also identification
authenticating users, 102–106
authorizing access, 106–107

creating strategy, 108–109
defined, 298
implementing, 110–112
overview, 95–96
icons, explained, 4–5
identification
access tokens, 98–99
behavioral, 101–102
biometric, 99–101
defined, 297
overview, 96
passwords, 97–98
Identity and Access Management (IAM).
See also identification
authenticating users, 102–106
authorizing access, 106–107
creating strategy, 108–109
defined, 298
implementing, 110–112
overview, 95–96
identity management, 45, 298
IDS (intrusion detection system), 35,
256–257, 299
IEEE 802.11, 298
iFCP (Internet Fibre Channel
Protocol), 154
image-based deployment, 62–63, 244
IMAP (Internet Messaging Access
Protocol), 130–131, 298
implementation phase, SDLC model, 164
incident management, 73
industrial espionage, 86
infected computer, 247
information security planning
layered frameworks, using, 68–70
overview, 65, 67–68
protecting enterprise data, 66–67
security policy, developing, 72–75
security standards, implementing,
70–71
simplicity, 71–72

technology, using to support security, 75–79

viewing as program versus project, 71

workable programs, designing, 68

Information Technology Infrastructure Library (ITIL), 25, 298

information technology (IT) governance, 24–25, 298

informational token, 98

initiation and planning phase, SDLC model, 164

input, unsanitized, 249

insourcing, 79

instant messaging (IM), 131–132, 298

instruction detection software (IDS), 35

instruction set, 241

integrity, 159, 298

intellectual property identification, 35

interface, portal, 125

internal IP address, 298

international character set, 35

International Organization for Standardization (ISO), 298–299

Internet
accessibility technologies, 173
defined, 298
open standards on, 38
sustained connections for groupware, 122

Internet Fibre Channel Protocol (iFCP), 154

Internet Messaging Access Protocol (IMAP), 130–131, 298

Internet Protocol address. *See* (IP Internet Protocol) address

Internet Protocol Security (IPSec), 103, 299

Internet Relay Chat (IRC), 129, 248

Internet Small Computer System Interface (iSCSI), 154, 299

intranet, 299

intrusion detection system (IDS), 256–257, 299

intrusion prevention system (IPS), 256–257

inventory, 144

IP (Internet Protocol) address, 250, 257–259, 298

IPS (intrusion prevention system), 256–257

IPSec (Internet Protocol Security), 103, 299

IRC (Internet Relay Chat), 129, 248

iris detection, 101

iSCSI (Internet Small Computer System Interface), 154, 299

ISO (International Organization for Standardization), 299

ISO/IEC 27000 series, 70

ISO/IEC 38500:2008, 25

IT governance, 24–25, 298

ITIL (Information Technology Infrastructure Library), 25, 298, 299

• J •

justification of changes, 19

• K •

Kerberos, 103, 105–106, 299

kill pills, 188

Kryder's Law, 155, 299

• L •

L2TP (Layer 2 Tunneling Protocol), 299

LAN (local area network), 300

laptop
ad-hoc replacement strategy, 239–240
cutting-edge replacement strategy, 236–237
full replacement cycle, 233–234

laptop *(continued)*
  LoJack, 188–189
  overview, 176
  partial/staged replacement cycle,
    234–236
  trickle-down replacement strategy,
    237–238
  using technology as employee
    rewards, 238
Layer 2 Tunneling Protocol (L2TP), 299
layered framework, 68–70
LCD system, 225
LDAP (Lightweight Directory Access
    Protocol), 103, 299
lead architect, 21
leadership, 10–11, 16, 280
leased equipment, 161
legacy system
  integrating, 277–278
  layered security around, 70
  planning for technology end of life, 50
  tech refresh, 232
  using encryption with SOA, 68
legal mandate. *See* mandate
liability for loss of mobile devices, 190
licensing, 30, 201, 206
life cycle of technology, 37, 49–50
lighting, 224
Lightweight Directory Access Protocol
    (LDAP), 103, 299
limitations, recognition of, 280
line-of-business (LOB) applications, 299
link to master copy, 156–157
load balancing, 60, 198, 300
LOB (line-of-business) applications, 299
local area network (LAN), 300
locking, mobile device, 187
log
  files, storage requirements, 148
  IM, 132
  purpose of, 72
  regulatory mandates for, 82
  reviewing, 63

logical unit number (LUN), 153
Logon permission, 107
LoJack, laptop, 188–189
long-range wireless technology, 177–178
LUN (logical unit number), 153

• *M* •

mailing list, 131
maintenance phase, SDLC model, 164
malware. *See also* botnet
  defined, 300
  electronic threats, 85
  overview, 247–248
  protection against, 250–251
  security policy for, 73
  spyware, 248, 306
  Trojans, 248
  viruses, 248
  worms, 248
Managed security services model, 78
mandate
  compliance with, 278–279
  discovery and retention, 83
  generalized, 83–84
  identity management, 108–109
  increase in complexity from, 46
  legal requirements, 82–83
  overview, 81–82
man-in-the-middle attack, 189, 252, 300
mapping data resources, 83
matrix, risk, 89
maturity models, 15
Message Passing Interface (MPI), 213
messaging technology, 128–132
metadirectory, 104
Metcalfe's Law, 115–116, 301
microblogging, 133, 300
microwaving optical media, 227
mirroring, disk, 158
mitigation, risk, 92
mitigation strategy, 89
mobile access policy, 189–191

mobile technology
  Bluetooth, 177
  boosters, 179–181
  cell phones, 177
  dead zones, 179–181
  device interaction, 179
  fixed stipend for, 279–280
  laptops, 176
  long-range wireless, 177–178
  mobile access policy, 189–191
  mobile network access to
    organizational resources, 182–185
  netbooks, 176
  overview, 175
  security, 178–181
  smartphone computing, 186–189
  synching media files and storage
    issues, 150, 151
  tablets, 176–177
modernization of technology, 50
monoculture, technology, 55, 307
Moore's Law, 155, 235, 300
MPI (Message Passing Interface), 213
multimedia files, 147
multiplexing, 259, 300
multitiered architecture, 171–172, 300

• *N* •

Nagios, 260
naked hypervisor, 198, 199
NAS (network attached storage), 153, 301
NAT (network address translation),
    257–259, 300
National Association of State Chief
    Information Officers (NASCIO)
    Enterprise Architecture Maturity
    Model v1.3, 15
National Vulnerability Database, 62, 86
natural threat, 85
navigation in extended network, 182
netbook, 176

network. *See also* collaboration solutions
  attacks on, 250
  culture, developing with portals, 126
  image based deployment over, 244
  mobile access to, 182–185
  monitoring, 260
  nursery, 244
  stateless packet filtering, 255–256
  test, 242
network address translation (NAT),
    257–259, 300
network attached storage (NAS), 153, 301
network interface card (NIC), 200
network mapper, 35
network of trust, 113–116
network-based IDS, 256
New object creation permission, 107
news feed, 139
NIC (network interface card), 200
notebook, 176
notification laws, data breach, 66–67, 76
n-tier application architecture,
    171–172, 173, 301
nursery, 244, 259

• *O* •

obscurity of password, 97
obsolescence, 49–50
offshoring, 23, 79, 301
on-device encryption, 187–188
Open Group Architecture Framework
    (TOGAF), 26
Open Records requests, 190
open source software
  benefits of, 34–35
  versus closed source, 276–277
  defined, 301
  drawbacks, 35–36
  overview, 33–34
open standards, 38–39, 301
operating cycle speed, 225

operational planning, 48, 301
outsourcing
  alternative site management, 269–270
  defined, 301
  destruction of media, 160
  risk management, 92
  of security, 78–79
  of supporting architect roles, 23
overwriting, 159, 160, 301

• P •

packet, 301
packet-filtering firewall, 255–256
pair programming, 168
palm sensor, 100
PAN (Personal Area Network), 301
pandemic, planning for, 265
paper, use of, 223–224
parallel processing, 210, 301
Pareto Principle
  applying, 48–49
  defined, 289
  Scrum programming, 170
  SSO projects, 105
partial replacement, 234–236, 301
partner organizations, 32, 77–78
password
  frequent changes in, 71
  identification systems, 97–98
  management with IAM, 112
  minimum standards for, 99
  in security policy, 73
PAT (port address translation), 302
patch
  automated management of, 283–284
  defined, 301
  management of, 62
  regular application of, 251
  software maintenance, 245

Payment Card Industry Data Security
    Standards, 46
PDA (personal digital assistant), 302
permission
  assigning within portals, 124
  user account, 107
Personal Area Network (PAN), 301
personal digital assistant (PDA), 302
personal sites, 125
personalization features, portal, 125
personalized portal interfaces, 125
personally identifying information (PII), 83
personally owned equipment, 279–280
petaflop, 209
phased implementation of groupware, 122
phishing e-mail, 85
physical-to-virtual (p2v) process, 201
PKI (public-key infrastructure), 253, 303
planned obsolescence, 49–50
planning, enterprise. *See* enterprise
    planning
planning levels, 48
platform
  defined, 302
  excess of, 12–13
platform architecture, 29–30, 302
platform standardization
  benefits of, 30–31
  closed source software, 33, 36–38,
    276–277
  consideration of business needs, 39–40
  open source software, 33–36, 276–277
  open standards, 38–39
  overcoming challenges in, 31–33
  overview, 29–30
PMO (Project Management Office), 27
podcasting, 139, 302
PoE (Power over Ethernet), 224
Point of View ray-tracing (POV-Ray)
    application, 213

Point to Point topology, 154
Point-to-Point Tunneling Protocol
    (PTPP), 302
policy. *See specific policy by name*
POP (Post Office Protocol), 130–131, 302
port address translation (PAT), 259, 302
portable computer, 175–176
portal
    authentication and access control,
        123–124
    business intelligence tools,
        integrating, 126
    collaboration and communication
        technologies, 124
    content aggregation, 124
    content management, 124
    defined, 302
    document management, 124–125
    enterprise search, 125
    file storage requirements, 152
    network culture, developing with, 126
    overview, 123
    personalization, 125
portfolio management, 28
portlet, 123, 302
Post Office Protocol (POP), 130–131, 302
POV-Ray (Point of View ray-tracing)
    application, 213
power consumption, 219
Power over Ethernet (PoE), 224
power requirements, data center, 61
power settings, hardware, 225–226
power supply, mobile device, 184–185
power-saving features, 287
Preboot eXecution Environment (PXE),
    196, 201
preventing failure, 15–16
printing, 286–287
prioritizing threats, 89–90
privacy laws, 84

privacy-related certification, 122
private cloud, 205
private IP address, 257–259
probability
    defined, 302
    determining, 88
    reducing for threats, 90–91
    of threat, 87
processing speed, 209
processor, upgrading, 240–241
product stack, single-vendor, 30
productivity, effect of standardization
    on, 54
profile, user, 125
program, 28, 71
programming
    agile, 169, 289
    extreme, 170, 295
    Scrum, 170–171, 305
programming language
    effects of choosing, 14
    reducing complexity in use of, 45
    source code, 33
programming phase, SDLC model, 164
project management, 27–28, 303
Project Management Office (PMO), 27
protection, data, 66–67, 157–161
protocol, client, 130
prototype, 303
prototype iterative model, 166–167
proxy server, 60
PTPP (Point-to-Point Tunneling
    Protocol), 302
public-key encryption, 252–253, 303
public-key infrastructure (PKI), 253, 303
purging, 160, 303
PXE (Preboot eXecution Environment),
    196, 201

• Q •

qualitative analysis, 88, 303
quality settings, printing, 286
quantitative analysis, 87, 303

• R •

RAD (rapid application development),
    169–171, 303
radio-frequency identification (RFID)
    proximity cards, 98
RAID (redundant array of independent
    disks), 60, 158, 304
rapid application development (RAD),
    169–171, 303
RCRA (Resource Conservation and
    Recovery Act), 221
reactionary replacement strategy,
    239–240
Really Simple Syndication (RSS),
    139–140, 303
real-time collaboration, 120
recovery plan
  developing scenarios, 264–265
  overview, 264
  testing, 267
  updating, 267–268
  virtualization strategies, 265–267
recovery point objective (RPO), 263, 303
recovery time objective (RTO),
    263–264, 304
recycling, 226–227
Red Hat Network (RHN), 284
redesign challenges
  compliance, 278–279
  hardware replacement, 278
  lack of executive support, 275–276
  legacy systems, integrating, 277–278
  opposition to change, 276
  overview, 275–280
  personally owned equipment, 279–280

platform standardization, 276–277
  recognition of limitations, 280
  resource silos, eliminating, 277
  separate revenue streams, 279
redundancy, 18, 47, 60, 304
redundant array of independent disks
    (RAID), 60, 158, 304
registration, software, 240
regulatory mandate. *See* mandate
Rehabilitation Act of 1973 (Section 508),
    83, 174
reliance on technology, 31–32
Remember icon, 4
remote access policy, 190
remote desktop, 184, 203, 304
removable media, 144
render grid, 216
replacement, hardware
  ad-hoc, 239–240
  cutting-edge, 236–237
  cyclic, 50
  defined cycles for, 232–236
  extended cycles, 220
  overview, 231–232
  surplus technology, relying on, 238
  technology as rewards, 238
  trickle-down, 237–238
  upon failure of system, 232
replacement, warranty, 161
repository, file, 145–146
requirements analysis and definition
    phase, SDLC model, 164
resource, integration of existing, 18
resource allocation, 249
Resource Conservation and Recovery
    Act (RCRA), 221
resource silo
  defined, 304
  eliminating, 57, 277, 281
  excess of, 12
retention, 83
retinal detection, 101

reuse of password, 99
revenue stream, 279
RFID (radio-frequency identification)
    proximity cards, 98
RHN (Red Hat Network), 284
risk, defined, 304
risk acceptance, 304
risk assessment
    business continuity planning, 264
    defined, 304
    impact, determining, 88–89
    overview, 87–88
    probability, determining, 88
    results, using to find vulnerabilities, 285
    risk matrix, 89
    tool in security policy approvement, 74
risk avoidance, 304
risk homeostasis, 91, 305
risk management
    addressing risk, 89–92
    assessing risk, 87–89
    defined, 305
    threats, identifying, 84–86
    vulnerabilities, identifying, 86–87
risk matrix, 89
risk mitigation, 92, 305
risk transference, 305
roles, 20–23
root access, 13
RPO (recovery point objective), 263, 303
RSS (Really Simple Syndication),
    139–140, 303
RTO (recovery time objective),
    263–264, 304

• S •

SaaS (Software as a Service) model, 122
SAN (storage area network), 153–155, 306
Sarbanes-Oxley Act (SOX), 82
scale, economy of. See economy of scale
scale of need, 32

SCCM (System Center Configuration
    Manager), 283
scenario, 264–265
schema, 111
Scrum programming, 170–171, 305
SDLC (Software Development Life Cycle),
    164–168, 306
search, portal, 125
search engine, 182
secret-key encryption, 252, 305
Section 508 of Rehabilitation Act of 1973,
    83, 174
secure application development, 251
Secure Sockets Layer (SSL),
    183–184, 253, 305
security. See also information security
    planning
    application development, 251
    backup and recovery, 159
    CIAs, 159
    of cloud computing, 205
    in community-created code, 35
    consolidation, improving with, 58–59
    data loss prevention, 251
    defined, 305
    diversity as factor in, 55
    in embedded systems, 18
    encryption, 252–254
    firewalls, 254–256
    IAM, 109
    identifying data users, 18
    intrusion detection and prevention,
        256–257
    malware protection, 250–251
    mandates, 46
    mobile device, 187–188
    NAT, 257–259
    network monitoring, 260
    overview, 247
    reducing complexity in identity
        management, 45
    remote desktops, 184

security *(continued)*
  SaaS providers, 122
  threats, identifying, 247–250
  wireless transmission systems, 179, 180
Security as a service model, 78
security policy, 72–75
security standards, 70–71
security update, 245, 251
security utilities, FOSS, 35
self-serve recovery, 58
self-service mechanism for password
    resets, 112
sensitive data
  in e-mail, 130
  encryption of, 252
  improved security with
      consolidation, 58
  layered security around, 70
  limitations in offshoring, 23
  multiple firewall protection for, 254
server
  ad-hoc replacement strategy, 239–240
  cutting-edge replacement strategy,
      236–237
  data center consolidation, 283
  failover capability, 60
  five-year replacement cycle for, 236
  full replacement cycle, 233–234
  load balancing, 60
  partial/staged replacement cycle,
      234–236
  proxy, 60
  security policy for installations, 73
  TFTP, 196
  trickle-down replacement strategy,
      237–238
  updating, 231
  VDI, 202–203
  virtualization of, 59, 149–152, 197–201

service, 305
service pack, 245
service rights, 107
service set identifier (SSID), 305
service-oriented architecture (SOA), 68,
    111, 172–173, 305
shared account, 109
SharePoint Unified Logging Service (ULS)
    logs, 148
sharing
  desktop, 138
  of resources, 57–58
Shibboleth standards, 103
Short Message Service (SMS), 132, 306
shutdown permission, 107
signature identification, 102
Simple Mail Transfer Protocol (SMTP), 306
Simple Object Access Protocol (SOAP), 306
simulation testing, 267
single sign-on (SSO), 104–105, 123–124
site survey, 179–180
skill concentration, 51–52
smartphone
  device locking, 187
  familiarity with, 186
  kill pills, 188
  laptop LoJack, 188–189
  on-device encryption, 187–188
  overview, 186
  planning ahead, 186–187
SMS (Short Message Service), 132, 306
SMTP (Simple Mail Transfer Protocol), 306
snapshot, copying, 62
SOA (service-oriented architecture), 68,
    111, 172–173, 305
SOAP (Simple Object Access Protocol), 306
social engineering, 73, 97, 306
social media, 73, 116–120, 132–135

software. *See also* anti-malware software; application development; closed source software; open source software
  authorized, 73
  cost compared to complexity, 47
  development, 45–46, 78
  firewalls, 254
  fixing vulnerabilities in, 62
  groupware, 120–122
  image-based deployment, 62–63
  incompatibility due to standardization, 54
  licenses, 30
  malware, 247–249
  patch management, 62
  platforms, 12–13
  registration issues with component upgrades, 240
  settings, configuring green, 225–226
  tech refresh planning, 199–200
  updates, 62, 200, 242–245
  virtualization, 203–204
  VPNs, 184
software architect, 21–22
Software as a Service (SaaS) model, 122
Software Development Life Cycle (SDLC), 164–168, 306
solar energy, 223, 287
solid-state drive (SSD), 225
source code, 33
SOX (Sarbanes-Oxley Act), 82
spam, 249, 306
spiral model, 167–168, 306
spoofing, IP address, 250
spyware, 248, 306
SSD (solid-state drive), 225
SSID (service set identifier), 305
SSL (Secure Sockets Layer), 183–184, 305

SSO (single sign-on), 104–105, 123–124
stack, single-vendor product, 30
staged replacement, 234–236, 306
Stallion visualization cluster, Texas Advanced Computing Center, 214–215
standard base deployment strategy, 243
standardization. *See also* platform standardization
  in closed source software, 37
  cyclic replacement of technology, 233
  for data center automation, 62
  decreased productivity, 54
  and desire for bleeding edge technology, 278
  incompatibility with existing applications, 54
  of open-source software, 36
  overview, 53–56
  of platforms, 12–13
  preparing for opposition, 55–56
  reduced functionality, 53–54
  requirement for image-based deployment, 62
  risk of technology monoculture, 55
standards
  authentication, 102–103
  cloud computing, 205
  defined, 306
  defining technical, 18–19
  open, 38–39, 301
  security, 70–71
Startup permission, 107
stateful packet filtering, 256, 306
stateless packet filtering, 255–256, 306
stipend for mobile device use, 279–280
storage area network (SAN), 153–155, 306
storage configuration, 152–153

storage grid, 215–216, 306
storage policy, 149–152
storage survey, 144, 307
strategic planning, 48, 307
streaming media, 140, 307
strength, password, 97–98
subnet, 307
sub-system update, 240–242
supercomputer, 207–211, 307
superuser access, 13
supervisor access, 13
support skill alignment, 52
surplus technology, relying on, 238
survey, storage, 144
Switched Fabric topology, 154
symmetric encryption, 252, 307
synched media files, 150, 151
synchronous communication,
    127–128, 307
System Center Configuration Manager
    (SCCM), 283
system memory, upgrading, 240–241
Systems Development Life Cycle (SDLC).
    See Software Development Life Cycle
    (SDLC)
Systems Security Engineering Capability
    Maturity Model, 70

• T •

tablet, 176–177
tactical planning, 48, 307
tasks, 17–19
tax credit, energy, 221
TCP/IP (Transmission Control Protocol/
    Internet Protocol), 307
team creation, 114
tech refresh, 199–200, 231, 285, 307
technical standards, defining, 18–19
Technical Stuff icon, 5

technology. *See also specific types of
    technology*
  collaborative, 76
  effect of change on connected, 13–14
  life cycle of, 37, 49–50
  monoculture, 55, 307
  reviewing for IAM strategy, 108
  as rewards strategy, 238
  using to support security, 75–79
technology architect, 21
technology stack, 44, 308
telecommuting, 220, 308
teleworking, 220, 308
terrorism, virtual, 136
test network, 242
testing phase, SDLC model, 164
tethering, 308
text messaging, 132, 308
TFTP (Trivial File Transport Protocol)
    server, 196
Thawte, 254
theft of hardware, 66
thick client, 202, 308
thin client, 202, 308
threat
  application vulnerabilities, 249
  countermeasures for, 90–91, 250
  defined, 308
  directed network attacks, 250
  electronic, 85
  human, 86
  malware, 247–249
  mitigation, 92
  natural or environmental, 85
  overview, 84–85, 247
  prioritizing, 89–90
  reducing impact of, 91
  reducing probability of, 90–91
  risk assessment, 87–89
three-tier architecture, 171

three-user network, 115–116
tiered data storage, 156, 157, 308
timebox, 308
Tip icon, 4
TOGAF (Open Group Architecture Framework), 26
token, access, 98–99, 289
topology, 154
Toxic Substances Control Act (TSCA), 221
training, employee, 75, 117
transference strategy, 89
Transmission Control Protocol/Internet Protocol (TCP/IP), 307
transparency, 206
trickle-down replacement, 237–238, 308
Trivial File Transport Protocol (TFTP) server, 196
Trojan, 248, 256, 308
trust, network of, 113–116
TSCA (Toxic Substances Control Act), 221
tunneling, 309

• U •

ULS (SharePoint Unified Logging Service) logs, 148
unsanitized input, 249
update
  automated management, 283–284
  disaster recovery plan, 267–268
  management of, 62
  security software, 251
update strategy. *See also* hardware update strategy
  overview, 231
  software updates, 242–245
  sub-system updates, 240–242
upgrades, software, 37, 38
USB fingerprint biometric reader, 100
user account, 107, 109, 112
user feedback, prototype model, 166

• V •

VDI (virtual desktop infrastructure) server, 202–203
vendor, virtualization, 198
vendor-specific certification, 25
vendor-specific protocol, 130
versioning, file, 58, 124–125, 146
video card upgrade, 240–241
videoconferencing, 135–136, 309
virtual desktop, 202–203
virtual desktop infrastructure (VDI) server, 202–203
virtual machine, 197, 198–199, 309
virtual private network (VPN), 183–184, 309
virtual reality, 136
virtual server, 149
virtual terrorism, 136
virtualization
  applications, 203–204
  cloud computing, 204–206
  and cost saving, 286
  defined, 309
  in disaster recovery planning, 265–267
  of hardware for environmental reasons, 226
  overview, 195–197
  reducing complexity through, 59
  servers, 197–201
  update deployment strategies, 244
  workstation, 201–203
virtualization host, 309
virtualized application, 309
virtualized desktop, 309
virus, 71, 248, 309
virus creation kit, 248
visualization cluster, 214–215
voice analysis, 102

Voice over Internet Protocol (VoIP), 137, 310
volunteer computing, 216–217
VPN (virtual private network), 183–184, 309
vulnerability
  in applications, 249
  defined, 310
  identifying, 86–87
  using risk assessment to find, 285

• W •

wake-on-LAN functionality, 226
walkthrough testing, 267
WAN (wide area network), 310
wardriving, 189
warm site, 269, 310
Warning icon, 5
warranty replacement, 161
waste disposal, 73
water consumption, 220
water cooling, 287
water microturbine power generation, 223
waterfall model, 165, 310
Web conferencing, 137–138, 310
Web feed, 139
Web service, 310
Web Services Description Language (WSDL), 310
Web site
  accessibility technologies, 173
  Chief Information Officers Council, 26
  community sites, 132–135
  containing warnings about software flaws, 249
  point of contact, 270–271
  social networking, 117–119
  wiki, 134
webinar, 138, 310
wide area network (WAN), 310

Wi-Fi (Wireless Fidelity), 179, 185, 310
Wi-Fi Protected Access (WPA/WPA2), 183, 311
wiki, 134–135, 311
WiMAX (Worldwide Interoperability for Microwave Access), 177
wind turbine power generation, 223, 287
Windows Server Update Services (WSUS), 283–284
wiping mobile devices, 188, 189
Wired Equivalent Privacy (WEP), 311
wireless access point, 189, 311
Wireless Fidelity (Wi-Fi), 179, 185, 310
wireless local area network (WLAN), 311
wireless transmission, 177–178, 183, 189
wireless use policy, 191
workable program, designing, 68
workflow, IAM, 112
workstation
  ad-hoc replacement strategy, 239–240
  cutting-edge replacement strategy, 236–237
  full replacement cycle, 233–234
  high-performance computing cycle, 217–218
  partial/staged replacement cycle, 234–236
  replacement, 285
  security policy for installations, 73
  standardization, 282
  trickle-down replacement strategy, 237–238
  updating, 231
  virtualization, 201–203
Worldwide Interoperability for Microwave Access (WiMAX), 177
worm, 311
WPA/WPA2 (Wi-Fi Protected Access), 183
WSUS (Windows Server Update Services), 283–284

• X •

X.500 suite, 102
XML (Extensible Markup Language), 295

• Z •

Zachman Framework, 26
zero-day threat, 311
zettaflop, 209

Apple & Macs

iPad For Dummies
978-0-470-58027-1

iPhone For Dummies,
4th Edition
978-0-470-87870-5

MacBook For Dummies, 3rd
Edition
978-0-470-76918-8

Mac OS X Snow Leopard For
Dummies
978-0-470-43543-4

Business

Bookkeeping For Dummies
978-0-7645-9848-7

Job Interviews
For Dummies,
3rd Edition
978-0-470-17748-8

Resumes For Dummies,
5th Edition
978-0-470-08037-5

Starting an
Online Business
For Dummies,
6th Edition
978-0-470-60210-2

Stock Investing
For Dummies,
3rd Edition
978-0-470-40114-9

Successful
Time Management
For Dummies
978-0-470-29034-7

Computer Hardware

BlackBerry
For Dummies,
4th Edition
978-0-470-60700-8

Computers For Seniors
For Dummies,
2nd Edition
978-0-470-53483-0

PCs For Dummies,
Windows
7 Edition
978-0-470-46542-4

Laptops For Dummies,
4th Edition
978-0-470-57829-2

Cooking & Entertaining

Cooking Basics
For Dummies,
3rd Edition
978-0-7645-7206-7

Wine For Dummies,
4th Edition
978-0-470-04579-4

Diet & Nutrition

Dieting For Dummies,
2nd Edition
978-0-7645-4149-0

Nutrition For Dummies,
4th Edition
978-0-471-79868-2

Weight Training
For Dummies,
3rd Edition
978-0-471-76845-6

Digital Photography

Digital SLR Cameras &
Photography For Dummies,
3rd Edition
978-0-470-46606-3

Photoshop Elements 8
For Dummies
978-0-470-52967-6

Gardening

Gardening Basics
For Dummies
978-0-470-03749-2

Organic Gardening
For Dummies,
2nd Edition
978-0-470-43067-5

Green/Sustainable

Raising Chickens
For Dummies
978-0-470-46544-8

Green Cleaning
For Dummies
978-0-470-39106-8

Health

Diabetes For Dummies,
3rd Edition
978-0-470-27086-8

Food Allergies
For Dummies
978-0-470-09584-3

Living Gluten-Free
For Dummies,
2nd Edition
978-0-470-58589-4

Hobbies/General

Chess For Dummies,
2nd Edition
978-0-7645-8404-6

Drawing
Cartoons & Comics
For Dummies
978-0-470-42683-8

Knitting For Dummies,
2nd Edition
978-0-470-28747-7

Organizing
For Dummies
978-0-7645-5300-4

Su Doku For Dummies
978-0-470-01892-7

Home Improvement

Home Maintenance
For Dummies,
2nd Edition
978-0-470-43063-7

Home Theater
For Dummies,
3rd Edition
978-0-470-41189-6

Living the
Country Lifestyle
All-in-One
For Dummies
978-0-470-43061-3

Solar Power Your Home
For Dummies,
2nd Edition
978-0-470-59678-4

Internet

Blogging For Dummies,
3rd Edition
978-0-470-61996-4

eBay For Dummies,
6th Edition
978-0-470-49741-8

Facebook For Dummies,
3rd Edition
978-0-470-87804-0

Web Marketing
For Dummies,
2nd Edition
978-0-470-37181-7

WordPress
For Dummies,
3rd Edition
978-0-470-59274-8

Language & Foreign Language

French For Dummies
978-0-7645-5193-2

Italian Phrases
For Dummies
978-0-7645-7203-6

Spanish For Dummies,
2nd Edition
978-0-470-87855-2

Spanish
For Dummies,
Audio Set
978-0-470-09585-0

Math & Science

Algebra I
For Dummies,
2nd Edition
978-0-470-55964-2

Biology For Dummies,
2nd Edition
978-0-470-59875-7

Calculus For Dummies
978-0-7645-2498-1

Chemistry For Dummies
978-0-7645-5430-8

Microsoft Office

Excel 2010 For Dummies
978-0-470-48953-6

Office 2010 All-in-One
For Dummies
978-0-470-49748-7

Office 2010 For Dummies,
Book + DVD Bundle
978-0-470-62698-6

Word 2010 For Dummies
978-0-470-48772-3

Music

Guitar For Dummies,
2nd Edition
978-0-7645-9904-0

iPod & iTunes For
Dummies, 8th Edition
978-0-470-87871-2

Piano Exercises
For Dummies
978-0-470-38765-8

Parenting & Education

Parenting For Dummies,
2nd Edition
978-0-7645-5418-6

Type 1 Diabetes
For Dummies
978-0-470-17811-9

Pets

Cats For Dummies,
2nd Edition
978-0-7645-5275-5

Dog Training For Dummies,
3rd Edition
978-0-470-60029-0

Puppies For Dummies,
2nd Edition
978-0-470-03717-1

Religion & Inspiration

The Bible For Dummies
978-0-7645-5296-0

Catholicism For Dummies
978-0-7645-5391-2

Women in the Bible
For Dummies
978-0-7645-8475-6

Self-Help & Relationship

Anger Management
For Dummies
978-0-470-03715-7

Overcoming Anxiety
For Dummies,
2nd Edition
978-0-470-57441-6

Sports

Baseball
For Dummies,
3rd Edition
978-0-7645-7537-2

Basketball
For Dummies,
2nd Edition
978-0-7645-5248-9

Golf For Dummies,
3rd Edition
978-0-471-76871-5

Web Development

Web Design
All-in-One
For Dummies
978-0-470-41796-6

Web Sites
Do-It-Yourself
For Dummies,
2nd Edition
978-0-470-56520-9

Windows 7

Windows 7
For Dummies
978-0-470-49743-2

Windows 7
For Dummies,
Book + DVD Bundle
978-0-470-52398-8

Windows 7 All-in-One
For Dummies
978-0-470-48763-1

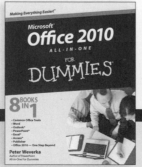

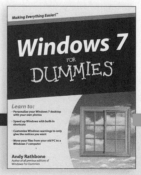

Available wherever books are sold. For more information or to order direct: U.S. customers visit www.dummies.com or call 1-877-762-2974.
U.K. customers visit www.wileyeurope.com or call (0) 1243 843291. Canadian customers visit www.wiley.ca or call 1-800-567-4797.

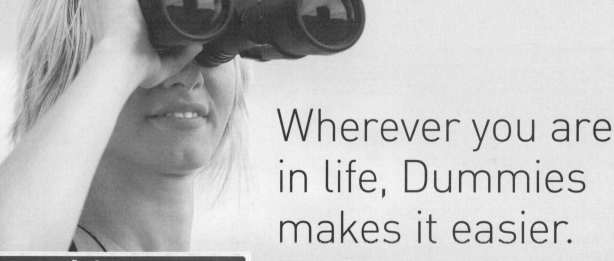

Wherever you are in life, Dummies makes it easier.

From fashion to Facebook®,
wine to Windows®, and everything in between,
Dummies makes it easier.

Visit us at Dummies.com

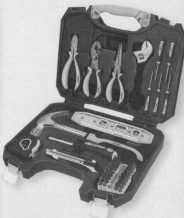